George Trumbull Ladd

George Trumbull Ladd
Pioneer American Psychologist

Eugene S. Mills

1969
The Press of Case Western Reserve University
Cleveland and London

Library
Southwestern State College
Weatherford, Oklahoma

Copyright © 1969 by The Press of Case Western Reserve University,
Cleveland, Ohio 44106. All rights reserved.

Printed in the United States of America.

Standard Book Number: 8295–0150–9.

Library of Congress Catalogue Card Number: 69-17683.

To Dotty

132236

Preface

In 1961, during a summer teaching appointment at the University of Victoria, I began to think seriously about a problem that had lain dormant in my mind for a decade. The problem concerned the marked contrast between the early prominence and the current obscurity of George Trumbull Ladd. My interest in it had arisen from a general remark by the late Professor F. Theodore Perkins of the Claremont Graduate School. In conversation about the history of the field, Professor Perkins had observed that a number of early figures in psychology seem to have suffered an obscurity that is altogether out of proportion to their contributions to the field. "How much of this," he had asked, "is due to the psychologist's small appetite for history?" Later, as I pondered the question, it struck me that perhaps Ladd was the best example of the phenomenon. I knew of his great influence in the last two decades of the nineteenth century, although at that time I certainly was not aware of the singular range and intensity of his career. I also knew that Ladd was a person of marginal importance for the modern psychologist. Predictably, I went to E. G. Boring's *History of Experimental Psychology* to read again the section on American functional psychology. I found that Boring had written appreciatively of Ladd's contributions, observing finally that there was no adequate account of his distinguished life and work. Apparently Ladd was deserving of more attention than he had received. It was the kind of problem that I looked forward to considering after the completion of my graduate studies, when an academic career would afford ample leisure time for playing with the fruits of curiosity!

Ten years later, the ample leisure time having been filled with other interesting problems, I found that Boring's assessment was still true; there was no adequate account of Ladd's life and work and no known bibliography of his writings. I began to compile a bibliography and to read systematically the books and articles that I could locate. At first the endless stream of dry prose made me impatient, and though perhaps I should not confess it, when weary of the solemn style I would turn to William James for relief; but gradually I found that the Ladd of the written word began to come alive. I became increasingly curious about the life and personality of the author. There was a compelling itch and urgency in Ladd's writings and a strangely self-confident nobility, a sense of high mission, about the entire life plan from which they were derived. One wondered how the man, the writings, and the times had merged to produce this influential, but now remote, oracle of the new mental science.

After I had decided to undertake a biography of Ladd, two developments occurred that were to be of crucial importance for the project. First, I made the acquaintance of Ladd's daughter, the late Mrs. Elisabeth Ladd Barrett of Fort Wayne, Indiana. Mrs. Barrett was a friendly, gracious woman whose reminiscence about her father can only be described as "affectionately critical." In addition, Ladd's granddaughters, Miss Cornelia T. Ladd of Cleveland Heights and Mrs. William B. Hunting of Cincinnati, as well as his grandson, Dr. Louis W. Ladd, Jr., of Cleveland Heights, provided friendly assistance and made available letters, personal copies of books, and other pieces of Laddiana for which I am greatly in their debt.

A second development of importance was a two-year grant from the National Science Foundation in support of the research project. Among other advantages, the grant made it possible for me to spend the summer of 1964 in Japan, tracing Ladd's faint footprints from lecture to lecture and collecting the publications by and about him that inevitably were left in his wake. I wish to record my gratitude to the National Science Foundation for its timely assistance.

A word now about the autobiography. In early correspondence Mrs. Barrett asked whether I might be interested in an unpublished manuscript by her father that she was keeping "splendidly intact but unread in an upstairs closet." I was interested. When made available it turned out to be a 794-page autobiography that had been written in the years from 1910 to 1912. It was a poorly typed document, edited by Ladd and including a number of long passages handwritten into the original text. The paper was crisp and delicate and the ink rather faded, but clearly it was a document of great importance for my biographical studies. Mrs. Barrett generously presented the manuscript to me for whatever use I might wish to make of it.

After Ladd's death in 1921, his wife had moved from New Haven to a farm in upstate New York, carrying with her a vast collection of her husband's books and papers. The autobiography was stored in the barn, where for over thirty years it lay undisturbed by the new psychology that had so little time for history and for Ladd. In settling Mrs. Ladd's estate after her death in 1954, the executors had sent the document to Mrs. Barrett. Unfortunately, other papers and documents that might have been of historical value were destroyed.

In the years from 1913 to 1916 Ladd had made two unsuccessful attempts to publish his autobiography. It is not difficult to understand why he failed in this effort. For one thing, the work is inordinately long, of uneven quality, and repetitious. In certain chapters he drew heavily upon previously published works; this practice may have made it a useful summary of his writings and experiences, but it diminishes the value of the document as a fresh piece of scholarship. In addition, the spirit of the work frequently suffers from a rather vainglorious style. Ladd was not as delicate as he might have been in stating for the record his own unusual achievements. Several chapters, otherwise of good quality, contain page upon page of quotations from appreciative letters written by former students. A small amount of this testimony goes a long way, but apparently the author did not want to risk losing any of these precious tributes.

Toward the close of his life Ladd must have concluded that the autobiography might not be published. The last book that he wrote, *Intimate Glimpses of Life in India*, contains much of the material from the chapters that deal with his sabbatical of 1899-1900. He did not give up completely, however, for at his death his will was found to contain instructions concerning publication of the book.

The autobiography has provided valuable background material for the present book, but I have made it a practice to check other sources concerning the details that I have cited from Ladd's manuscript. While I have quoted the autobiography in those sections in which it has seemed appropriate to let Ladd tell the story in his own words, it will be apparent to the reader that on a number of occasions I have taken issue with the spirit or the letter of his account. Confused pagination and a disorganized narrative, particularly in those sections containing extensive additions in Ladd's own hand, have made direct reference to the original document extremely difficult. To clarify references to the autobiography I have had the entire manuscript retyped and bound. My footnotes use the pagination of this newly bound version.

I have acknowledged my great indebtedness to the Ladd family and to the National Science Foundation. I wish also to express my appreciation for the kind assistance that has been provided by Professor Koji Sato of Kyoto University and Professor S. Okamoto and

Miss J. Moriyama of Okayama University. Professor Okamoto traveled with me on most of my research trips in Japan in the summer of 1964. Miss Moriyama provided valuable translations of Japanese documents, and all three assisted in a most selfless manner in assembling relevant Ladd materials in Japan. Their interest in the project has been a great satisfaction to me.

Professor George W. Pierson and former President Charles Seymour of Yale University were helpful in the early stages of research. Professor David Lyttle of Syracuse University read the manuscript and made a number of constructive suggestions, as did my colleague Professor Robert I. Watson of the University of New Hampshire. Professor Watson also was generous in granting me access to a number of documents in his personal collection on the history of psychology. It is a pleasure to record my appreciation to the cooperative staff of the Yale University Library. The chief reference librarian, David R. Watkins, was helpful in arranging access to special collections at Yale. Mrs. Ruth W. Helmuth, university archivist of Case Western Reserve University, provided files and friendly assistance.

I appreciate also the valuable assistance of Joseph Trimble and L. Jackson Newell of the University of New Hampshire. Mrs. Mary E. Wyatt of Whittier College and Mrs. Marion Gould, formerly of the University of New Hampshire, were of great help in typing project correspondence and in organizing and retyping the original copy of the autobiography. Finally, I want to acknowledge the constant support and encouragement that has been provided by my wife, Dorothy W. Mills. Across six years, from Boston to Tokyo, she has shared it all with me. My gratitude is inadequately expressed in dedicating this book to her.

E. S. M.

Durham, New Hampshire

Contents

George Trumbull Ladd

". . . a summons is issued to the forces
of the soul to rally, to marshal themselves, to submit
to discipline, to do in a definite and purposeful
way a certain piece of work."

G. T. LADD, Psychology: Descriptive and Explanatory

Chapter · 1 ·

The Philosopher as Scientist

At the close of the nineteenth century George Trumbull Ladd was one of the most prominent and influential scholars of the new mental science that was pushing its way into American academic life. After a long, slow start, psychology was beginning to make its move toward identity and respectability, and Ladd was generally acknowledged to be one of the prime movers of the field. Today, nearly a half-century after his death, the American Psychological Association that he helped to establish in 1892 lists approximately 25,000 members, most of whom undoubtedly have only a meager knowledge of his intense and productive career. They may know that he taught at Yale University, that he wrote an important textbook, and that historically he is to be considered as a functional psychologist who stressed metaphysics. Beyond these general impressions, however, his life and work have been of interest principally to those who maintain an active acquaintance with the origins of the field. Ladd's career is a challenging problem for the historian because of the marked contrast that exists between his early prominence and his current obscurity.

If Ladd is little known today it is not because he failed to leave a record of his ideas or because he confined his activities to a limited

George Trumbull Ladd

geographical region. He published thirty-five books and innumerable articles, both professional and popular; he served ten years as a minister in two cities in the Midwest and preached and lectured in hundreds of communities across the country and abroad; for twenty-five years he held academic appointments at Bowdoin College and Yale University, and also was a special lecturer at Wellesley, Columbia, Harvard, the University of Iowa, Western Reserve, and Andover Theological Seminary; he founded the Yale Psychological Laboratory, was the second president of the American Psychological Association, and served as a delegate of the A.P.A. to the World's Congress of Psychologists in Paris in 1900, and to the International Congress of Arts and Sciences that was held during the St. Louis Exposition in 1904; he made three lecture trips to the Far East, spent several months in 1907 as a special adviser to Marquis Ito, the Japanese Resident-General in Korea, and was awarded the Third and Second Degrees of the Order of the Rising Sun by the Emperor of Japan; and he received honorary doctorates from Princeton and Western Reserve universities.

The range of Ladd's activities, the quantity of his writing and lecturing, and the intensity with which he enumerated and defended his views were extraordinary. His zeal for work approached fanaticism. Troubled throughout his life by nervous and dyspeptic ailments, he characteristically responded to illness with self-denial and increased labor. He believed, and it would seem to have been a reasonable conclusion, that his frail health and his professional zeal were somehow related. Whatever may have been the personal dynamics of his health and scholarship, he lived for nearly eighty years and continued productive almost to the end.

One hundred years ago the man with scholarly interests was often drawn into the study of theology as a preparation for the ministry. This was the path that Ladd chose. His strong preference for classical learning served him well in college and seminary studies. Following formal training at Western Reserve College and Andover Theological Seminary, he spent ten years in the ministry,

2

briefly in a small rural community in Ohio, and then for eight years in a large church in Milwaukee. Throughout this period he continued his studies and followed a steady program of writing. With the passing of each year it became increasingly evident that the intellectual commitments required by the ministry and the limited time available for serious scholarship prevented the personal and scholarly development that he craved. Perhaps he would have continued an unhappy and rebellious career in the ministry had it not been for his conviction that the cherished values of culture and religion were being seriously challenged by the onrush of a scientific age. Ladd decided that he must play a part in the great drama that was enveloping the scientist and the theologian, and in characteristic fashion he set out upon a mission that was both reasonable and audacious. Through teaching and scholarship he would serve as the mediator between the old and the new so that the best of both worlds of learning and experience might be preserved.

By training and by temperament, Ladd was a classicist and a philosopher. He had steeped himself in the study of language, and his recreational as well as professional reading was concentrated upon the Latin, Greek, German, and Hebraic editions of classical literature and philosophy. With an attitude that was both reverent and critical, he toiled over the great works and ancient problems of man. He believed that the truths of human history were likely to be twisted or diluted by repeated inspection and that, wherever possible, the scholar should immerse himself in the study of original documents. The immersion process required objectivity, restraint, a passion for detail, and enormous creative energy. But the passion for detail should not become an end in itself. Ladd was strongly inclined toward what might be termed the abiding generalities of belief. He was an inveterate metaphysician, seeking always to make the details of learning consistent with an assumed grand design of order and reality.

Upon entering the academic world in 1879, Ladd began for the first time to read extensively in the literature on mental science. He collected all the books he could find concerning psychology, and in his deadly serious and systematic way prepared to become master of the new field. His entry into psychology was a reflection of his intellectual interests and his curiosity, but it also resulted from a desire to know all that he could of the new science so that he might defend with understanding the accepted values and beliefs of classical learning and of religion. When he began his study of psychology, he began as well to read the rapidly accumulating literature concerning science and naturalism. He was caught up in the excitement of the new age and, like many of his learned contemporaries, was influenced by Darwin's remarkable theories. It was a time to try out ideas; for those who were interested in man and his social problems, it was a time for asking what science could do when applied to the mind. Ladd's early conception of the methods and goals of science was rather quaint and ill defined, but it is to his credit that he was discerning and flexible enough to appreciate the importance of this new opportunity for learning about man. There were many men with a theological background who prejudged and thoroughly rejected the notion that science could be used to shed light on human behavior.

Excited by his new mission, Ladd read again the writings of McCosh, Porter, Bain, J. S. Mill, Lotze, and Locke. He was familiar with the philosophical literature concerning such topics as reason, emotion, memory, and perception; however, he started his quest by reconsidering these old problems in the light of science. It is not clear whether he made much progress, but soon there came an acquaintance with the works of Weber, Fechner, Helmholtz, and Wundt. Here was an exciting new hope. The methods of psychophysics offered a means for exploring the relation between mind and body, and as a mediator he was eager to settle the mind-body question in order to avoid what he considered to be the ravages of a rampant materialism. With considerable talent for systematization, he began to compile the fruits of his study into a handbook of physiological or, more accurately stated, experimental psychology. In 1887, after six years of intense scholarship, he published his enormous work under the title *Elements of Physiological Psychology*. He had not settled the mind-body problem, but he did feel that *Elements* was a major step in the right direction.

With the publication of *Elements of Physiological Psychology*, Ladd moved out of the philosophical and theological roles that were so appropriate to his interests and training and into a new role as psychologist—a role that was new for him and relatively new for the American academic scene. The strange thing is that he began his contributions to psychology by publishing such a large and complex book on the basis of an informal program of self-training in the field. He was good at this sort of thing and undoubtedly found reading original sources and making a systematic summary of his study a congenial task. American psychology was ready for just such a definitive interpretation of the literature, and he was hailed as one of the leaders of the new science. He was proud of his accomplishment, optimistic about the future, and ready now to call himself a scientist. The years to come would make painfully evident that the new role was but a mask drawn over the unaltered inner life of a committed philosopher.

While Ladd continued his interest in psychology until his death in 1921, his chief contributions to the field were made between 1887 and 1905, the year of his unhappy dismissal from the Yale faculty. In addition to *Elements of Physiological Psychology* his most important books were *Primer of Psychology* (1894) and *Psychology: Descriptive and Explanatory* (1894). He published many psychological articles, most of which were theoretical rather than experimental, and the topics showed the breadth of his interest and the extent of his confidence that psychology could be applied usefully to important questions. He wrote on the psychology of the novel, legal aspects of hypnosis, the development of attention in infancy, color illusions, control of the retinal field, psychophysical

George Trumbull Ladd

parallelism, cerebral surgery without anesthetics, multiple personality, and "why women cannot compose music!" In all these efforts he was expressing, as were others such as William James at Harvard, G. Stanley Hall at Clark, and James Mark Baldwin at Toronto, Princeton, and Johns Hopkins, the zeal of the early psychologist who was hard at work exploring both the central problems and the still uncertain boundaries of a new field.

Exhilarated by the fresh approach to old problems that science provided, Ladd played an important part in launching psychology, but he was more interested in studying the philosophy of science than he was in being a scientist. A preoccupation with metaphysics and ethics colored everything that he did as a psychological theorist. He shared with James an impatience with laboratory work and a tendency to speculate rather than experiment. The delineation of theory was much more interesting to him than the application of methodology. Perhaps it could be said without injustice that the philosopher who so warmly welcomed the new science and so effectively argued for it, especially in debate with his theological friends and colleagues, never became a scientist at all.

If Ladd failed to become a scientist it was not because he spurned the title; indeed, he believed that his function as a mediator required that he understand and employ the methods of science and that he be accepted as a scientist. Whether or not he can be appropriately labeled a scientist is both debatable and of little consequence. The important point is to recognize, as he could not, that what he chose to call science was merely a necessary historical precursor of American psychological science. It was still philosophical analysis, largely based upon speculation and infused with some of the terms and some of the spirit of science.

Ladd should not be criticized unduly for his limitations as a scientist. Most of the tendencies and reservations that he possessed were present also, in one degree or another, in his psychological colleagues of the day. James's attitudes toward the "nasty little sub-

6

ject" are well known, and G. Stanley Hall, in spite of his enormous contributions to the field, had some metaphysical doubts about the methods and limitations of science when applied to man. While recognizing these misgivings in Ladd's colleagues, we do not wish to imply that the personal characteristics of his position were any less his own or are made unimportant in assessing his contributions to the field. James and Hall had similar attitudes, but these did not as fully precondition their psychology; both men based their work on the assumption that the discipline was one of the natural sciences. Ladd tried, but his heart was not in the effort. Behind his arduous labor there was always to be found a sometimes nibbling but often flagrant doubt that psychology was indeed a natural science.

His principal reservations about psychology were metaphysical. A confirmed dualist, Ladd believed that, whatever might be revealed by the methods of science, there was still a psychological reality immune to scientific method which could be known only by immediate experience. He was philosophically astute enough to realize the problems that this position created for mental science, but he was not to be shaken from his belief merely because it created unresolvable issues for the field. He argued skillfully and repeatedly that there was no true knowledge in science without an open acceptance of the limitations inherent in its methods. He insisted that "the development of Mind can only be regarded as the progressive manifestation in consciousness of the life of a real being, which, although taking its start and direction from the action of the physical elements of the body, proceeds to unfold powers that are *sui generis* according to laws of its own."[1] With this statement he set himself apart from scientific materialism. He would have science in psychology, but he would have it on his own terms. The philosopher as scientist could not ignore that larger reality which "surely must encompass the tough methods of the scientist

[1] *Elements of Physiological Psychology* (New York: Charles Scribner's Sons, 1887), p. 632.

7

and the misty vistas of philosophy." He died an unrepentant dualist, until the end cautioning psychology to beware of the pitfalls of materialism.

Ladd was a man of deep convictions. He was sensitive to contrary evidence and occasionally showed surprising flexibility in abandoning a previously hardened position; once the elements of proof were fixed in his mind, however, he was reluctant to change a belief. His position on most issues was infused with a strong tone of morality. Scholarship was a moral quest, and science (and therefore psychology) was never to be separated altogether from its moral ends. While most psychologists conceded the moral and ethical claims that he made, they insisted that these issues be kept separate from the methods and goals of science. One could believe what he wished concerning science and morality, but science itself was amoral. Ladd was always troubled by the reluctance of scientists to admit the moral and ethical context within which they worked. He tirelessly pointed out the metaphysical and ethical naïveté of his fellow theoreticians in psychology who, no matter how sterling their efforts on behalf of science, seemed consistently to confuse experimental reliability with philosophical truth. But then, he was more interested in truth and reality as philosophical problems than he was in the evidence that might be marshaled by science for the dependability of a relation between variables.

Ladd's preoccupation with truth, reality, free will, and the moral consequences of behavior established his primary interest in philosophy as it embraced psychology, rather than in psychology as a separable discipline. His concern with these questions was considered appropriate in the early days of psychology, but it became less fashionable as the field gained confidence in its scientific legitimacy. As his colleagues grew more impatient with his metaphysical complaints, he began to strengthen his ties to professional philosophy. Where previously he had argued his case from within psychology, toward the close of his career he began to restate his position as a philosopher who had looked across all science and found it to be seriously limited and unduly ambitious. Because he was fervid in his belief about important issues and unable to resist the urge to publish, his arguments occasionally became unimaginative and redundant.

Ladd's psychological theories were consistent with the American theory development of his time. They were functional in their stress upon the active and purposeful nature of mind. The individual was viewed as a dynamic organism that was self-aware, and mental life was considered to have a useful function in the solution of practical problems of living. Though he did not develop a tightly knit pattern of theory positions that could have been identified as a unique psychological contribution, the exhaustive treatment of topics was distinctly his own. It was a classic effort to blend psychology and philosophy. No other writer of his time expressed so resolutely and so well the interrelated issues of these two fields.

In the course of a professional life that spanned a half-century, American psychology grew out of the preliminary stages of mental science; it eschewed philosophy and religion, became more mechanistic and experimental, and found new pride in being a psychology without a soul. The changes that occurred during these decades carried the field away from the values and beliefs that were to remain the central argument that Ladd directed to psychological problems. He moved into and with American psychology, contributing significantly to its infant development, but he could not, by reason of both interest and conviction, follow the development of psychology into its vigorous adolescence. He stood unbending before the tide that obviously was running against him, and his claim to fame in the 1880's and 1890's became grounds for obscurity after the turn of the century.

Ladd's reputation as a professional philosopher was based upon his influential role as a Yale teacher and author. His writings were critical and synthetic; they were more useful as texts than as books to turn the direction of philosophical thinking. He was known as a translator of the work of the German philosopher Hermann

George Trumbull Ladd

Lotze and often was considered erroneously to be one of Lotze's disciples. While he ranged widely in his scholarship, his philosophical writings drew most heavily upon the literature of the new mental science, the theories of Kant and Lotze, and principles of Christian theology. Theologians distrusted him because of his advocacy of science, psychologists became impatient with him because of his preoccupation with metaphysics, and professional philosophers, who might have been the most tolerant of his breadth of interest and mixed loyalties, were generally unenthusiastic about his efforts to crowd so many kinds of reality into one grand view. Ladd was a man of many countries, but a citizen of none. His failure to achieve professional citizenship was the major tragedy of a long and productive career.

In summary, then, Ladd was a persistent scholar who had deep convictions concerning man's purpose and destiny as both a physical and a spiritual being. He was early attracted to the study of theology, moved professionally into philosophy, was drawn into an active role in the new mental science, and finally, in ways that appropriately expressed his personal and temperamental characteristics, directed his efforts to social and political criticism. In five decades of strenuous work his personal and professional development became an expression of, and a comment upon, the philosophical, psychological, and cultural life of his time. A study of the force and the limitations of his ideas highlights his personal achievements as a thinker and scholar, but also it illuminates the modes of development of intellectual life and of academic institutions. His current obscurity reflects the changing intellectual and social conditions within which each scholar labors, hoping to insert something of value into a human history that may enhance or diminish the importance of his own contributions. Ladd lived long enough to experience the painful transition from early recognition to partial eclipse of his life and work.

Chapter · 2 ·

A Son of the Western Reserve

Throughout his long life George Trumbull Ladd considered himself a citizen of the Western Reserve. As a psychologist he acknowledged the importance of the learning and experience of his more mature years, but he held nonetheless that his personal characteristics and professional achievements were directly influenced by the sturdy virtues of life within the New Connecticut. Ladd's sense of identity with the problems and fortunes of his native region was little diminished by fifty busy years of professional life outside the Reserve. As he was fond of telling others toward the close of his life, he was born in the wilderness frontier of Ohio, spent a half-century surveying the forests of philosophy and psychology, and finally found contentment only in the quiet culture of Japan.

The appearance of the Ladd family in the Western Reserve in the early part of the nineteenth century was the particular manifestation of a large and significant frontier movement. The creation of the New Connecticut was a tribute to the courage and persistence of the Old Connecticut Yankees who sought to fulfill the royal charter which had been granted to Connecticut in 1662 by Charles II. That charter gave the colony the land contained within the borders of the present state and, in addition, all the land to the west "from sea to sea." The confusion concerning American geography was to be the source of continuing strife as many Connecticut Yankees attempted to find the basis for a more abundant life. Following tragic efforts to establish a foothold in Pennsylvania, highlighted by heavy battles with Indians and early Pennsylvania settlers, the Western Reserve was created in 1786.

The wilderness life of the Reserve further developed, and in some degree refined, many of the themes that were evident in Old Connecticut society. Puritanism, Congregationalism, and patriotism were woven into the personal lives of immigrants and their immediate descendants. They tried to establish a peaceful and lawful society which would provide each individual with an opportunity for development. Thrift and hard work were matters of morality; and moral principles were serious business.

> The savor of conscience and courage was in most of the measures which enlisted their sympathies. Seriously speaking, the colonists, like the older Puritans, were a serious people. They had "convictions," and with them convictions amounted almost to organic things. They performed functions in the moral life of these people and were forces in all their greater private and public achievements.[1]

If life in the Reserve was frugal, and certainly it was for most early settlers, the bounteous wilderness offered hope of improvement to those who were willing to work hard. Undoubtedly it was comforting to realize that God expected His children to labor righteously and to avoid the sins of sloth and ease; when existence required hard work, it was helpful to know that labor was a necessary ingredient of morality. The conviction that labor and morality were intertwined was commonly held by the settlers of the Re-

[1] Alfred Matthews, *Ohio and Her Western Reserve* (New York: D. Appleton & Co., 1902), p. 176.

serve and became one of the themes stressed in the educational and religious training of children.

The early decades of the Western Reserve were years of shared hardships and opportunities. The hard-won right of access, upon which was superimposed the rigor of earning a livelihood, created a basis for regional consciousness and regional pride. The introjection of the values and scruples of frontier life carried with it a sense of regional destiny. Here in the undeveloped wilderness were those who sought a new freedom, and while they were highly independent and resourceful people, they were joined by a bond of purpose and hope.[2]

The Ladd family first settled in the Reserve when George's grandfather, Jesse Ladd, made an exploratory visit to Painesville in the winter of 1811–1812. He left his large family in Connecticut to find a place where he might make a fresh start in new surroundings. Lured by the promise of abundant crops, he later returned to New England to move his family to the small community of Madison, a few miles east of Painesville.[3] Jesse Ladd established a stagecoach stop on the main road between Erie and Cleveland, and the Ladd Tavern is today an old farmhouse only slightly changed from the days when it served as a point of rest and refreshment for travelers into the Western Reserve.

> With a single exception, I have no records of the doings or fortunes of my Grandfather Ladd's family from the time he brought them out of the Mountains of Becket to the land that promised such abundant crops of Indian corn, until his death about fifteen years later. The farm which he cleared was situated directly upon the main highway between Erie and Cleveland and Toledo; during and after the War of 1812 this be-

[2] See F. L. Paxson, *History of the American Frontier, 1763–1893* (New York: Houghton Mifflin Co., 1924), pp. 95–122.

[3] See A. G. Riddle, *History of Geauga and Lake Counties, Ohio* (Philadelphia: Williams Brothers, 1878), pp. 232–233.

came a principal thoroughfare for officials, traders and settlers of the Western Reserve and further West. After regular stages were run, it was not infrequently necessary for the passengers to alight from the vehicle, procure rails from the nearest fence, and pry it out of the mud into which the wretched corduroy roads of the forests of the Maumee and other swamps had allowed it to sink up to its axles or beyond. Along this highway at intervals of about ten miles more or less, the homes of the principal settlers became houses of entertainment; and I have heard my father say how many of the boys in his day learned to their ruin the drink-habit through the pernicious privilege of sipping the whisky and sugar left in the glasses of the customers at the bars. With all the goodly things of the region, there were compensating evils in the form of prevalent fevers and an abundant supply of rattle-snakes.[4]

Ladd was born in Painesville, Ohio, on January 19, 1842. Through his father, Silas Trumbull Ladd, he was of Norman-French extraction and a descendant of Elder William Brewster. His mother, Elizabeth Williams, was of Welsh derivation and a descendant of Governor William Bradford. The family took pride in its relation to two notable figures of New England history; in fact, Ladd seemed to consider his heritage a built-in call to sturdiness and accomplishment.

From the time of Jesse Ladd's emigration to the Reserve the Ladds were known and respected as independent, resourceful citizens. A great deal was expected of them, and their views were given weight in community affairs. The birth of a son as the first child of the marriage of Silas and Elizabeth Ladd promised a continuation of the family line, and of course family lineage was a matter of great importance to the citizens of the region. What could better justify the optimism of the community than the natu-

[4] G. T. Ladd, "The Autobiography of a Teacher" (unpublished manuscript, written 1910–1912), pp. 18–19; hereafter referred to as "Autobiography."

ral inheritance of frontier virtues by the offspring of known and tested family stock? Silas Ladd was a prominent member of the community, but certainly it was a prominence untainted by financial success. From 1837 to 1842 he spent five busy and unprofitable years in the lumber business. In the year of his son's birth he and a colleague dissolved their partnership and Silas assumed the position of treasurer of Western Reserve College in Hudson. He was in Hudson when his son was born, and though there were occasional journeys from Hudson to Painesville, it was not until the autumn of 1844 that the family was reunited in Hudson.

The position of treasurer of struggling Western Reserve College was one of heavy responsibility and meager pay. In his autobiography Ladd commented that "very strict economy, an economy which was not far removed from pinching poverty, was necessary for all those connected with Western Reserve College between 1842 and 1850."[5] There was little money available to pay the faculty and staff of the college, but the resources of the school did permit payments in food and goods. The records maintained by Silas Ladd were a quaint but complicated accounting of transactions, and an entry for November 16, 1842, quoted by his son, reveals something of the financial basis of family life that was shared by the Ladds and other college employees.

> "F. D. Matthews owes sixteen dollars and ten cents on former term bills. He had a cow given or loaned to him by Drake Fellows of Tallmadge, with which he wishes to pay this debt. As Mr. Matthews is poor, it is thought best in consultation with Prof. Hickok, to take the cow and balance the account. I have exchanged the above cow with Prof. Long for his cow, and it is agreed that he shall be charged two cows as estimated by H. Baldwin. The Long cow was then butchered and what he did not retain was sold to others."[6]

[5] "Autobiography," p. 40.
[6] "Trials of an Old-fashioned College Treasurer," *Yale Review*, 5 (1916), 385.

George Trumbull Ladd

Though Silas Ladd was a hard-working treasurer, the college's financial condition was dismal, and the years in Hudson were colored by the constant fear that the college would have to disband. The seriousness of the situation is evident when one considers that in 1853, after Silas Ladd had returned with his family to Painesville, there was no graduating class, the faculty included the president, one professor, and one tutor, and there were only twenty-three students.[7]

After returning to Painesville in 1850, Silas Ladd continued his interest in business and education. He entered the grocery and provision business, and though he had more success with groceries than he had had with lumber, he was never a prosperous businessman. He remained helpful in the struggles to preserve Western Reserve College and also joined five other Painesville men in founding Lake Erie Female Seminary. Some years later he served as treasurer of the seminary.[8] A painting of Silas Ladd hangs in a prominent place on the Lake Erie College campus; one can well imagine from this portrait that the subject was an upright and serious man of character.

Silas and Elizabeth Ladd had four daughters.[9] Mary Elizabeth was born in the winter of 1844 while George and his mother were still living in Painesville. Two daughters were born in Hudson, Martha Brewster in 1846 and Laura Williams in 1849; a fourth daughter, Clara Baldwin, was added in 1851 after the family had returned to Painesville. Silas Ladd was heavily burdened by his business and social responsibilities, and there is reason to believe that George was strongly influenced by the constant feminine attention of his sisters and his mother. While he was not a priggish

[7] *One Hundred Years of Western Reserve* (Hudson, Ohio: The James W. Ellsworth Foundation, April, 1926), p. 33.

[8] He also served as treasurer of the Lake County Agricultural Society and was a "depositor" of the Lake County Bible Society. See Riddle, *History of Geauga and Lake Counties, Ohio*, pp. 43–44.

[9] Silas Ladd's first wife, Mary Evelina Hills, died in giving birth to Jesse Brewster in August, 1838. The infant son lived only a few weeks. Silas married Elizabeth Williams in 1841. (From a genealogical summary compiled for the writer by Mrs. Barbara Cooper of the Lake County Historical Society, Mentor, Ohio.)

boy, his early experiences were markedly quiet and internal with little of the hard physical diet which characterized the life of boys in the community. He developed a fondness for quiet games, and his interest in books and reading became the dominant passion of his life.

> It seems to me that I remember much less than ought to be the case, of the first eight years of my life which were spent in the College town of Hudson, Ohio. I have no recollection of learning to read, or of acquiring the elements of any subjects customarily taught to children of eight years and under, in those days. I remember playing on the floor with blocks, upon which my mother had pasted the letters of the alphabet; and I know that I read fairly readily in the New Testament at morning prayers, when I was scarcely more than three years of age. I know also that I did read books on geography, history, and Biblical stories—not only in the Bible itself but in form supposed to be especially adapted to children, such as "Peep of Day," "Line upon Line," "Here a Little and There a Little." But I have no recollection of having tasks set me or of getting lessons. The first large sum of money I ever earned was a gold dollar for committing to memory the Shorter Catechism. This dollar and another which I had somehow managed to scrape together, were spent in buying two books at an auction sale which seemed to me to afford an unexampled opportunity for desirable bargains in that line. The books were *The Works of Flavius Josephus* and *Plutarch's Lives*. These books, and *Pilgrim's Progress*—a copy of which someone had given to me— were an inexhaustible source of pleasure and information. I love them all today, and they are among the most cherished books in my library.[10]

The reflective traits that developed early in Ladd's life were due in part, perhaps, to the necessary restraints which were imposed by his physical condition. Frail and prone to exhaustion from unusual exertion, subject to dyspeptic attacks, and harassed by eye troubles

[10] "Autobiography," pp. 35–36.

when, as was usually the case, he had spent long hours reading and writing, Ladd began early in life to cultivate the rewards and pleasures of learning. He read widely and tried with alternating agony and delight to record his ideas in written form. But his scholarly pursuits were to be both a release and an affliction. From boyhood until the final years of his life he had difficulty in establishing a workable regime which would serve his powerful intellectual and literary needs and also preserve his frail health.

In order to strengthen his health, Ladd's parents were advised to take him on rides in the open country and to insist upon long periods of rest. An uncle, Dr. Andrews Merriman, who lived and practiced medicine near the Ladd home in Painesville, believed that George's indwelling and studious manner was injuring his health and prescribed a summer of outdoor life on a farm. The confusion, loneliness, and desperation which resulted from one such experiment is poignantly expressed in Ladd's own words:

> But when, toward the end of summer, the home-sickness became desperate, scarlet fever broke out in the neighborhood, and appetite, digestion and strength began to give way, even my uncle concluded that the farm was no place for me to recover health; my father relented and I came home. It was my first lesson in the important physiological truth, that maladies incurred by one species of over-work are not best treated by another species of over-work. The incident which stands out most prominently in all the experiences of this Summer is the reminiscence of how, in a fit of desperation brought on by exhaustion and nostalgia I raised the axe with which I was splitting kindlings, determined to split open my foot, as by accident, when the voice—"It would be wicked"—prevented me from carrying out the determination.[11]

The restraining voice that saved his foot from the axe was a powerful companion of childhood and a compelling force for pro-

[11] *Ibid.*, p. 53.

priety throughout life. Religion was a continuing theme in the lives of the citizens of the Western Reserve, and the Silas Ladd family was committed to religious principles and beliefs that were both personal and familial. Family religion, with daily prayer and Bible reading added to Sunday and midweek services, was an unquestioned accompaniment of life. As a boy, George experienced the doubts and strains of religious confusion and disbelief, but at the age of thirteen, when exhorted by the mother of a friend who had just died, he "went thoughtfully home, and leaning my head upon my arms on the table, by a deliberate choice settled the thing once for all between God and myself."[12] It is significant to note that the matter was settled "by deliberate choice," for Ladd maintained throughout his life that religion should be subjected to the rational and deliberative powers of the individual and that, to be meaningful, religious commitment must be an exercise of free will. Later in life he was severely criticized by some Congregational ministers for insisting upon the right to subject religion to rational and critical scholarship.

As an adult, Ladd believed that the character and lives of the men and women of the Western Reserve in the first half of the nineteenth century were made pure and strong principally through family religion. He felt that the latter part of the century produced an increase in moral debility within the Reserve, and this he attributed to the deterioration of family religion. The question of regional morality and the purity of life may be argued, but at least it is evident that family religion was a powerful conditioner of Ladd's own life. He expressed in his daily work the goals and constraints which were enunciated by the religion of his childhood, and carried into the extensive scholarship of his professional years the search for rational proof of the efficacy of the simple virtues of family religion.[13] In the effort, the extent of his success and the courage of his struggles are more impressive than are his failures.

[12] *Ibid.*, p. 58.
[13] An interesting parallel is to be observed in the early life of James A. Gar-

George Trumbull Ladd

Four elements of Ladd's character were vividly drawn from childhood in the Reserve. First, he developed a strong sense of the sacredness of truth. As a boy he may have experienced this most directly as a matter of not telling lies, but nevertheless the basis for a lifelong loyalty to truth was established. Second, his life was infused with a sense of moral restraint—a restraint that was expressed by the recognizable inner voice of conscience. A dialogue with his own conscience became a primary relationship in his behavior. Third, he developed a lasting belief in the virtue of hard work and began to experience a marked feeling of guilt associated with any sign of indolence in his daily life. There were to be few signs in the years ahead! Fourth, he developed an almost physical revulsion to profanity and rudeness. He became a person of self-conscious propriety, and though in later years he sometimes seemed rude and insensitive to others, especially when they encroached upon his time for serious work, it was a rudeness born of impatience rather than of boorishness.

Unstable in physical health, mentally curious and discerning, driven to his own devices as the only male child in a family circle of girls and women, and imbued with the power of a Puritan morality daily reinforced through family prayer and Bible study, Ladd became a serious adult while yet a child. He felt that it was naughty to have too much fun, or, to put it in a more positive way, he believed that the joys and satisfactions of hard work and serious commitment were superior to those of humor and amusement.

Ladd's boyhood was quiet and reflective, but it was not unhappy. He loved and respected his parents and his sisters; although Silas and Elizabeth Ladd were restrained and undemonstrative, George

---

field. While Garfield was born in the Reserve a decade before Ladd, many of the same social and religious influences were brought to bear upon his formative years. Both men had a lifelong interest in religion and tried to apply and to extend the faith that was developed during boyhood and adolescence in the Reserve. Garfield was a member of the Disciples of Christ. See W. W. Wasson, *James A. Garfield: His Religion and Education* (Nashville: Tennessee Book Co., 1952), chaps. 1 and 2.

considered himself a loved and fully accepted member of the family. At ease concerning his own role in the life of the family, and stimulated by the broad interests of his father and a close association with college faculty and students, he was free to develop thoughtful and studious habits early in life. By the age of eight, when he began more intensive studies with the aid of private tutors, George was irretrievably lost in a world of books and ideas.

Chapter · 3 ·

The Controlling Passion

For the Silas Ladd family, the move from Hudson to Painesville in 1850 was an expression of both despair and optimism. After eight years of struggle and poverty, highlighted by strong disagreement over policy with the faculty and staff of Western Reserve College, the "old-fashioned college treasurer" reached the conclusion that his future in Hudson was entirely too bleak for the head of a growing family. While the future of the college was in doubt, the future of the Reserve was not. With the itch and optimism of the businessman in a developing land, Silas Ladd prayed for divine guidance and entered the grocery business in Painesville. The move was a significant change for the entire family; but for George it was a bright beginning. With the move to Painesville came a more rigorous formal schooling and, through private tutoring and disciplined study, the intensification of what was to become the controlling passion of his life.

Silas and Elizabeth Ladd returned to Painesville with hope and a joyous feeling of homecoming. The move was to be a permanent one and they began immediately to search for a home that would be appropriate for a prominent but rather poor family of the Reserve.

In 1851 Silas purchased an unfinished two-story brick house on South State Street, not far from the center of town. When completed, the large, well-constructed house became a special delight to George. Most of his Painesville experiences were centered upon the quiet and studious life that unfolded within the ivy-covered walls. The house continued to be owned by the Ladd family for fifty years and is today known locally as "Ivy House," one of the loveliest in the town.

George ranged widely from the State Street house, walking quietly around the town in a thoughtful and retiring manner. The family continued to encourage open-air activity as a way of combating his tendency toward illness. While he did play with other boys his own age, explore the forests and rivers of the area, build tree houses, and get properly dirty, there was little doubt that his chief interest was intellectual and that he preferred solitude to the distracting and demanding company of others. By the time he entered the village high school at the age of twelve, study had become so interesting to him that he had lost the distinction between study and reading for pleasure. He must have seemed a bit unusual to his more robust and active friends. There is no evidence that he was an unfriendly or overbearing boy, but the fervor of his intellectual interests and his always unsatisfied hunger for books and instruction probably set him apart from most of his peers.

Silas Ladd did not have a large library, and unfortunately for the young scholar Painesville was without a public library. Books were borrowed wherever they could be found, and George continued to build and cherish the personal library he had started in Hudson.

> We read most of Scott and Dickens; and Halliwell's *Complete Works of Shakespere, Revised from the Original Editions, with Historical and Analytical Introductions to Each Play,* was taken as it came out in serial numbers. *Uncle Tom's Cabin,* as it ap-

peared in serial form, in *The National Era*, was also eagerly devoured; it served to perpetuate and increase my hatred of slavery as derived from the example and precepts of my father. Other works of fiction which I remember reading during this period are *The Lamp Lighter*, *The Wide Wide World*, and that moving story of the sufferings of "the women of Israel" at the hands of the Spanish inquisition, as told by Grace Aguilar, the daughter of a Jewish merchant in London, and entitled *The Vale of Cedars*. Everything available and permissible in the line of books for reading was eagerly sought and faithfully improved. Beside these legitimate indulgences, I have to confess a few which cannot be so classed. For I can still recall the mingling of pleasurable excitement with pains of conscience, as I lay on the sunny roof of the stable, going through the histories of those celebrated and gallant English highwaymen, Dick Turpin and Sixteen-Strong Jack. A fair but not complete substitute for these tales of adventure were *Robinson Crusoe* and *Settlers in Canada*; and these were not tabu. For the Rollo and Jonas Stories I never had much appetite.[1]

While still a young boy, Ladd seemed to have understood that he would one day go to college. His father's position at Western Reserve College, association with college students and staff, and the strong interest in education that was so characteristic of the more cultured families of the Reserve and that was forcefully represented in Silas Ladd's attitude toward life—all of these were encouraging influences on the young bookworm. An even more compelling consideration, however, was Ladd's own devotion to study. College attendance was an exciting prospect, but the absence of preparatory schools or academies was a difficult obstacle to surmount. It is to Silas Ladd's credit that he recognized and encouraged the abilities and interests of his son and arranged college preparatory studies under the guidance of private tutors.

[1] "Autobiography," p. 48.

In the 1850's college preparation required mastery of grammar, the study of history, and competence in mathematics; but the most important index of adequate preparation was the student's background in language and classical studies. Often the only test of a student's readiness for matriculation was a test of his knowledge of Latin and Greek. By the time Ladd was eleven years of age, he was self-consciously preparing for college entrance with the aid of a private tutor in these two subjects.

The Reverend Mr. Brayton, a retired Episcopal clergyman who ran a boarding school for boys in Painesville, certainly was no scholar in classical studies, but he had an amateur's interest in Latin and Greek and, fortunately for George, a deep feeling for the aesthetics of classical literature. As a tutor he provided guidance in the rudiments of Latin and Greek and a sympathetic interest in the progress of his young charge. There was no problem, of course, in gaining the interest and commitment of his pupil, for George brought to the relationship his characteristic seriousness and sense of purpose. In responding to his tutor's interest he began to love these two languages and the literature which they conveyed. He was fond of reciting passages, experimenting with the rhythm and tone required for the strongest possible poetical effect. Given the intelligence and enthusiasm of his pupil, the Reverend Mr. Brayton taught better than he knew.

Ladd's devotion to classical studies became the single passion of his adolescent years, but it was a devotion to the aesthetics, history, and literature of the languages with little interest in the rules and prescriptions of grammar study. As an adult he argued that a knowledge of the structure and use of language was best obtained through the study of classical languages and that he was fortunate to have been relieved, through such study, of "the most irksome and profitless of all the tasks put upon youthful minds; I refer to the study of English grammar."[2] Latin and Greek were never

[2] *Ibid.*, p. 49.

George Trumbull Ladd

"dead" languages to Ladd; he saw in them poetry and life, as well as the fundamentals of proper communication.

Ladd's precocious interest in scholarship is revealed in the only document that has been preserved from this period of his boyhood, an optimistic little essay entitled "The Present and the Past." The opening and closing paragraphs capture the sense of progress that was so indelibly present in the minds of citizens of the Western Reserve.

> The present and the past—a little reflection will I doubt not convince the most skeptical that the present is an age of Progress. Compare the enlightened state of the world at this period with the darkened and superstitious ages that are past. Everything has changed. Science that has lain buried in oblivion is roused to action and man has discovered that he was made for a nobler and better purpose than the gratification of his will. He has not only thought, but he has acted, and improvement has marked his efforts. In the place of the rude bark-canoe of the savage, the majestic steamer, with its precious burden, ploughs its way, upon the face of the deep waters. The miserable hut of the Indian has passed away, and the habitation of the white man marks the place where it then stood. Ponderous, shapeless vehicles creeping at snail's pace have given place to the swift movement of the rail-road car, and news flies as on the wings of the wind. Instead of inkhorn and musty parchment, the steam printing press supplies its millions with books.

> . . . .

> But should men falter, and draw back, because much has been accomplished; nations are still in heathen darkness, and thousands are dying daily, without the knowledge, of the true God. Science has not found its way into every corner of this vast globe, and millions there are, who never saw the precious Bible. The sun of Science does not leap at once into its Meridian: No, it steals upon men gradually; it has been brought,

where it now is, progressively, line upon line, precept upon precept as the human mind could receive it. Rapid indeed has been America's progress. What was she? nothing. What is she? a great nation. Aye sons of freedom, cherish forever your liberty, let it be next to your God, and as for thee, America, may thy motto ever be, press onward, and upward.[3]

The high-school years provided a steady diet of formal classes and private tutoring. Ladd enjoyed his classwork and recitations, but the real excitement of his life was provided by study under the guidance of his tutors. He began to read more widely with each passing year, and his confidence in his own intellectual abilities began to rise. The breadth of his reading is revealed in a carefully wrought 1,600-word epic poem entitled "Earth's Battle Fields."[4] The poem treats in a rather elevated manner the wars and tragedies of human history from biblical times to the American Revolution, and it is evident that Ladd was deeply impressed by man's valor in the face of threats to his ideals. He glorified the struggle of righteous man against worldly evils. The poem reveals a sensitive eye for history.

By the age of sixteen Ladd felt ready to qualify for college admission, but recurring illness, which was characterized as "nervous dyspepsia," and to which were added severe eyestrain and a general physical weakness, unfortunately made it necessary to defer entrance. Medical consultations once more prescribed open air, exercise, and as small a dose of reading and study as was necessary to maintain his morale in the face of a bitter disappointment. The two years of delay were not entirely lost. Buggy rides in the open country and light work in his father's grocery store (with considerable unofficial reading in the back room) left Ladd with two certainties—first, that the glory of God is most impressively found in

[3] Original document in the possession of Mrs. William Hunting of Cincinnati, Ohio.
[4] *Ibid.*

nature when uncontaminated by man and, second, that he was not temperamentally suited to enter the grocery business.

In the summer of 1860, a few months after his eighteenth birthday, Ladd journeyed to Hudson to take private examinations for entrance to Western Reserve College.

> After two years of somewhat fretful delay, a few months following my eighteenth birthday and in the summer of 1860, I was thought fit to apply for admission to Western Reserve College. In order to save expense and because I had no fear of not meeting all the conditions in respect of scholarship, permission was asked and obtained to take a private examination, after the regular entrance examination had been held. On arriving in Hudson I went first to the house of Professor Nathan P. Seymour to be examined in the classical languages, and was shown up to his study. I was questioned rather minutely on the Latin and Greek grammars, and made to read passages from all the books required for entrance. I seemed to acquit myself fairly to the satisfaction of myself and my examiner. When this testing was finished the Professor took the Virgil from my hand and walking back and forth in the study, gave me a striking example of how classical poetry, *as poetry*, might be translated. The Latin ran: *Et tuba commissos medio canit aggere ludos* (Aen., V, 113). As with sonorous voice my teacher, by example, declaimed "Mid rampart now the trumpet sounds a note of sports begun," I opened my eyes to the aesthetical side, the aspect of beauty, of the literature of ancient Greece and Rome. They have never since been closed to the fair and comforting vision of what I glimpsed at that time.[5]

". . . a note of sports begun!" As if to keynote his college years, Professor Seymour spoke to Ladd of the poetry of classical studies. The self-prepared scholar was examined, admitted, and once more challenged on familiar ground to open his eyes and mind to the

[5] "Autobiography," p. 39.

beauty and glory that are found in literature when it speaks of life. After six long years of study and delay, the interests first aroused by the Reverend Mr. Brayton in his quiet study in Painesville were now to be given an opportunity for expression in the formal discipline of college scholarship. Ladd was excited and eager to begin his studies, though he realized that undoubtedly he would work himself too hard and once more suffer from his various ailments.

In the fall of 1860, Ladd moved into the home of family friends, Mr. and Mrs. Harvey Baldwin of Hudson, and began immediately a regime of study which was so intense that it aroused his dyspepsia and made continuation uncertain. In addition to thorough preparation of assignments for the courses in which he was enrolled, he filled every spare hour with reading and writing on subjects that were self-assigned. He studied Latin, Greek, mathematics, and philosophy, but he also read widely in history and religion, soon discovering a special excitement in the effort to relate these two areas in a systematic theoretical pattern. He was determined to test the assumptions of every subject he studied and to accept nothing without critical examination. He read the works of Reid, Kant, Sir William Hamilton, and John Stuart Mill, and he explored the philosophical foundations of religion, an interest that was destined to continue throughout his life.

While the study of Greek and Latin filled most of his spare hours, when "the unlimited and misty vistas of philosophical speculation began to open before me, the time was divided pretty equally between the ancient classics and philosophy." The "unlimited and misty vistas" apparently were unveiled initially by reading Thompson's *Outlines of the Laws of Thought*, Hamilton's *Lectures on Metaphysics*, Butler's *Analogy*, and Locke's *Essay Concerning Human Understanding*.

> I found myself, as it were, in my native element. I found too, that these are the studies which furnish the keys without the

use of which no human mind can unlock the door to any form
of science or species of literature far enough to get even a
glimpse of its highest values and deepest meaning.[6]

In the decades ahead, Ladd's insistence that philosophy provided
the keys to all other forms of human inquiry was to become a familiar, and to some a tiresome, refrain.

The excitement of personal growth and discovery at Western
Reserve was tempered by persistent health problems and by the
uncertainties of the Civil War period. The campus community was
deeply affected by the daily war bulletins, and classes were dis-
rupted and demoralized. Ladd drilled in a company of "Western
Reserve Cadets" and volunteered for duty only to suffer "inex-
pressible mortification and grief" when he was rejected because of
his physical condition. His service was limited to two days when, in
September, 1862, he was a member of an informal band of "Squir-
rel Hunters" which had been hurriedly assembled for the protec-
tion of Cincinnati. The group got as far as Columbus before it was
recalled. Ladd was enormously proud of a citation which he received after his brief service.

> Cincinnati was menaced by the enemies of our Union. *David
> Tod*, Governor of Ohio, called on the Minute Men of the State
> and the Squirrel Hunters came by the thousands to the rescue.
> You, George T. Ladd, were one of them and this is your *Hon-
> orable Discharge*.
> September 1862.
> approved by
> *David Tod*
> Governor[7]

The unstable financial position of Western Reserve College was
made even more precarious during the Civil War as students and

[6] *Ibid.*, p. 43.
[7] Document in possession of Dr. Louis Ladd, Jr., of Cleveland Heights, Ohio.

faculty withdrew for service. It was extremely difficult to maintain the variety of course offerings needed for a liberal education. The curriculum was reasonably well suited to the study of classical languages, mathematics, and philosophy, but it offered very little instruction in modern languages and in the natural and biological sciences.[8] With the aid of special tutors, Ladd began the study of French and German. While his knowledge of French was always limited, in time he was able to develop a mastery of German. In later years he published a six-volume English translation of the works of Hermann Lotze.

The curriculum deficiency in the natural and biological sciences was not easily remedied by private study. Though it is doubtful that Ladd was temperamentally suited to a career in science, it is interesting to speculate what might have been the effect upon his career of scientific training during his college years. He always considered the absence of an early training in science a major handicap in his later professional life. His capacity for systematic study in science was amply demonstrated when, twenty years later, he began to organize materials for his enormous *Elements of Physiological Psychology*. With virtually no background in physics and physiology, he digested the evidence available in the German, French, and English literature on the subject and, in a period of six years, produced his highly regarded book. Though never devoted to laboratory work, he did have an impressive talent for scholarship in scientific areas, as well as in philosophy and classical studies. A good background in science during his college years might have helped him avoid some of the blind spots that were to characterize his work in scientific psychology.

[8] In 1855 the college offered a "Scientific Course" leading to the Bachelor of Science degree, but the effort failed because of the lack of faculty competence in necessary scientific areas. See F. C. Waite, *Western Reserve University—the Hudson Era* (Cleveland: Western Reserve University Press, 1943), pp. 342–344. Materials describing "The Course of Study" for this period are available in the Office of the University Archivist, Case Western Reserve University. See *Catalogue of Western Reserve College, 1863–1864*.

George Trumbull Ladd

The classical education that Ladd received at Western Reserve suited his abilities and interests and provided at a crucial point in his life the inspiration to dig more deeply into language and philosophy.[9] It broadened his knowledge and taught him some of the problems of scholarly research. For years he had been trying to write essays on topics that interested him, but it was in college that he first had the advantage of constructive criticism. Book in hand he had entered college and book in hand he would leave it; but the college years had added an instrument for expression of his ideas. With the same immoderation that characterized his reading and study habits, Ladd became addicted to the use of pen and paper.

Writing became as necessary to his personal fulfillment as reading and study had been for a dozen years. He desperately wanted to grow in understanding, and he wanted with an equal urgency to order his thoughts so that he could express them in some lasting form. For one who was rather quiet and withdrawn, there was a natural challenge in serious writing; better the solitary battle with pen and paper than the unpredictable social adventures of the spoken word.

As Ladd's devotion to writing increased with the passing of each college year, his professors must have followed his development with some mixture of feeling. He wrote many more papers than were required by class assignments and faithfully submitted them to his professors for comment. When the response was friendly and constructive he moved on with excitement to other topics, but when the response was delayed or unduly critical he would worry and sulk until once more overcome with the need to begin a statement of his ideas. His papers were long, dry, detailed, and painfully faithful to the light as he saw it. The writing which has been

[9] A record of Ladd's four-year program of studies is available in the Office of the University Archivist, Case Western Reserve University. While the college graded on a scale of eight during this period, in his senior year he received a grade of nine in metaphysics! Perhaps it was an early sign of his peculiar devotion to this subject.

preserved from this period is remarkably similar in style to the work of his more mature years. Ladd's writings plod before the reader, devoid of the thrust and sparkle that grace the work of William James. The aesthetics of ideas, a matter close to his heart as a classicist, seems peculiarly absent from his literary style. Whether the critical evaluation of his college essays contained any advice concerning graceful literary style and the virtues of a reasonable brevity we cannot know; but if the advice was offered it was never heeded.

The crisp, faded documents of one hundred years ago reveal a steady hand and an earnest style. The young scholar was not afraid to tackle difficult topics. He wrote papers on "The Gnostic Philosophy," "The Advantage of a Collegiate Education," "Truth as an End," and "The Constitution of Human Nature as a Guide in Morals."[10] Of collegiate education, Ladd commented that "going to college will not make a man of anyone not fully determined to be a man, and it cannot unmake one who possesses that determination. . . . There is something in the straight forward regular routine of discipline which cannot fail to have its good effect." The view that there were intellectual and moral benefits to be derived from disciplined study was consistent with the prevailing philosophy of education, and this theme remained at the center of Ladd's own educational philosophy throughout his life. Forty years later he would argue for this viewpoint in a controversy over the proper design of a college curriculum, moving dangerously close to the notion that education is good if it hurts.

"The Constitution of Human Nature as a Guide in Morals," written in his senior year, provides an early foretaste of the theme that was to characterize his later professional mission. He began by contrasting history, with its warmth and spirituality, and astronomy, representing an impersonal and material reality. Between the

[10] Original documents in the possession of Mrs. William Hunting of Cincinnati, Ohio.

spiritual and material orders of reality, the choice was clear: man must look to his own constitution as a spiritual being if he is to find a guide to moral behavior. But how may one proceed to study the basis for morality? Two methods are possible. First, one may decide what God's plan *must* be and then decide how best to serve it. Ladd rejected this plan in favor of a second approach. "I choose the humbler method, to see, whether amidst all that is in me, there is any principle, whose nature marks it as the law of my nature. It is our task then to search amid the ruins of the soul's temple to find out its structure, and from fragments discover the style of its architecture." The rejection of the first method and the adoption of the second represented a surprisingly independent and analytical approach to the problem. A willingness to search for principles and laws of nature as a basis for belief and action was as close as he could have come to advocating a psychological investigation of human problems. For the young son of a devout Congregational family of the Reserve it was no small matter to reject the first method in favor of a search for principles "amid the ruins of the soul's temple."

Professor Nathan Perkins Seymour was especially helpful to Ladd during the college years of intense study and experimentation. Seymour was professor of Greek and Latin languages from 1840 to 1870 and emeritus professor from 1870 to 1891. A kindly but demanding teacher, he praised and encouraged Ladd; but his encouragement always contained a challenge to carry the inquiry one step beyond the paper which had been submitted. He quietly pressed for still more perspective. He understood the desperate seriousness of Ladd's interest in scholarship and took time to share with him the trials and delights of an intellectual life. Seymour was one of a small company of men who launched Ladd's career by providing him with a personal response at a time when he needed encouragement. Many years later Ladd became a close friend of Seymour's son, Professor Thomas Seymour of Yale University, and it was in the son's home that he sat by the bedside of his old teacher during the final hours of his life. Still later, he had a friendly relationship with Thomas Seymour's son, Charles, who was to become president of Yale, thus continuing an intimate friendship with the Seymour family across three generations.

Convinced that he had a talent for scholarship, and impatient to begin advanced study, Ladd hurried through his final year of college eagerly anticipating three years of seminary. The decision to enter Andover Theological Seminary was a natural consequence of a strict Congregational upbringing, a deeply religious academic experience under the influence of Christian scholars, and a strong personal bent toward classical languages and philosophy. Perhaps even these powerful conditions would have been insufficient to direct him into ministerial training, however, had it not been for one further consideration—namely, Ladd's uncompromising belief that his scholarship must be an influence for good in society. It was Professor Nathan Seymour who patiently guided Ladd toward theological study, principally through inculcating in him a belief that scholarship was a moral exercise and that man's moral life was in dire need of that illumination which could only come from competent Christian scholarship. Ladd was enthusiastic about his future as a theological scholar, but the personal struggles which would be required for effective public speaking in the ministry, and the precise mission which he was to undertake as a basis for all his scholarship in the years ahead, were unknown to him when he finished college.

The final year at Western Reserve was not a happy one. Ladd was deeply distressed by the death of his mother and was plagued by physical weakness and a number of other familiar troubles. Excited by the prospect of entering seminary, he was graduated from college in July, 1864, only to find that his nagging complaints would make further study impossible.[11] Once again the ea-

[11] Ladd delivered a commencement speech and valedictory, choosing as his topic

gerness to push ahead with his education was blunted by illness, and the painful two-year delay which had preceded college was to be re-enacted before the family physician would permit him to enter seminary.

Dutifully, but without heart, Ladd went to work in his father's business. For two years his life was a mixture of Greek and groceries:

> The arrangement of help in the store was such that I had to take my meals alone. My regular companion was a book lying beside the plate, to which quite as much time and attention were customarily given as to the food. Enough Greek learning was remembered to make anything more than an occasional use of the dictionary unnecessary. In this way all of Herodotus and all of Thucydides were read twice; and besides, Xenophon's *Historia Graeca*, and, since I was specializing in history, the twelve volumes of Grote. These excesses—connected with, but not exactly of, the gastronomic order—were certainly foolish, not to say fool-hardy. I remember little of what I then learned, whether of Greek language or Greek history; but I confirmed the habit of pursuing an object steadily in the face of both physical and mental obstacles and difficulties.[12]

In August, 1866, Ladd left Painesville to begin his long-delayed seminary studies in Andover, Massachusetts. Traveling by way of New York City, where he was most impressed by Central Park and a three-hour concert by Dodworth's mighty band of eighty pieces, he arrived in Andover and began immediately to introduce himself to members of the faculty. He soon met Professor J. Henry

---

"Inner and Outer Reform Contrasted." He discussed the relation between personal and social conflict and advocated reform in both areas as a necessary element of progress. A basic point in his speech was psychological in nature: "Who is so wanting in shrewdness as not to have observed that no assumption of scholarlike talk and ways can serve the intellectual man, if symmetry of mind be wanting?" Original document in the possession of Mrs. William Hunting of Cincinnati, Ohio.

[12] "Autobiography," pp. 55–56.

Thayer, who was destined to become the Reverend Mr. Brayton and Professor Seymour of his years at Andover. Thus, from the beginning of his strenuous seminary life, he was fortunate to have the understanding of a teacher who appreciated his intense, groping ways. At each stage of his life Ladd needed a close personal relationship with someone he could respect; Thayer's role in making his seminary years such a scholarly success cannot be overestimated.

What had been a serious commitment to studies at Western Reserve became an almost desperate assault upon the curriculum at Andover. Ladd entered his professional training with an appetite sharpened by two years of annoying delay. He was determined to waste no time in his progress toward the ministry, even if it meant a sacrifice of the few non-academic pleasures which he permitted himself. He and his fellow seminarians, many of whom had been sobered by service in the Civil War, were an earnest lot, and Ladd would yield to none of them in the discipline and singlemindedness of his efforts. He began his last three years of formal study as a deliberate and self-conscious preparation for the "learned ministry." Later years would reveal that Andover made him far more learned than ministerial.

The seminary training of Congregational ministers in the middle of the nineteenth century involved a prescribed curriculum of classical studies with emphasis upon Latin, Greek, Hebraic, and German sources. The Andover curriculum was designed to produce a "learned ministry" which could educate and enlighten congregations on theological issues, as well as inspire individuals to lead moral lives. Church doctrine was clear on most major issues, and students were expected to understand both the accepted doctrine and its theological and biblical proof. Though united in basic educational purpose, the Andover faculty was not at all of one mind concerning the finer points of theology; and, of course, the finer points often were the ones most zealously debated in classes. A class with Professor Edwards A. Park was a network of arguments in support of the Edwardian theory of the will. Professor Egbert C. Smyth taught ecclesiastical history from a doctrinal position traceable to the views of the German Schleiermacher. From Professor Charles M. Mead the students learned Hebrew and Old Testament exegesis. And, of course, there was Professor J. Henry Thayer:

> Of all my teachers in Andover Theological Seminary the one to whom I owe most, as expressed in our relations as teacher and pupil, and also by a warm friendship lasting his entire life, was Professor J. Henry Thayer. An ardent temperament, a high sense of honor which excluded all pretence of knowledge and every species of hypocrisy, warm feelings of humanity which had been quickened by several years of service as a pastor and a chaplain in the army, unbounded patience and enthusiasm in study, controlled by a conscientious regard for every kind of verity, whether in the large matters or appertaining of minute details—all these characteristics combined in a rare degree to make Professor Thayer an admirable type of Christian gentleman and scholar. Withal, he was perhaps not popular with the entire class; but he was beloved and admired by those who knew him best.[13]

Throughout his life Ladd considered Thayer to be a highly personal model of the Christian gentleman and scholar, and there is reason to believe that his own characteristics and ambitions were brought into focus around the figure of his seminary teacher. Thayer was a living example of what Ladd thought he wanted to be; it was Thayer's intellectual and professional influence that most directly set the course of Ladd's career. Thayer's patient ways, Ladd's zeal for scholarship, and the tendency of the faculty to settle issues by an "argument from Scripture" combined to launch the young seminarian upon a course of research that was to require a major portion of his energy for fifteen years.

[13] *Ibid.*, p. 71.

In characteristic fashion Ladd studied subjects rather than lessons. He prepared his assignments, of course, but he did so as a part of a larger self-imposed assignment to get at the heart of an entire subject. His long preparation in classical languages began to pay dividends, for he found that he had direct access to source materials and did not need to depend upon the word of his professors. In the study of systematic theology under Professor Park, he was fascinated by the "arguments from Scripture" that Park used to defend his own position. Ladd checked the biblical sources that Park cited and discovered that they often were of doubtful relevancy, at least in their function as a "proof" of Park's point of view. He began to feel that the Bible was often misused, through either personal bias or plain carelessness, and that this rich and suggestive human document deserved an exhaustive and critical scholarship.

Undoubtedly he was a rather difficult student for any professor, for his earnestness and contentiousness made it impossible for him to let issues slide by in class. Thayer was a comfort to him and encouraged him to continue on an independent course of research. He wrote papers on biblical and historical subjects and showed them to Thayer for criticism. One such piece of research involved the problem of the Synoptic Gospels. Ladd was enthusiastic about the so-called modern or higher criticism of biblical literature that was becoming more prevalent in theological circles, and he undertook a scholarly analysis of the authenticity of claims concerning the origins of the Gospels. He was enormously proud of the fact that these studies were accepted for publication in the *Bibliotheca Sacra*, appearing anonymously in the numbers for January and April, 1869. The research and writing which he started at this time grew in scope through the next decade and ultimately were expressed in his two-volume *The Doctrine of Sacred Scripture*, published in 1883.

Though Ladd was never at ease socially, he did participate in some extracurricular activities. He played croquet, went to the seminary bowling alley, took part in two spiritualistic experiments, attended teas in nearby homes, and "stood by" at a number of coeducational parties. There were long hikes in the surrounding countryside, but apparently most of these were lonely, brooding efforts. His autobiography refers to a number of exciting events that he attended during his three years in Andover—a lecture by Charles Dickens in Boston, a public reception for General Sheridan in Lowell, and the famous Peace Jubilee in Boston in June, 1869. He knew that recreation was important, especially for one with chronic afflictions brought on by overwork, but his obsessive traits made diversions more a trial than a relief.

Fortunately, the overwork was tempered by one diversion that was destined to become permanent therapy. In 1868 Ladd attended a Western Reserve College commencement and, through a friend's efforts on his behalf at an otherwise forgettable game of alumni croquet, met Cornelia Ann Tallman of Bellaire, Ohio. After only two further visits, and several dozen letters between Andover and Ohio, they made definite plans for marriage following his graduation from seminary.

Ladd's health broke in February of his second year at Andover when chronic digestive and visual troubles were complicated by a severe cold. An acute inflammation of the eyes made it impossible for him to continue. Returning to Painesville, he spent three months reading philosophy and studying the class notes sent to him by Andover friends. Early in May he was able to go back to Andover and began immediately to plan a summer at sea on a Cape Ann mackerel schooner. With a seminary friend, Cyrus Richardson, he proceeded to East Gloucester in July and set sail for Nova Scotia. For six weeks Ladd and his companion struggled to match the efforts of hardened seamen on a fishing boat. By prior arrangement they were discharged at an appropriate point and made their way to Prince Edward Island. There followed a 160-mile walk from Point North to Charlottetown with memorable visits in the homes of hospitable island fishermen and farmers.

The summer of sea air and exercise did not greatly improve Ladd's health; indeed, his complaints became even more serious. His autobiography quotes a letter to his father, written from East Gloucester, in which he speaks of "nervous trouble accompanied with many painful sensations in the head; such as great pressure at the back part of the brain and through the temples; with disturbance of the circulation."[14] He sent a detailed description of his condition to the family physician in Painesville. Though he began his studies with a mixture of hope and discouragement, he could not continue beyond Christmas. Once more he returned home for recuperation, and once more he read philosophy and followed class notes forwarded by friends.

The seriousness of Ladd's illness raised doubts about his ability to begin the duties of a full-time ministry. His physician believed that a regular out-of-door life away from books would be necessary in order to maintain his health. Silas Ladd helped him explore various employment possibilities, including a foreign consulship, but nothing came of these efforts. By the summer of 1869 he was ready to return to Andover for a final term. He went with the discouraging prospect of finishing seminary in a state of mind and body which would frustrate his plan for entering the ministry. To Ladd's surprise his last term was a pleasant and memorable one. He was able to follow his usual regime of studies, and with little evident damage he added the responsibility of preaching in a number of churches which had vacant pulpits. He was considered for pastorates in Portland, Maine, and in Lawrence and Plymouth, Massachusetts, but no offer was made. His poor health record and nervous and strained habits of speech must have made him seem a rather risky candidate. He completed his seminary studies with no immediate job prospect and with little confidence in his ability to withstand the demands of regular employment. There was no way of knowing then that he was about to enter upon a fifty-year period of

[14] *Ibid.*, p. 90.

intense professional and scholarly work and that, while he would be troubled by physical complaints all his life, there would be fewer interruptions because of poor health in the time ahead.

The years at Andover confirmed in Ladd the belief that he would be a scholar. They sharpened his interest in biblical and philosophical problems and started him on a program of research that would successfully launch his career. He was caught up in the trend toward modern critical scholarship and was deeply influenced by the general move toward a more naturalistic interpretation of human problems. While ten years passed before he began the study of psychology, his view of man was becoming more liberal. It is to his credit that he recognized the developing struggle between the old and the new learning. In spite of a classical education largely devoid of instruction in science, and a traditional theological training, Ladd was able to see the coming intensification of a battle between the classical and the modern, naturalistic views of man. He had read Darwin and he was astute enough to know that much of the old learning would have to give ground to new and robust principles. He was determined to play a part in the great confrontation yet to come.

> It was during the Andover years . . . that my peculiar and very own life-plans took shape and became the object of intelligent and deliberate choice. With a clearness which, as it still (1910) seems to me, was quite unusual among the theologies of more than forty years ago, I saw that my generation was to be one of rapid and great changes in every form of knowledge and of thought; it was to be a *transition age*. This transition could not fail to reach and profoundly disturb and greatly modify every form of biblical learning and every statement of doctrine in the theological creeds. I resolved to give my life— whether by leadership in the pulpit and by my ministrations in the pastoral office, or if called to some other form of essentially the same service—to the making of this transition in a way to

secure the old truth, while adding to it the new truth, both as respects substance and as respects form. Both for the life of the Christian Church, and for its influence in control of the thought and life of the public, it seemed to me that the thing, then most important, was that new and truer views of what the Bible is, and of how it should be used should prevail. I wished to be a mediator in this, and other respects. It was in accordance with the life-plan thus formed that I continued the studies which were published fifteen years later in my "Doctrine of Sacred Scripture."[15]

By assuming the role of mediator in an age of transition, Ladd condemned himself to a life of perpetual conflict. Aligned by his education and temperament with classical scholarship, he might have lived comfortably and productively within it had he not been so receptive to some of the issues and methodologies of the newer learning. He began by taking issue with existing biblical scholarship and was criticized for his liberal and unorthodox views. Later, when he moved into the scientific arena, particularly through his efforts in psychology, his classical assumptions prevented an enthusiastic acceptance of many of the major tenets of science; he was forced to attempt a reconciliation between matters that were basically uncongenial. He would always be a metaphysician and he would never quite understand or forgive science for its lack of interest in metaphysical questions.

[15] *Ibid.*, pp. 98–99.

Chapter · 4 ·

Edinburg and Milwaukee

Through a violent blizzard, Ladd and his bride of three hours drove a team of horses and a sleigh into the rural community of Edinburg, Ohio, on the evening of December 8, 1869. With an annual salary of seven hundred dollars, the free use of a small parsonage and eight acres of land, a coop of chickens and a bag of corn, and a woodshed full of fresh beef, the newly married, newly ordained Congregational minister was at last ready to begin his professional career.[1] The violent storm that ushered Ladd into Edinburg was an appropriate symbol of the future. After two years he would leave the town with impatience and disappointment, and for decades still to come he would know the loneliness and frustration of a career that mixed defeat and sorrow with achievement. But Edinburg was a beginning, and for Ladd the joy of overcoming illness and delay must have made his entrance into town a triumphant ride.

The decision to become a country parson had been made in near desperation. Sick and dispirited, Ladd had returned to Painesville

[1] See *Book of Records*, Edinburg United Church, November 1, 1869; also, "Autobiography," p. 103.

with little hope of entering upon his life's work. Week after wretched week passed with no improvement in his condition. Finally, while riding the train into Cleveland to see his physician, he resolved to begin his work no matter what the hazards might be. After a long consultation the physician agreed to permit a single year of experiment, provided a quiet pastorate could be found which required only a single sermon each week and allowed a great deal of leisure and open-air activity. Ladd was recommended for the Edinburg position by two former Andover classmates who had preached in the community. Following two trial sermons and some hesitation by the trustees, the quiet pastorate so reluctantly prescribed by the physician was made available.

The village of Edinburg was thriving in a quiet, rural way. At the center of the community were a store, a blacksmith shop, a small cluster of houses, and three churches. The Congregational Church was the largest and most influential, with a membership of approximately one hundred fifty.[2] The most prominent people in the community were farmers of New England descent, sober, honest, uncultured citizens who shared a strong interest in the moral welfare and religious training of their families. In sobriety, honesty, and strength of belief in moral and religious principles Ladd was congenially suited to his parishioners; substance of belief was another matter, however, and the pastorate which began so quietly was destined to become, in a period of two years, a noisy impossibility.

Once established in Edinburg, Ladd launched his now familiar regime of fierce self-discipline. While the demands of the pastorate were not severe, the demands of the pastor were unfailingly stringent. Morning chores were followed by work on the next Sunday's sermon and visits to the homes of sick or erring members of the congregation. Weddings, funerals, and guest appearances in

[2] Personal communication from the office of the minister, Edinburg United Church, October 10, 1961.

45

other rural churches in northeastern Ohio were a regular feature of each week's work. Ladd was painfully earnest about his responsibilities. He abhorred the slipshod and uncaring practices of some ministers and early determined to give his office the fervor, if not the grace, of competence.

One of the problems that dogged him during these early years concerned the development of an effective style and technique of public speaking. His predecessor in the pulpit had been a vigorous revivalist, and the Edinburg congregation had come to expect impressive sermons.

> The anaemic Andover-bred student soon found his congregation would not keep awake, if he read to them the polished essays which had been commended to him by his admired instructor in the art of sermon-making. But this would have been a discomfiture, little short of an intolerable disgrace, to which, in spite of physical weakness and inexperience, he had no intention to submit. It was indeed fortunate that he was placed in such a situation at the very outset of his ministerial career. For he adopted promptly a plan from which he never afterward departed. The plan was this: To keep his mind filled, and his heart aglow, with the great truths of religion; to communicate with his people so constantly and intimately as to know what of these truths was best adapted to their present needs, to arrange the thoughts in logical order and then, with proper temper, with moral earnestness mingled with much sympathy, and with plain yet carefully chosen speech, to drive straight for the people, with a view to informing their minds, quickening their feeling, and getting truth applied to the control of life. To the stimulus of this farming community I largely owe whatever success I may have had as a preacher in the later years of my ministerial life.[3]

In driving straight for the Edinburg people, Ladd may have informed their minds and quickened their feeling, but he also raised their ire. He knew the life and people of the Western Reserve and

[3] "Autobiography," pp. 104–105.

gloried in the history and culture that he and his parishioners shared. He wanted desperately to be one with his people and to be appreciated as their priest and teacher; but he wanted even more to serve the master of his own mind and learning. It is significant that, with all his love for the Western Reserve, he characterized himself as "Andover-bred." He belonged to the world of ideas in a time when that world was undergoing rapid change and he had set out to mediate between the old and the new. But how was he to fulfill this role in the Edinburg of 1869?

In his steady, self-assured manner, Ladd tried to educate his parishioners, to make them aware of the new forms of learning and of the fruits of modern biblical scholarship. It was not to be an especially successful or happy assignment. The farmers of Edinburg wanted inspiring and reassuring sermons that emphasized the immutable principles of religion and of daily life; but Ladd was more interested in heuristics than he was in homiletics. He wanted his congregation to breathe the air of liberal Protestantism, to open their minds to new ideas, and thereby to experience the fresh exhilaration of an informed faith, as well as the quiet comfort of time-tested principles. The good people of Edinburg listened while the young parson explained and urged upon them the bounty of his years of intense study and reflection. They respected him, but increasingly they came to believe that he was too high-powered and pretentious for a community that made a virtue of simple faith. As the months passed, Ladd began to feel the growing irritation within his flock. Faced with the tormenting situation, he responded characteristically—he drove straight for the people with increased intensity, mustering to the full a moral earnestness born of total conviction. Apparently it did not occur to him that he was preaching more philosophy than he was religion and that the congregation would not pay seven hundred dollars a year for Immanuel Kant and Hermann Lotze.

The Ladd, Kant, and Lotze pastorate was provided with its first real test after one full year. At the annual meeting of the Society, the governing body of the church, it was moved and seconded "that we instruct our Trustees to retain the present incumbent of pulpit. After long discussion, a motion was made to lay the motion on the table one week. Carried."[4] It would seem a safe assumption that the matter was discussed informally during the one-week interval. At the next meeting of the Society the original motion was passed without difficulty, though there were dissenting votes.[5]

The young parson was having his troubles, but life in Edinburg was still a great improvement over the life of an invalid in Painesville. There were two special reasons for satisfaction. First, Ladd was happy in his home life and drew strength from the supporting love of a good woman, and, second, his scholarly work was proceeding, slowly but well. Each day he devoted several hours to religious and philosophical studies. He continued an exploration, begun during the Andover years, of the claims for the origins and authenticity of the Bible. The quiet, pastoral, and altogether non-academic Edinburg environment was a congenial setting for progress on this large task. These studies were to continue for many years and eventually result in the large two-volume edition of *The Doctrine of Sacred Scripture*, published in 1883.

> Yet there were many hours when both body and mind were incapable of any exertion. (Perhaps this is the best place to say that, so far as my experience is any criterion whatever, it is just the details of the arrangement of work which enable the man of moderate ability to do most work.) If the mornings were given to the study, the afternoons, whenever the weather permitted—and I soon came to pay little attention to weather—were given to the parish which, with its twenty-five square miles afforded my pony exercise enough, and more than enough, when the Spring thaws made the clay mud much over hock-deep. I have several times spent an hour and a half getting over two or three miles of these roads. But the evenings, with the

[4] *Book of Records*, Edinburg United Church, January 3, 1871.
[5] *Ibid.*, January 10, 1871.

exception of Sunday and one week-day evening, when a little handful gathered in the vestibule of the meeting house for conversation and prayer, were spent in the one living-room of the parsonage. Here especially in the winter time, there were no distracting noises on the outside, few calls to receive or to pay, and no shows to entice one away from home. But there was a coal fire in a Franklin stove (the best quality of coal cost three dollars a ton at the mine five miles away); there were plenty of good books to read, and duets on the piano and flute to play. And the parson was gaining experience, self poise and trust in God; and was constantly improving in health.[6]

Early in his second year at Edinburg, Ladd realized that he would have to find a position which offered a greater opportunity for his talents as scholar and intellectual mediator. He needed the challenge of a more demanding pastorate, one in which he could feel the interest and response of a diversified community. His desperate need to speak and write on philosophical and social questions was frustrated by the firm certainties of a small, rural population, and both his scholarly interests and his ambition suffered under the restraint. The birth of a son, George Tallman, in May, 1871, made the meager salary insufficient, and of course the attitude of the congregation toward their pastor made an increase in salary unlikely. There were two possibilities for immediate action— a professorship of Hebrew at Oberlin College and the pastorate of the Congregational Church in Kent, Ohio. In commenting upon these positions, Ladd wrote in his autobiography, "For the former I had no inclination; for the latter the time did not seem particularly opportune in view of the interests of my people at Edinburg."[7]

The interests of the people at Edinburg certainly were a factor. Things were not going well, and it is possible that Ladd would have been asked to leave had he not resigned. Writing in his autobio-

6 "Autobiography," pp. 106–107.
7 *Ibid.*, p. 108.

graphy in 1910, he looked back across the decades with benignity and stated that "we parted with regrets but with no weakening of respect or of affection."[8] Apparently he left hurriedly, though he did not yet have another position—a surprising move for one who was so concerned to find greater financial support and security for his growing family. When he left Edinburg the church owed him eighty-eight dollars. As late as November 11, 1872, a motion to pay this amount lost twice in the church Society.[9] In 1873 the trustees instructed the treasurer to "seek a settlement with Rev. Ladd," and ultimately he was paid twenty-five dollars.

Unemployed, and concerned about his future in the profession for which he had prepared with such zeal, Ladd left his family in Painesville and preached his way from pulpit to pulpit in a north-westerly direction. He got as far as Minneapolis when a seminary friend recommended him for the vacant pulpit at the Spring Street Congregational Church in Milwaukee. On trial, and virtually pen-niless, he rose before the Spring Street congregation on August 20, 1871, to deliver the first of some six hundred sermons to the people of Milwaukee. Following a number of weeks of delay by the offi-cials of the church, he was formally called to his new position on October 9 at a salary of two thousand dollars. The country parson had become a city minister, trading the quiet life of rural Ohio for the brash energies of a city which featured, among other chal-lenges, what was known as "a wide-open Sunday." It was a city ideally suited to an energetic preacher who had a passion for social justice. Ladd wasted no time in "driving straight for the people."

The church was organized in 1847 as the Free Congregational Church, the original name reflecting an intention to remain open to those who were not able to "hire accommodations" in other churches, as well as a testimony against slavery as "a great sin

8 *Ibid.*
9 *Book of Records*, Edinburg United Church, November 11, 1872.

against God and man, a palpable outrage on human rights."[10] The name was changed to the Spring Street Congregational Church in 1852 and again in 1881 to the Grand Avenue Congregational Church. Founded on a strong note of protest against injustice, throughout its early years the church remained a vital force in the public conscience of the city and region. Members of the congregation were active on behalf of abolition and temperance and entered into most of the legislative struggles of the growing community. The tradition of the church was an appropriate one for Ladd who, after the staid society of Edinburg, needed a forum for the release of his deep convictions about man.

Early in his ministry at the Spring Street Church, Ladd introduced the two themes that were to characterize his years in Milwaukee and ultimately force him to abandon his profession in favor of an academic life. The first theme, a natural extension of his years in Edinburg, was a continuous effort to apply the fruits of his scholarship to the requirements of the pulpit. He made the pulpit a public forum for the discussion of religion and the new modes of rationalism and natural philosophy. His sermons were the lectures of a teacher rather than the comforting and inspirational offerings of a preacher. The faith that he upheld for his congregation was a faith in the human and social value of an informed and critical mind. While he subscribed to most of the essential doctrines of Congregationalism, his testimony usually contained a reservation or interpretation which was peculiarly his own. He was not the kind of minister to gladden the hearts of the dogmatic.

The second theme of Ladd's ministry was not as easily predictable from his earlier behavior. Faced with the human and civic problems of a large city, and struggling always against his own natural reticence, Ladd became a social actionist and a public cham-

---

[10] O. B. Blix *et al.* (eds.), *One Hundred Years of Christian Service, 1847–1947* (Milwaukee: Grand Avenue Congregational Church, 1947), pp. 8–9.

pion of justice. Milwaukee gave him the opportunity to speak to social issues that were irrelevant to the good people of Edinburg. The
impurity of his faith and the austerity of his personal manner
would have alienated the Spring Street congregation had it not so
openly admired his great learning and his courage in the battle
against civic devils. He might speak above their heads, question
precious beliefs, and become restless when others engaged in small
talk, but to the people of the congregation the Reverend Mr. Ladd
was a man of impressive integrity, fearless in battle. What they
lost in the dry forests of the Sunday sermon they gained in daily
identification with a man of principle and candor.

If Satan resided in Milwaukee between 1871 and 1879, then
surely he must have earned his dishonest living as a newspaperman
or politician. The minister of the Spring Street Church preached
love, charity, and the nobility of human learning, saving his wrath
for the press and the Common Council. The columns of the *Milwaukee Sentinel* bristled with long reports of his sermons, editorial
comments upon the sermons, and rejoinders by Ladd. The press
was upbraided for its lack of Christian morality and for its gossipy
exaggerations. Newspapermen were reminded that "God marks
the man who pens filthy smutch and sends it out into the world to
blacken whom it touches."[11] The stinging accusations were met by
detailed arguments to the contrary and by counterattacks:

> The men who wield the pen do not tell more lies than the
> men who wag the tongue, and we doubt if they tell half as
> many. . . . If you wish to see an exhibition of "Christian morals
> applied to the press" that has some fun in it as well as instruc-
> tion, set two religious newspapers by the ears over some doc-
> trinal point, and the necessity of Mr. Ladd's discourse will be
> illustrated in a few minutes with living apparatus. Such wicked
> irony, such bitter sarcasm, such merciless logic, such scalping

[11] *Milwaukee Sentinel*, March 17, 1873.

as will be carried on by those religious gladiators! Why, it is enough to drive a political editor crazy from pure envy of their eminent ability and skill in the business.[12]

The struggles which began on March 17 with Ladd's sermon on "Christian Morals for the Press" continued throughout the year, and as late as December 5 he was still writing letters of rejoinder to the editor of the *Sentinel*. It is little wonder that the congregation was impressed by the courage and provocative skills of their dry Sunday lecturer.

Although Ladd continued to attack the press, and to be attacked in return (all of this to the glory of God, the edification of his congregation, and the health of newspaper circulation—for he was good "copy"), his relationship to the press was one of Christian charity compared to his bitter struggles against "immoral politics." As the years passed, his preoccupation with Milwaukee political life increased to a point where it became a dominant theme of his ministry. He resented the condescending attitude of politicians who felt that moral and religious principles have little to do with politics and that ministers should confine their attentions to "proper" religious topics. Convinced that religion was relevant to human and governmental affairs, he insisted that Milwaukee politics be purified by "the application of right principles." From the pulpit, he proclaimed that "the true view is that moral and religious principle should entirely permeate, and utterly control politics. Politics ought to be just as pure as the family life, as the prayer-meeting in the churches."[13] Reaching across the centuries, he brought Jesus, Plutarch, Cicero, and Oriental philosophers into Milwaukee and urged the election of candidates who stood for "right principles." It is not known whether the politicians were led, thereby, to read these primary sources; probably they preferred to stand on local issues.

12 *Ibid.*, March 19, 1873.
13 *Ibid.*, April 1, 1878.

George Trumbull Ladd

When Ladd felt that politicians were not supporting "right principles" he was capable of strong language. In 1878 he assailed the
Common Council for its resolution instructing the Milwaukee de-
legation to the legislature to work for the abolition of religious
services and instruction from state educational institutions. In a
letter to the *Sentinel*, which was given the title "Skinning Them
Alive," Ladd stated:

> We remind you finally of the fact that you are overreaching
> yourselves. This thing is quite too coarse and open. You have
> not drawn your lead fine enough for such game, gentlemen.
> You should take some lessons in serpentine procedure from that
> old serpent. He will teach you better in another lesson. . . . As
> pastors, we observe that even men of your stripe, when death
> comes to themselves or their family, begin to think that man is
> a religious animal. . . . We will fight you and your resolution
> to the very last, by speech and by writing, by ballot and by law,
> by every legitimate means. We will not despair of the State,
> though we have no hope of, or from, such as you.[14]

Ladd's position on religious education in the public schools was a
strongly held, and frequently defended, belief throughout his life.

Perhaps the finest example of Ladd's political pen is the long
letter to the editor of the *Sentinel* protesting the failure of the
municipal government to deal adequately with the sewage-disposal
problems of the rapidly growing community. The letter was given
the title "No Ague in Milwaukee—Consequently Reverend George
T. Ladd Must Be Shaking With Some Other Disease." Such com-
positions must have made him one of the *Sentinel*'s most useful un-
paid writers.

> I have had the ague. To the initiated the question at once
> arises, what kind of ague? Was it quotidian, tertian or quartan,

[14] *Ibid.*, January 11, 1878.

or was it the erratic ague? Was it the shaking or the dumb ague? My kind can be best described by the following anecdote. A gentleman in the city of Cleveland found himself not in very good condition and concluded to recuperate by paying a visit to his children, who lived in one of the malarious regions of Ohio. The visit was socially enjoyable, but in the matter of recuperation it was not a success. On his return he felt different, but very queer. The doctor was summoned and found his patient shivering and grumbling over a glowing coal fire. When the man of healing came out from the sick room he was met by his patient's daughter, who asked eagerly for the cause of her father's strange experiences. "What is the matter with him?" said she. The doctor looked thoughtful but made no answer. "He hasn't got the ague, has he?" A faint smile was the only reply. "Well, if he has got the ague it's the dumb ague," she said. "It's the very dumbest kind of ague," said the sympathetic doctor.

.   .   .   .

I hope the City Fathers will do all they can to preserve in this regard the reputation of Milwaukee. They have done tolerably well the past year. I hope they will not grow weary of well doing. Indirectly they have made a good many die, and a far greater number more than usually willing to die. They are thus a great assistance to the minister. I hope they will have more sewers constructed like those already made. I love to see the white, low-lying reek, which like the "reek o' the rotten fens" pours up on a frosty morning from the manholes along Spring Street. It reminds me of things I would gladly avoid. It warns every thoughtful man to flee from the City of Destruction and from the wrath which is to come. I hope they will have as much dirt as can be turned up to lie as long as possible in the summer's sun. I hope they will pour still thicker and fouler streams into our river, for the spring rise has left it a little too clear. It's a good way to show one's independence to run counter to the experience of the civilized world. Sail, on, O Ship of State.

> Excellent pilots have you, though the scum on the waters may
> get too thick to bring the gallant craft through, and though all
> on board but the pilots have to hold their noses during most of
> the passage. But an alarming thought occurs to me. Some of
> the City Fathers may themselves have the ague, what then? If
> they could only have the typhoid fever they might go off with-
> out much time for reflection. This would work no injury to the
> schemes of their comrades for preserving the reputation of the
> city. But should they have the ague, they would have a new
> basis and ample time for reflection.
>
> But a consoling thought now comes to my mind. They say
> that beer is an antidote for ague. We are safe; the reputation
> of the city will be preserved.[15]

Ladd was convinced that his parishioners were unduly preoccupied with the church as an institution and that Christianity was
most vitally expressed in and through the "church invisible." He
was small comfort to those who were concerned about the material
forms of religion and the social status of the congregation. To the
dismay of some, he spent a great deal of time working with the
lowly and unchurched people of the city. He viewed the church not
only as a human creation for the fulfillment of private, spiritual
life, but also as an instrument for social action. Believing that the
public testimony of the church should bring it into direct contact
with sick and sinning men on the margin of society, Ladd took
more joy in the restoration of one erring drunkard than in the
weekly satisfaction of his regular flock.

Milwaukee was a living challenge to one who preached temperance and meant abstinence. At this early stage of his career, Ladd
was an outspoken enemy of tobacco and liquor; however, at a later
period, when he had become accustomed to the habits of a rising
university professor, he was to enjoy the "medicinal" effects of liquor followed by a good cigar. While in Milwaukee he preached

---

[15] *Ibid.*, July 8, 1875.

the usual temperance sermons, but it is clear that his concern about the use of liquor was related more to possible social and psychological effects than to moral prescriptions. He held that stricter laws should be enacted to deal with the drunkard. His attitude was plainly punitive rather than therapeutic:

> I would have more strict laws for the central criminal, the drunkard. He is a criminal, and while I would not shut him out from mercy, I would have him justly punished. They say the saloon-keepers make drunkards. They do, but the drunkards make the saloon-keepers. I would have a law making each person found drunk once on the street finable. The second offense should be more heavily fined; for the third offense he should have his name posted in every saloon in town, and all saloon-keepers should be forbidden to sell to him.[16]

While the drunkard was to be punished, his offense was principally a matter of contributing to potential social deterioration. Society was justified in punishing the criminal in its own self-defense. Some independence of mind was required for a minister of rigidly non-alcoholic background to preach a temperance sermon on sociological and psychological bases. Though Ladd was not yet able to formulate the scientific basis of his argument (and perhaps a temperance sermon was hardly the place to attempt it), he was struggling to find an over-all point of view concerning man, and he was astute enough to realize in his dissatisfaction that predigested religious viewpoints were insufficient.

Ladd's belief that drunkards should be punished as criminals was in marked contrast to his position on insanity. His surprisingly enlightened attitude toward mental illness is well expressed in an impassioned sermon analyzing the murder trial of Mrs. Willner. The case drew his fire for a number of reasons—the poor woman was a member of his own congregation, she was a defenseless figure

[16] *Ibid.*, September 4, 1876.

who was threatened by the official forces of society, and there was a strong suspicion of political chicanery in the treatment that the case received. A chance to continue the public spanking of politicians who did not behave according to right principles would have sufficed to bring Ladd into the controversy; however, there was one additional very important reason for his deep interest in Mrs. Willner's fate. Ladd's extra-ministerial scholarship had aroused his interest in the function of the human mind. He had read W. B. Carpenter's *Mental Physiology*, some works by Maudsley, and items of interest concerning the McNaghten rulings. While it would be several years before he set himself the task of reading everything available in the infant field of psychology, the trial of Mrs. Willner represented the first evidence of his exposure to psychological literature. The scholar who wished to mediate between the old and the new was to find in psychology the point of entry for his mediational efforts.

Ladd held that Mrs. Willner was clearly guilty of murder, that the crime was the result of insanity, and that insanity was a disease. Disease, he argued, required treatment rather than punishment. Citing the McNaghten and other legal rulings applying to insanity, he quoted from Chief Justice Ladd of New Hampshire, "who ridiculed the theory that the mind is like a vessel with water-tight compartments, and that the insanity could be squeezed into one of them. . . . The wisdom of all the law asserts that the person is not responsible for an act done by him if his mind is insane and the act is the result of the insanity."[17] Ladd visited Mrs. Willner in the city prison, urged his parishioners to clamor for justice in the case, and charging that "the foul stream of American politics is polluting public life" advocated that the jury system be modified to permit trial before three judges rather than a lay jury of "ignorant fellows."

With the passing of the years in Milwaukee, Ladd became more absorbed in his own scholarship. Two or three mornings each

17 *Ibid.*, May 29, 1876.

week he withdrew to his study for several hours of hard study and writing. The intensity of his work is revealed in the following remarks:

> At that time I enjoyed powers of concentration which have long since weakened or wholly passed away. In my study, which was just above one of the busiest streets of the city, I have often heard the city clocks strike for nine in the morning, and have known absolutely nothing of what was going on outside until I was wakened to hear them striking three or four hours later.[18]

The Sunday "lectures" to his congregation were products of hard labor and revealed an increasing reliance upon reason as the only true basis for religious and moral progress. He stressed the need for an intelligent faith, arguing that an uninformed faith was an empty and undependable guide for action.[19] Life was to be tested by action, and the course of man's activity was established and given meaning by a reasoned faith. Ladd's pre-psychological development was clearly functional. He was interested in the sweep of behavior as an ongoing process that was illuminated by reason and purposeful in nature.

A rather thin and tentative theoretical position began to emerge during these years in Milwaukee. While it was neither psychology nor theology, it was an early expression of Ladd's groping movement toward a position of his own. Although he was not yet able to think in psychological terms (this would come a few years later when he had completed his study of all available psychological literature), he realized that something important was missing in his understanding of mental life. It is to his credit that he recognized the need for a new frame of reference when, by training, temperament, and profession, he would have found the rigid adherence to a theological system an easier way out of the dilemma.

[18] "Autobiography," pp. 133–134.
[19] *Milwaukee Sentinel*, June 22, 1874.

Preaching did not satisfy Ladd's strong need to express his thoughts. From his study over the busy street there flowed a steady stream of letters, newspaper and magazine articles, and reviews. He published articles on such churchly topics as charity, almsgiving, and the doctrine of Christian song. While he was undoubtedly serious about these matters, they made relatively little demand upon him, and as unimpressive and dutifully written essays they must be considered as mere bread-and-butter productions. They do tell us that he was in favor of charity and almsgiving and that Christian song is sweet consolation when selected with intelligence and sung with appropriate regard for its meaning. It was not enough to sing joyously; one must sing intelligently and well!

Preaching, politics, and Christian song were time-consuming elements of Ladd's Milwaukee years, but it is clear that he committed only a small part of himself to these activities. He was most keenly alive when, alone and undistracted at the writing table, he could abandon himself to the "veiled and misty vistas" of philosophy, religion, and history. With all of the distractions of a busy public career, he was in fact a deeply motivated, practicing scholar. In a very real sense, he was supporting himself and his family through the ministry to the end that he might continue his more important work as a scholar. Ladd took pride in his ministerial work and was delighted that he was succeeding in Milwaukee, after his failure in Edinburg; however, the ministry never claimed him and he was increasingly impatient with the shallow, repetitive, and essentially non-intellectual aspects of his life in the church. He was impatient for a number of years before it became apparent that he would have to leave.

Year after year Ladd faced almost daily the mounting manuscript of his *Doctrine of Sacred Scripture*. He began to fear that he was not equal to the task; that the manuscript might be burned or lost; that someone else might publish a similar book before he was finished; or, even more appalling in a Laddian chamber of literary horrors, that the finished work might not be thorough enough. He worked and worried his way through eight years, finally leaving Milwaukee with an incomplete manuscript and a full-blown obsession.

Among the materials published during the Milwaukee years, two items reveal the early efforts that Ladd made to fulfill his self-assumed role as mediator between the old and the new learning. Over a period of several years he published in the *Bibliotheca Sacra* and the *New Englander* a series of articles dealing with theological questions. This series provides a sample of the dry, thickly wooded forests of theology in which he was such a devoted explorer. He ranged from the history of the concept of God, to the origin of the concept of God, to the difficulties of the concept of God, with intermediate stops to undertake a detailed study of the word "cherubim." In this huge effort, the man's delight in elaborate writing based upon elaborate analysis challenges the reader's interest and will. The consummate piece of elaboration was an article on systematic theology containing a twenty-three-page list of definitions and abbreviated schema into which the theologian may "fit his discoveries of truth, his speculations upon truths, and indeed all the fruits of his thinking, reading, and study."[20] It was a bold creation, but there is no evidence that theologians rushed to fit their discoveries, speculations, and fruits into the framework.

Among the articles in this series, "The New Theology," published in 1876, was a singular expression of the new Ladd. It was a brave and successful effort, revealing for the first time that Ladd was capable of writing in an interesting and highly readable style when inspired by his subject and filled with fresh ideas. But even more important, the article signaled the beginning of what was to be a permanent break with the old theology and a lasting but unhappy marriage with naturalism and science. With the publication of this article Ladd began his career as a heretic. The extent of his

[20] "An Essay in Systematic Theology," *Bibliotheca Sacra*, 36 (1879), 706.

heresy was evidenced by the fact that while he was *persona non grata* in many church circles, he was invited with increasing frequency to speak before college audiences.

In "The New Theology," Ladd argued that a progressive science of theology was possible and that it would of necessity rest upon the sciences of nature, language, history, and consciousness. Ministers and theologians were taken to task for their failure to assimilate the new discoveries of science:

> So far as we have any time and brains for scientific study, we are too apt to be engaged in theologic battle-dore and shuttle-cock. To borrow a somewhat undignified figure of speech from the gold, stock, and wheat exchange—we are engaged in acting the part of bears and bulls of orthodoxy. This wresting of nature, the Bible, history, and consciousness, in the interests of a polemical theology, must give way before the more patient and exhaustive study of all these sources by means of the improved helps which have recently been furnished.[21]

Enter the mediator! With the above statement Ladd criticized the past practices of orthodoxy and pointed the way toward the exciting and progressive modes of "the new learning." The nervy argument of the article was carried beyond the limits of ministerial good sense by suggesting that ministers should "trust the eyes of Darwin while examining the orchids."[22]

The article lamented the lack of recognition and reward for students in theological seminaries who wished to pursue science, pointed optimistically to future great developments in the study of consciousness, and advocated research that is docile, patient, minute, and untrammeled. Ladd closed his argument on a theme which was a central conviction of his mediational life work: "The old truths will not be lost or damaged but will be invigorated

21 "The New Theology," *New Englander*, 35 (1876), 679.
22 *Ibid.*, p. 667.

when more thoroughly separated from errors."[23] The remaining decades of his life were a self-conscious effort to fulfill the promise and the central theme of this article.

By 1876 Ladd was fully launched upon his career of scholarly writing, and publications began to appear with impressive regularity. While he continued to flay the Common Council on behalf of right principles, he was beginning to devote a larger percentage of his time to the preparation of serious manuscripts. He published the material from two major lectures on "The Unknown God of Herbert Spencer" and "The Promise and Potency of Professor Tyndall," wrote an article on "Final Purpose in Nature," began work on a book concerning church polity, and scribbled away on the seemingly endless *Doctrine of Sacred Scripture.*

The lectures on Spencer and Tyndall were the first of many public complaints about "starring." Ladd defined starring as "the method of propagating opinions in philosophy and religion upon the mere authority of some recognized teacher in the natural sciences."[24] He accused Spencer of advocating an empty reconciliation of science and religion based upon the fact that both deal with a power in the universe which is utterly inscrutable, and he criticized Tyndall for holding that the promise and potency of every form and quality of life is to be found in matter. Though Ladd wanted to mediate and reconcile, he resented any effort to oversimplify the conflict; his resentment was likely to be especially bitter when he detected a condescending attitude on the part of scientists. He felt that the basic reconciliation required was metaphysical, and throughout his life he made it perfectly clear that he considered scientists to be poor metaphysicians.

The minister turned scholar did all that he could to make the Spring Street Church both a force for social betterment and an edu-

[23] *Ibid.*, p. 693.
[24] *The Unknown God of Herbert Spencer and the Promise and Potency of Professor Tyndall* (Milwaukee: I. L. Hauser & Co., 1878), p. 36.

cational institution. It is significant that Ladd chose to involve the young people of the church in a new literary organization, the Philozetians, or Lovers of Learning. He attended meetings of the group, smiled, and applauded the music, tableaux, shadow pictures, and recitations, and he must have enjoyed especially a recital which contained these lines:

> Rogers, Myers, Booth or Johnson,
> What are they when we compare them,
> Hold them up in contrast with him,
> Him who figures very largely—
> Is the all-commanding figure—
> As in that tale of Nights Arabian,
> Figures with the Lamp of Wonders?
> And the query comes straight to us—
> Irresistibly comes to us—
> Where were we without a-Ladd-in?[25]

But the Spring Street Church was a church and not an educational institution, and Ladd was increasingly aware of his strong need to communicate to others the fruits of his private scholarship. As his reputation, both scholarly and heretical, increased, he received and gratefully accepted numerous invitations to address audiences in other parts of the city and region. He was particularly responsive to requests from colleges, and the interest in his ideas which was displayed at Carleton, Beloit, and Ripon made him impatient with the limitations he faced in the Spring Street congregation. As a minister, "what he willed was done,"[26] but he could not convert the church into a college, and it was toward the colleges that his interests and talents irresistibly inclined him. He knew that he must change not only his position, but also his profession.

[25] M. A. Boardman, *Historical Sketch* (Milwaukee: Grand Avenue Congregational Church, 1907), pp. 26–27.
[26] O. B. Blix *et al.*, (eds.), *One Hundred Years of Christian Service*, p. 21.

> During the last two years of the Pastorate in Milwaukee I experienced a growing dissatisfaction with myself and with my work, and a longing for something different and more closely related to my life-plan. This dissatisfaction seemed unreasonable; it was not to be accounted for by anything in my relations to my people or any detectable, not to say conspicuous, lack of congenial and successful work. It was a sort of temperamental and internal, but significant and finally compulsory, "vocation" addressed to the individual soul.[27]

Enough of sermons, weddings, and funerals—he must teach and write and he must find a forum within which to carry forward his self-assigned role as mediator.

Ladd accepted a three-year appointment as Southworth Lecturer on Congregationalism at Andover Theological Seminary, and to his surprise, in June, 1879, received news of his appointment as professor of philosophy at Bowdoin College. His ten-year ministry had come to a close. For the next forty years he would speak, write, travel, and in general live the life of an articulate and argumentative scholar.

On September 21, 1879, Ladd resigned from his pastorate, stating among the other reasons for his action that

> my constitutional instincts and preferences, my early desires and education, my more recent development of tastes and pursuits, lead me toward a life of study and authorship; in a manner and degree very difficult to acquire and maintain in the pastorate of a large and growing church in a city.[28]

The resignation was accepted with official and apparently genuine regret. Farewell teas and receptions were duly held and a gold watch and a solid silver soup tureen were presented to Ladd and his

27 "Autobiography," p. 135.
28 *Book of Records, 1866–1894,* Grand Avenue Congregational Church, Milwaukee, September 21, 1879.

wife. On October 26, 1879, he rose to offer his final sermon from the Spring Street pulpit. After a brief preliminary expression of affection for the members of the congregation, he drove straight for the people in a final assault on the political machine that was drawing the city away from right principles.[29]

[29] *Milwaukee Sentinel*, October 27, 1879.

Chapter · 5 ·

Bowdoin and the Call to Yale

Laden with books on theology, philosophy, and language, but not psychology, and worried about his own unfinished manuscripts, Ladd arrived in Brunswick, Maine, certain in the knowledge that he would now have a proper atmosphere for serious scholarship. The mediator had cast his lot with the academicians, believing that the college campus was the congenial forum he had sought for over a decade. He was to find that the academic profession was made to order for a man of his interests and temperament, but that the struggles it provoked were similar to his battles with the Milwaukee political machine.

Bowdoin provided a busy but relatively quiet two-year interlude between the civic stresses of Milwaukee and the academic storms at Yale. It gave Ladd a chance to complete two books on religious topics, try his wings as a classroom teacher, and begin an intensive period of self-education in psychology. By the time he left Bowdoin in 1881, he had put aside all doubt about the direction that his life would take; he would be a scholar-scientist in a university setting, arguing the difficult case for a universe of natural law infused with an Intelligence that was supra-human.

George Trumbull Ladd

The move to Bowdoin was a successful one for Ladd. From both a personal and a professional standpoint, he was pleased by what he found at this small New England college. President Joshua Lawrence Chamberlain had been a well-known officer in the Civil War, and he carried to his administration of the college the same vigor and forthrightness that had characterized his military career. He gave Ladd the freedom that had been promised for the organization of the Department of Philosophy and supported him in his efforts to improve the curriculum.

Ladd's fellow professors accepted him and did what they could to help him and his family settle into the life of the college and town. The new professor of philosophy was inclined to be severe in his judgment of others and found it hard to understand or accept professors who did not devote themselves to the advancement of their fields. It was not enough to teach effectively; the college professor was engaged in a moral effort, one crucial aspect of which was the extension of knowledge. Apparently some members of the Bowdoin faculty were living quiet, easy lives, and for them Ladd found little time. The Ladd family was entertained socially by many members of the faculty and community, but it soon became evident that certain professors were likely to be embarrassed by the intensity of Ladd's commitment to learning.

An account of Ladd's relationship with one Bowdoin colleague, which also reveals something of his early interest in psychic phenomena, is contained in this comment in his autobiography:

> While I was on the best of terms with all the professors, I had at first most familiar daily intercourse with Professor Carmichael, who at that time held the chair of physics. We were near neighbors and used to take our walks together. Professor Carmichael was a great stickler for the unimpeachable verities of *science*, and even went so far as to claim that his chair was the only one in the College of "science," properly so-called. Relatives of mine who had occupied the house in Rochester

where the "Fox girls" had lived just before them, had been having great trouble with some of the physical phenomena of so-called spiritualism, such as table-tipping and table-walking, things thrown about the room or down the stairs, when no hands were visible to throw them, etc., etc. These affairs had become seriously annoying but had made absolutely no impression toward converting any member of the family to spiritualism. I amused myself by narrating these performances to my colleague, the hard-headed man of science; but for a long time I could make no impression upon him. It was all pure fraud, unmixed superstition or even a bit of lying. Until one day, he told to my astonishment the story of how, in his mother's house, a heavy table had followed his aunt part way up stairs and had got stuck in the banisters. "Do you believe such nonsensical stuff as that?" was my question; "Do you think that my mother and aunt would tell a lie?" was his indignant reply. As we know more about this mysterious entity which we call matter, and especially as we know how immeasurably more there is about it which we do not know, and probably never shall begin to know, we may properly be rather more cautious in affirming or opining just what must be and what cannot possibly be in the way of physical phenomena. There is vastly more direct testimony affirming the facts of table-tipping, etc., than there is for the facts of radio-activities; and the time may not be far away when the former, *as facts*, will admit as readily of experimental demonstration.[1]

In 1879 Bowdoin College offered a rather loosely organized set of courses on philosophy and mental life. In this respect it was no different from most other American colleges and universities. The new psychology was only beginning to make itself felt in higher education. European experimental psychology, still largely a matter of psychophysics but gaining in formal scope and purpose with each year, was a distant influence. Increasingly it was becoming evi-

[1] "Autobiography," pp. 144–145.

dent that a new and improved role for philosophy was needed in college and university curricula. While classical philosophy was the accepted root of philosophical learning, it was to be augmented by an analysis that paid attention to the naturalistic observation of human performance. Ladd was called to Bowdoin to organize and initiate a department of mental and moral philosophy, though undoubtedly the president and the members of the board were rather unaware of the new directions that were to develop within academic philosophy. They did seem to be aware of the need for a new emphasis upon philosophy, and certainly they realized the need at Bowdoin for a more formal development of the studies which already were offered by the college curriculum.

> With all this of favoring circumstance, the work of organizing and successfully initiating a Department of Mental and Moral Philosophy in Bowdoin College, thirty-five years ago, was no sinecure. . . . President Chamberlain had given in the year before some rather fragmentary and occasional talks on subjects lying within, or on the borders of, this Department. But he had made no claim to be anything more than an unsatisfactory *locum tenens*; or, to use a phrase which he would probably have preferred, "to hold the fort" until the proper commander arrived to take his place. The only real professor of philosophy within the memory of the oldest graduates had been Thomas Cogswell Upham, who had held that chair from 1825 for more than forty years. Professor Upham was an amiable gentleman and a writer of many books; most of which were more or less remotely connected with his views as to the nature of mental life. His one definite treatise on psychology was published in 1859 under the title "Elements of Mental Philosophy, embracing the two departments of the Intellect and the Sensibilities." This treatise was not unpleasant reading, but it bore no comparison with the work of Noah Porter on "The Human Intellect," as respects the acquaintance of the two with modern

European work or insight into the real nature of the psychical processes.[2]

Though Ladd's two-year period of initiation into college teaching at Bowdoin was, on the whole, a pleasant experience, the new role introduced some difficulties that were to plague him for the remainder of a long academic career. The unmixed sobriety of his presentation, a mode of lecturing which he preferred to characterize as one of "moral earnestness," may have been expected in delivering sermons, but college students were nevertheless restless and, even in that day, eager for some entertaining relief. He was remorseless in his serious delivery of lectures and, still worse from the students' point of view, inflexible and very demanding in making assignments.[3] A brief and unsuccessful student revolt occurred shortly after Ladd began his work at Bowdoin. It was a poorly organized complaint, published in the student newspaper, *The Orient*, that the new professor was making unrealistic demands upon his students' energies.

As for the professor's attitude toward all this fuss, he regarded it as a simple case of inadequate mental preparation for serious study. New student habits were called for and he demanded that they be established immediately. Academic study was too important a matter to compromise for the sake of an easy popularity. Ladd wrote a reply to *The Orient* stating that the best students appreciated his course and that only the lazy men objected to it. In 1910 he wrote:

> It will readily appear that any one proposing to break utterly with the tradition that regarded the study of psychology little

[2] *Ibid.*, p. 145.
[3] A key to the difficulty is provided in the following comment: "though an able thinker and investigator he [Ladd] was very minute and technical, too much resembling the learned Doctor Dryasdust. . . . It was probably for the best that in 1881 Professor Ladd accepted a call to Yale." Louis Hatch, *The History of Bowdoin College* (Portland, Maine: Loring, Short & Harmon, 1927), p. 179.

71

better than the pleasure of listening to an entertaining but irrelevant talk, or the good fun of exciting and watching the
eccentricities of the teacher, was sure to meet at first with considerable opposition. And in fact, before long the remonstrance
took the form of the round-robin, to which reference has already been made. But when it became known that the new professor proposed to work himself in behalf of his class, and for
their true good, much harder than he could hope to work them,
the class received him and their work with him in a praise-
worthy manner. And, indeed, the Bowdoin undergraduate was,
when I had experience of him as his teacher, an uncommonly
manly and well-meaning fellow.[4]

In the end that "uncommonly manly and well-meaning fellow,"
the Bowdoin undergraduate, conceded a point or two and resigned
himself to the inevitability of Ladd's "moral earnestness." The new
professor conceded, albeit thirty-two years later, that he had been
inadequately prepared for his teaching and had, when he began his
work at Bowdoin, "a deficiency of acquaintance with the tricks, the
conventions, the associations, of the college boy, both in and out of
the classroom."[5] In the years that followed he repaired the deficiency, but the student complaints continued.

The years in Brunswick were quiet and restful after the heavy responsibilities of a city ministry, but with his usual strong diet of
self-imposed work, Ladd found far less ease than he had expected.
He began immediately a regime of reading and research in psychology in order to overcome the handicap that was so apparent to him
when he undertook the formal teaching of the subject. He collected
all the books he could find on mental science and imported from
abroad the experimental literature that was beginning to accumu-
late in the field. But Ladd was a long way from having developed
a foundation in the psychology of his day. He had not yet become

[4] "Autobiography," p. 146.
[5] *Ibid.*, p. 147.

acquainted with the work of Helmholtz, Fechner, Weber, and Wundt; only gradually did he begin to realize how unprepared he was to make any formal contribution to the new field. His desire to contribute to the solution of psychological problems was strong, but at this point it was achievement enough to read for understanding and for the enrichment of his teaching.

Perhaps the heaviest drain upon his time and energy was brought on by his previous acceptance of an invitation to deliver a series of lectures on Congregationalism at Andover Theological Seminary. The burden of preparing these lectures, later published as a book entitled *The Principles of Church Polity*, contributed a great deal to the stress of his first year in Brunswick. The twelve lectures required extensive research, and the collection of relevant materials had a way of posing complicated questions that led him into serious debate with himself. His resolution of some of these questions helped to establish him as an unorthodox figure in Congregational circles.

In addition to these demands upon his energy there was "the threatening, almost spectral shape, the skeleton of the great work on Inspiration, on which I had been at work ten years, but which was as yet only about one-third clothed with flesh and circulated through and through with fresh life-blood."[6] This unclothed work was, of course, his growing book *The Doctrine of Sacred Scripture*, enormous and even more controversial than the work on church polity.

In December, 1879, Ladd's father became seriously ill. Though he left Brunswick as soon as he heard of the illness, his father died before Ladd reached Painesville. Ladd was strongly attached to his father and this sudden loss left him in depressed spirits for many weeks.[7] After spending two weeks in Painesville, devoted largely

---

[6] *Ibid.*

[7] It was a difficult period in Ladd's personal life. Two sons had been born in Milwaukee: Louis Williams on March 15, 1873; Jesse Brewster on July 28, 1876. At

to his service as executor of his father's estate, he traveled to New Haven, where he spent a week preaching at the Center Church and discussing the organization of the Bowdoin curriculum with members of the Yale faculty. He met a number of Yale scholars for the first time and had several conferences with President Porter. Ladd made frequent visits to New Haven in 1880 and early 1881, each time visiting President Porter for a discussion of their mutual interests in psychological and philosophical problems. The friendship and respect that developed from these conferences led ultimately to an invitation to join the Yale faculty.

While the two years at Bowdoin were important to Ladd as a time for completion of old commitments and adjustment to his new profession, it was the deeply personal and intellectual transformation of these years that made them so crucial for his later life. For the first time, he devoted himself to the serious study of psychology and to the claims that science made for itself. He threw himself into the scholar's role with characteristic urgency, but the issues were more personal than they had been before. He was no longer a minister sounding off, to the side of other issues, about the new learning and the new science. He was a professor in a field that embraced the new science of mental life, and he was largely without formal preparation in the field that he professed. Moreover, Ladd was now forced to face up to the consequences of his self-assigned role as a mediator. Was it possible that the old and the new were irreconcilable? Perhaps the learning so dear to him as a classically educated man was doomed by natural science. He must have known at least a few moments of doubt and hesitation as he sat in his Brunswick study reading the one hundred books he had ordered for his own re-education. But he was not a fainthearted man, and whatever doubts he may have had did not prevent him from committing himself publicly on several major questions.

the age of four, and not long after Silas' death, Jesse Brewster died suddenly of a childhood disease.

The intellectual development of this period of Ladd's life is best seen in two long articles. The first article, "Final Purpose in Nature,"[8] was published very early in his Bowdoin career; one must assume that he did much of the work on this article in Milwaukee. The article reveals a sensitive search for answers to large philosophical questions and shows also an abortive effort to handle these big issues at a level of physiological psychology. It is filled with Laddian pre-psychology, a collection of bits and pieces of reading in those areas that he felt would hold the key to his mediational success. It is clear that even before his self-education in psychology he saw that the most informative evidence concerning the questions that he must answer lay in the new mental science, and that a physiological approach to these questions would be necessary. It was this conviction, reinforced by additional reading at Bowdoin and at Yale, that launched him upon the enormous task of organizing the material of the new science in his *Elements of Physiological Psychology.*

"Final Purpose in Nature" contained references to Darwin, Bacon, Lotze, Hartmann, Volkmann, Du Bois Reymond, and Helmholtz. Though he referred to Helmholtz, it is not clear whether he had yet read the man's works. It seems more likely that his reference was built upon a reading of secondary sources. At any rate, a background of random reading was brought to bear upon a major question and the argument was audacious, if not convincing. The article had the effect of solidifying Ladd's position, of closing one very large door, before he had had the benefit of a formal study of the new psychology. Though his position was not an unusual one for that time, one wonders whether he might have seen the matter in a different light had he remained uncommitted for a few more years.

The door was closed in the following manner. Ladd argued that Bacon, Darwin, and others had done much, in the name of science,

[8] *New Englander*, 38 (1879), 677–700.

to discredit the ancient Aristotelian concept of final purpose, but that, when properly understood, the concept was seen to lie at the very root of science. With Lotze providing background for his position, he set out to demonstrate that science reveals final purpose at work as an explanatory principle; but before he got to the demonstration he declared that "the existence of final purpose in nature is simply an indisputable fact."[9] This was an early expression of an annoying Laddian trait—the tendency to prejudge issues in such a way that all subsequent discussion became merely a supporting argument for his position. The remainder of the article was a detailed exposition of this "indisputable fact," carefully wrought and surprisingly informed with respect to physiology, but inflexible and rather testy in tone.

Following several pages on the physiology and optics of the human eye, he concluded that every particle of living matter in the eye and all complex systems involved in its functions work for one final purpose, that of clear vision. In addition, however, the eye as a human organ fulfills its final purpose, at a higher level, by serving as an instrument of the mind. He held that "seeing without the mind is not real seeing" and that the mind of man is required as an instrument of meaning in the universe. There can be no doubt about the direction in which Ladd was heading with this argument. He was building toward a theory of final purpose that was metaphysically anchored in God. Thus, the "indisputable fact" of final purpose was but an expression of Ladd's indisputable prior commitment to Christian theology. It is not surprising that the budding psychological scientists of the 1890's found Ladd a difficult colleague. His contributions to the field were too important to dismiss lightly, but what could one do with a man who held that it was the duty of science to demonstrate already established principles?

> It is the work of science to acknowledge the fact of prevalent final purpose, and in light of this acknowledgement to discover

[9] *Ibid.*, p. 680.

and present the specific final purpose of all its objects as well as the means by which these final purposes are accomplished. We can excuse the natural sciences from making remoter inferences; we cannot excuse them from observing & rightly interpreting by first inference, the plain and abundant facts.[10]

Ladd closed a second door to his later theoretical development with the publication of "Nature, the Supernatural, and the Miraculous." The article was adapted from a speech that he had delivered at a religious conference in the summer of 1882. Acknowledging that the question of the supernatural is the fundamental issue in considering the conflict between scientific pursuits and religious faith, he argued that the modern conception may not be inconsistent with the truths of the "ancient notions." He wanted to show that science was unjustified in its assumption that nature is "a self-centred, self-contained, and self-competent whole," and that "we can have neither the complete idea of nature nor of the supernatural, without taking both points of view." Rejecting the carpenter theory of the origin of the universe, he argued that the forces of nature require the unceasing presence of a higher force—the force of the supernatural. He was impatient with "thin, cheap philosophy and poor, watery religion," and disavowed any belief in miracles detached from an orderly universe.

> It is only when a miracle is conceived of as in right relations to an order which is *both* natural *and* supernatural that it becomes tolerable to reason. . . . The miracle, in order to be believed, must be brought into right relations to an orderly system,—to a system in which natural and supernatural cooperate in an orderly whole; it must be one event which is ascribed to an agency recognized in some form as the cause of other events.[11]

[10] *Ibid.*, p. 692.
[11] "Nature, the Supernatural and the Miraculous," *Christian Philosophy Quarterly*, 2 (1882), 86.

George Trumbull Ladd

While miracles are in some special way acts of God, they are necessarily in and of nature.

Though the position that Ladd took on miracles and the doctrine of final purpose was consistent with his theological background and education, it must be remembered that the argument was no mere recital of traditional religious philosophy. The case for final purpose was not lightly adopted. There was evidence that a wide, though random, scholarship had preceded the article. He went far beyond most ministers of his day in the friendliness of his attitude toward natural science, and while he tried to "join" science in order to preserve the ancient learning, he did hammer hard on the theologians who were unable or unwilling to accept the contributions of science. His efforts at mediation cut both ways; on the one hand he began early to distrust the scientist's unsophisticated metaphysics (all his life he would be puzzled by the fact that so many others dismissed metaphysics as an unnecessary complication in science), while on the other he upset many religionists by dismissing cherished beliefs because they were not consistent with the findings of modern science and scholarship.

It may appear that Ladd was a poor scientist because of his efforts to force science into the service of philosophy and religion, and undoubtedly this is true; but at the same time it is necessary to appreciate the extent of his growth as an intellectual figure who was deeply and emotionally wedded to religion. As early as the Bowdoin years his career began to reveal a built-in tragedy—a battle of heart and head which, in spite of a devoted and relentless scholarship, could not be resolved. His effort at mediation was an externalization through his career of the desperate need for internal mediation between conflicting traits and interests.

At the close of his second year at Bowdoin, Ladd unexpectedly received a letter from President Porter inviting him to join the Yale faculty. The invitation was supported by a letter from Professor Thomas Seymour, the son of Ladd's beloved Western Reserve professor, Nathan Perkins Seymour.

YALE COLLEGE

(confidential)   New Haven, Conn., June 8, 1881

My dear Professor Ladd.

It has been decided that I ought to have some relief from the duties of teaching which have been assumed and to some extent expanded by my own choice for several years. The choice of the Faculty has fallen upon yourself. I write to propose the question whether you will allow your name to be proposed to the Corporation as the nominee of the Faculty. You will understand that there can be no reasonable doubt of your being elected in case you give this consent. You will be expected to take the whole of the required Psychology and the Philosophy which it implies.

It will be important that I should teach also, in order that I may know the members of the class personally; and I will teach the History of Philosophy, Natural Theology and the Evidences of Christianity—required for the first term, six exercises a week, and special electives in the same lines, two hours a week after the Christmas recess, with some general lectures on the choice of a profession, such as have been given for several years.

I propose this arrangement because I wish to leave you certain departments entirely free, as being more agreeable. Perhaps we might alternate between Ethics and the History of Philosophy in different years.

All this is on the supposition that you may be inclined to accept this offer. The salary is $3500 in case you keep house, or $3000 in case you board. You know our method substantially. We teach by text-books in the main, as you have done. There are some trials incident to large divisions and the duty of going over the same subject twice. Perhaps there are some attractions in the place connected with the presence of a large body of men interested in philosophy and theology. I think I can promise you a very cordial and honest reception, and a considerable degree of intellectual activity, and a promising field of usefulness. If there is any advantage in a personal interview, I will meet you in Boston at any time which you may prefer. I know you are bound to Bowdoin by special ties. Perhaps Mr. Hincks might be thought of to fill your place and relieve you of some of these difficulties in case you are inclined to come.

You will excuse the brief and dry presentation of the proposal. You will not be disappointed in your colleagues nor in a general spirit of harmony and zeal for their work, and you cannot be in the rare opportunity for useful instruction and influence, as also for personal encitement to improvement. Let me add, should you look forward to theology as your final chair in some department, this place even for a few years, with all the advantages which it brings, is not uninviting. You will please regard this matter as entirely confidential for the present, and be so good as not to decide in the negative, if you are so inclined, without a personal interview with

Yours very truly

N. Porter[12]

The call to Yale was complicated by a further invitation from Andover Seminary, received at virtually the same time as the letter from President Porter, to accept a lectureship on systematic theology. Having successfully delivered the Southworth Lectures on Congregationalism, he was now asked to give twenty lectures on the substance of his growing manuscript concerning the doctrine of biblical inspiration. It was proposed that he offer the lectures on inspiration for the "fourth-year men" in the seminary, the most advanced students.

Ladd attempted to get a postponement of his acceptance of the Yale offer, but President Porter indicated that he was in need of immediate relief and urged that a decision be made.

---

[12] The writer has been unable to locate the original copy of this letter. Presumably it was destroyed as a part of a much larger housecleaning after Ladd's death. It is quoted as recorded in the "Autobiography," pp. 153–155.

When I had received the permission, for which I was bound by both honor and courtesy to wait, I laid the case before President Chamberlain and the Hon. Peleg Chandler, then Chairman of the Board of Trustees at Bowdoin. The former deprecated my going; indeed, he afterward described the situation to a friend in nautical terms by saying that "just as the College was getting under full sail, the flying-jib gave way." He also disclosed the fact that the Trustees were looking to me as his successor in the presidency; and he even went so far as to offer to resign at once, if I would remain and take the place thus vacated. Mr. Chandler corroborated what the President had said with regard to the intentions of the Trustees; but he was also more concessive, and expressed the opinion that the offer from Yale was such as came to exceedingly few young men, and to them only once in a lifetime.[13]

Following a period of understandable indecision, during which time he worried about his unfinished organizational efforts at Bowdoin, Ladd accepted the professorship at Yale and made plans to move to New Haven in time for the fall term. He also accepted the invitation from Andover, thereby characteristically setting for himself a heavy schedule of teaching and writing—a schedule which was to drive him near the breaking point in the first year of his work at Yale.

For the second time in two years Ladd was unexpectedly drawn into new fields of labor. With the move to Bowdoin he had permanently abandoned the ministry and entered upon academic and scholarly pursuits which, while principally philosophical in nature, promised to satisfy somewhat his increasing appetite for psychological study. In accepting the call to Yale he moved into a more formal role as a psychologist, although again the work was cast in a philosophical mold. He seems to have been fascinated by the sequence of events into which he was so compellingly drawn. While

[13] *Ibid.*, pp. 156–157.

George Trumbull Ladd

it is not difficult to appreciate the role of his own interests and talents in creating these opportunities, Ladd felt that higher forces were wondrously at work upon his life. In a letter to his brother-in-law, Lewis Brastow, it is clear that he felt he was the recipient of divine guidance.

> My dear Lewis, is it not all like some strange dream? I have been dumb in the dust before God at the thought of his way with me. He seems unfolding my life before me with such rapidity, and causing it to run into such unexpected channels, that I almost fear he means to destroy me. When I look back only six years and recall how I was working without much courage or light, or—as it seemed to me—recognition, and how I prayed and complained that my mission might be made known, and sometimes quite distrusted the Eternal Wisdom; and then consider how, within a few years, I have been overwhelmed with work, and dragged by the Divine hand, rather than directed, where I had not thought to go, but have found myself at the happiest and best;—I am utterly amazed at what God has wrought. He has rarely given me anything which I have distinctly seen and craved: He has given me better and greater things unsought.[14]

14 *Ibid.*, pp. 158–159.

Chapter · 6 ·

The Heretic

During the last half of the nineteenth century it was not unusual for a clergyman of Ladd's temperament and belief to be considered heretical by the conservative Congregationalists who were determined to protect the faith against unorthodox forces. The church was feeling the effects of modern biblical scholarship and the sweep of science. Doctrinal assumptions were being examined with increasing fervor, and many cherished notions, previously accepted without serious question, were under heavy attack. Ladd's avowed purpose in life "to mediate between the old and the new, so as to conserve the unchanging truth that is in them both, in spite of changing forms and by virtue of the very laws of its development," quickly placed him at the center of an extended controversy. As was to be true throughout his life, he sought to mediate, but not by an easy compromise. His career as a heretic within Congregational circles lasted for a decade and was a significant part of his life in Milwaukee, Brunswick, and New Haven. A heretical reputation preceded him to Japan and India when he visited those countries as a traveling scholar and lecturer.

> My career as a heretic began when I was a pastor in Milwaukee. Its origin was in a lack of that self-interested caution which so

often induces us all to refrain from telling the truth when asked questions about matters of fact. This, indeed, it seems to me, has often been almost the sole ground on which men have been denounced and even persecuted for heresies,—scientific, social and ethical, as well as in matters of theological opinion. The "Indian Orchard Council" had been followed by a rather wide-spreading excitement among the churches of the Congregational order. This excitement would probably have died down without producing any of the ulterior evil results which actually followed it, if it had not been deliberately fanned by the "religious press,"—largely, one cannot avoid thinking, for advertising purposes. The point of controversy was as to the views on the doctrine of future punishment which should be deemed necessary to qualify a candidate for ordination in a Congregational church. Adherence to the doctrine from which the damnation of non-elect infants was a logical corollary had for some time either been abandoned or afraid to proclaim itself, both by the ministers and by the members of these churches. But the principal "organ" of Congregationalism had defined *orthodoxy* on this subject as requiring the belief that "all who die impenitent suffer conscious everlasting misery." It requires only a superficial analysis of this sentence to discover that it is rather skillfully devised so as to drag into light the two or three principal forms of dissent which its author deemed heretical. One could not be an annihilationist, for the misery must be "conscious"; or a restorationist, for the case was settled forever by an "impenitent death"; nor could one take refuge in a somewhat mystical interpretation of the word "eternal," for this word according to the definition, must be used in Scripture as the equivalent of the word "everlasting," however much more it might be held to include.[1]

As a leading Congregational minister Ladd pressed upon religious colleagues his view that the church needed an honest liberal-

[1] "Autobiography," pp. 236–237.

ism in the interpretation of the doctrine of future punishment. At the root of his position was a conviction that the doctrine of future punishment, if held in a literal way, was an absurdity. It was rationally unsound to believe that the young child and the idiot were to be consigned to eternal punishment. There was no evidence to support the doctrine as it was advanced by the self-proclaimed purists in the church, and as the controversy grew in intensity Ladd became more and more insistent that his opponents quit arguing from a base of authority and supply evidence that a rational man might respect. This was too much; by asking for evidence which could be recognized by others he seemed to be questioning the whole basis of revealed religion. To the orthodox he began to sound like a member of the enemy force, that company of scientists and disbelievers which was undermining religion and morality.

The controversy settled into a debate concerning requirements for ordination of ministers who were to represent Congregationalism in foreign missions.[2] With others of like mind, Ladd argued that an inflexible adherence to the doctrine would have ruinous effects upon the recruitment of intelligent and able young ministers and missionaries. He defended a number of young men who were judged to be too impure to represent the church abroad. Throughout these efforts he asserted that doctrine should be held open to the highest reflective scholarship of which man is capable, and that not even religious principle is immune to human error.

By aligning himself with those who would subject doctrinal questions to critical examination, Ladd incurred the distrust of many powerful members of his denomination. His position on the question of eternal punishment created the basis for the more

[2] An excellent account of the climate of transition and controversy within which Ladd and other liberal scholars argued their case is provided in G. G. Atkins and F. L. Fagley, *History of American Congregationalism* (Boston: The Pilgrim Press, 1942), esp. chaps. 11–13. Though Ladd's work is not considered in this history, the substance of his argument for modern biblical scholarship is sketched and the role of the liberals in changing Congregationalism is clearly documented.

intense and prolonged battle that was to be focused upon him as a theologian and philosopher. The storm that gathered during his early days in Milwaukee was to erupt following the publication of his *Doctrine of Sacred Scripture* and the more popular version of that book, *What Is the Bible?*

The Doctrine of Sacred Scripture was the fruition of ten years of scholarship. In undertaking this enormous project, Ladd gave expression to interests and plans which had been developing since his college days at Western Reserve. The blending of interests in religion, philosophy, and Greek and Latin studies formed the basis for early efforts to understand the origin and development of biblical literature. He wrote papers on biblical history at Western Reserve and, once established at Andover Seminary, began a concerted effort to understand the precise claims which the Bible makes concerning its own origin, with particular attention to the role of inspiration in the creation of biblical literature. Ladd was not one to accept uncritically the claims that others made for the Bible. He wished to approach this great work with a sympathetic but critical eye. In beginning his exploration into scriptural history he realized that the very act of examination would be an affront to many orthodox believers; however, he was determined to remain faithful to the standards and procedures of scholarship. He believed that an easy prejudgment of biblical claims, as presented by others, was as morally slack as was a violation of the major tenets of the Christian faith. And, of course, having begun this large and risky task, he characteristically announced and defended at every opportunity his conviction that the Bible should be subjected to critical scrutiny and that the evidence produced by sound scholarship should form the basis for belief.

The Doctrine of Sacred Scripture, published in 1883, represented an attempt to study the origin of the Bible by the techniques of modern biblical science. It stressed the importance of ascertaining the historical origins of the Bible without assuming its inspirational or mythical creation. Time and again Ladd compelled himself to face the question, what are the historical *facts*? He wished to bring the evidence "before the bar of common judgment on the ground of sufficient reasons." While earlier approaches to the study of biblical origins, especially those that assumed its inspirational basis, purported to show what the Bible *must* be, he wished to show what it *is*.

Ladd considered himself to be a Christian scholar. As he put it in his introduction to the book *What Is the Bible?*, "It is as *Christians* that we begin this examination; as Christians, with faith confirmed, enlightened, and enlarged, we expect to finish it."[3] He was convinced that the Christian, not to mention Congregational, faith could only be ennobled by the most probing analysis of the Bible. Obviously, his conception of Christian religion was not a slavishly literal one. He sought the spirit of religion rather than the letter of religious doctrine; however, he firmly believed that the spirit could be made vital in practice only if it was founded upon a careful and honest effort to discover religious truth. For Ladd, the scholar's role involved a self-conscious exercise of human morality.

In his effort to mediate between the old and the new, Ladd began early in his career to realize the difficulties and the opportunities that would face one who tried to embrace two worlds. While he held that reality was an encompassing, non-divisible realm that could only be enriched by the varying modes of study open to the scholar and scientist, he knew that there would be points of difference that could not be reconciled by mediation. His studies of biblical literature provide an early indication, however, that on most matters he would rest his case on evidence from science and reason. In retrospect we must conclude that he was often singularly incapable of accepting the evidence from science when it violated his previously established positions; the important point, however, is that from the beginning stages of his scholarly career he argued

[3] *What Is the Bible?* (New York: Charles Scribner's Sons, 1888), p. 16.

for the acceptance of scientific evidence. At times he spoke the language of science only to argue against scientific evidence, but for a theologian of his day and training he was remarkably advanced in his efforts to support science.

The Doctrine of Sacred Scripture provides an interesting foretaste of Ladd's later career in psychology. One must remember that his entry into these studies began in the early 1870's, well before psychology was firmly established in America and previous to his own reading in the field. He advocated a science of biblical study and urged a consideration of the historical evidence concerning the Bible; but he took one further step toward a psychological mode of study. He held that even so delicate a subject as the origin of the Christian Bible must be treated in the light of the strengths and frailties of individual human reason and emotion. He did not, of course, provide a systematic psychological framework for the analysis that he undertook, but he did show that he was aware of the psychological relativity of judgment and belief. It was his realization of this individual factor in judgment and in the perception of error that made him especially impatient with those who insisted upon a dogmatic definition of truth. For a young theologian newly graduated from formal seminary training, he began his first major study with a keen and surprisingly uninhibited mind. At this time he certainly was no psychologist, but he knew something of the problems of analysis that were to help make psychology necessary.

In *The Doctrine of Sacred Scripture* Ladd held that (1) the biblical writings themselves make no claim to a strictly verbal inspiration and a universal infallibility for their content; (2) with a single insignificant exception, no creed of Christendom makes such a claim; and (3) many of the most distinguished and pious scholars of both the ancient and the modern church entertained no such view as this claim implied. The heresy in this position is evident only when one takes into account the orthodox view of the day—a literal acceptance of verbal inspiration as the origin of the Bible and as a claim for the infallibility of the whole work. The biblical literalist had no trouble recognizing Ladd's heresy. The Holy Word was undermined by scholarly tricks. Of the Bible, Ladd held that

> many of its writings will indeed cease to be used in the future as they have been used in the past. The Old Testament will no longer be employed to feed the feeling of vindictiveness, to prove the rightfulness of slavery, polygamy, and the subordination of woman. The cosmogony of Genesis will not always be taken as a description of the actual process of world-building in accord with all the details of modern scientific evolution; nor will the Song of Solomon be made, by a mystical interpretation, to stimulate and praise the love of Christ and the Church. All attempts will be surrendered to frame a theory inconsistent with, or independent of, the facts, and then to employ the Bible in accordance with the demands of the theory rather than with either the nature of the Bible or the more refined needs of the redeemed soul. But the Bible will thereby lose nothing of its efficacy and honor as the means employed by the Spirit in the distribution of grace to the individual believer and to all mankind. For its efficacy and honor as a medium of divine spiritual gifts do not depend upon its infallibility or its perfectness in all regards. They depend chiefly upon a very few simple but unchangeable facts and truths.[4]

For many Protestants, Ladd's book was a splendid example of the apostasy that needed to be confronted and, if at all possible, destroyed before it undermined the fundamental beliefs of the church. From the time of its publication, and continuing for many years to come, he was subjected to a barrage of criticism, accused of evil ways, and—certainly this was personally most painful to him— believed to be unfit to teach and to guide the development of a

[4] *Ibid.*, pp. 482–483.

proper morality in young students. The religious press found a great deal worth comment in the positions that Ladd held, and commentary appeared for a long time. The issues and the debate were much larger than is shown merely by noting Ladd's role in this yeasty period of transformation, but it is apparent that he symbolized one side of the argument for the purpose of public debate.

The editor of the *Methodist Review* commented with unconcealed fervor: "When our clergy will wish to hear such a blatant egotist, or listen to his literary sophistries, or accept his rationalistic jugglery, it will be when they themselves have been caught in a snare as profane as infidelity itself."[5] This was strong language, but it was only part of the attack. The intensity of feeling that was expressed in the article is summarized with concern and apology by another Methodist publication, *Zion's Herald*.

> It is a pity that the controversy over "rationalism" and the orthodoxy of certain institutions of learning should have descended into a species of intellectual fisticuffs. This condition, however, it has reached in the last number of the *Methodist Review*. In an editorial entitled "Wounded Rationalists," the *Review* pays its respects to Professors Ladd and Harper of Yale, in a manner which revives the style of controversy in vogue a century ago. These gentlemen—one or the other of them—are accused of prevarication, "literary hypocrisy," "supercilious egotism," "gross temper," lacking all "manly sentiment" or "truth-loving or Christian spirit," "deceiving" their readers, of "intentional deception and falsehood (*he* [Harper] *knew he manufactured it when he wrote of it*)" of "double-dealing," of "guilt," of "playing a game of hide-and-seek" with their readers, of "hypocraiy" [sic] in the conduct of certain journals, of

[5] *Methodist Review*, September, 1889, p. 752. The attack resulted from an open letter concerning rationalism and orthodoxy that Ladd published in *The Christian Advocate*, July 4, 1889, pp. 3–4. He was answered from afar, as well as from his own country. See C. S. Long, "Professor Ladd Rebuked from Japan," *Methodist Review*, November, 1889, p. 910.

"literary sophistry," "rationalistic jugglery," etc., etc. This is both strange language to be used by a clergyman of his brother ministers, and a strange method of refuting supposed erroneous opinions. . . . The using of the language of the prize-ring in what ought to be a dignified and respectful debate between Christian scholars, is greatly to be deprecated. . . . The unusual license of language in personal accusation, which is afforded in this editorial, revives the objectionable features of the *odium theologicum*, that old theological hatred which has passed into a proverb, and must afford peculiar gratification to men of the stamp of Ingersoll.[6]

The two major expressions of Ladd's heresy, his position concerning the "American Board controversy" (the criteria for ordination of ministers) and his *Doctrine of Sacred Scripture*, resulted in personal attacks in the religious press; but even more troublesome were the rumors and unfounded criticism which persisted at religious meetings and in the day-to-day personal relations between ministers. He suffered many attacks without comment; others were met by friends and colleagues. Professor Thomas A. Thatcher, an old friend and teacher at Andover, and Dr. Robert Harper of Yale were faithfully helpful. Some of Ladd's former students defended him in informal conferences with others. Defense was needed; in various places around the country, he was cited as a person whose presence on the Yale faculty was dangerous to young minds, and a few advocated that students should not be sent to Yale until his influence was removed or until the university officially repudiated his position. Yale academic freedom was equal to the challenge and there is no evidence that thought was given to his removal from the faculty. That would come later and for other reasons.

Ladd's involvement in the debate concerning the ordination of ministers extended from his Milwaukee years until approximately

[6] "Dr. Mendenhall and Rationalism," *Zion's Herald*, September 11, 1889, p. 4.

91

1890. The official governing bodies of Congregationalism argued the doctrinal issues along conservative and liberal lines, and of course Ladd was closely identified with the liberal viewpoint. Though he did not hold an official position on the board, he took part in the debate because of his friendship for certain of the young men whose ordination was at stake and because, as a man who held strong convictions on the subject of theology, he could not sit idly by and permit the church to govern itself by what he considered to be medieval thinking. He participated in the regular meetings that were devoted to discussions of this issue, wrote articles announcing his beliefs, gave lectures and sermons in many Congregational churches, and wrote letters to friends and acquaintances in the church. In all of these efforts he expressed the themes that were so extensively treated in his book on the Bible. His book and his stand on ordination and other issues are clearly related; moreover, his career as a heretic resulted from the perceived relation between his scholarly claims and his public action. He was quite prepared to bear the criticism that came his way, but he was deeply troubled by the fact that so many of his critics had not bothered to read his book. The size and scholarly dryness of the book undoubtedly repelled most readers, but Ladd always maintained that the orthodox critic was not given to reading anyway when the subject under consideration seemed inconsistent with his beliefs.

Although the debate continued for several years, the sticky and painful heresy had reached a personal climax for Ladd when, writing from New Haven on March 1, 1887, he published a long open letter in the *Boston Advertiser*, asking questions of Reverend A. L. Chapin of the Congregational board. At that time, the basic question was still focused upon the belief of potential missionaries concerning whether "the fate of the entire heathen world is irrevocably fixed at death." He asked specifically whether Chapin had intended, in an earlier resolution passed by the board at its Des Moines meeting of 1886, that no missionary be sent into the field unless he subscribed to that tenet. In his public reply in the May 12 issue of the *Boston Advertiser*, Reverend Chapin discussed the background for the board's action and admitted that the resolution did not specifically forbid the appointment of missionaries who were unable to believe in the irrevocable fate of the entire heathen world. While there was much confusion about the implementation of this position in the appointment of missionaries, and while other related debates continued, Ladd seems to have been satisfied that he had won his point as a liberal theologian. He was less active in strictly theological debates, at least of a public, heretical variety, after this time. In the preceding years he had become preoccupied with studies in psychology and philosophy, and his great energy was now directed toward more formal writing in these areas and toward his developing interest in the Far East. In his autobiography he looked back upon his efforts as a theological liberal and commented:

> What I remember with most satisfaction is the unspeakable relief with which I finished my decade of experiences in the role of heretic. No one, in the Congregational churches of this country, can play the same role now; for times have radically changed. And although we may be obliged to confess that a part of this change is due to a lack of conviction and of interest in matters of theological doctrine, we may also claim, I think, that part also is due to a great improvement in Judgment as to what is most important in genuine religion, and as to the spirit which should characterize all the religious life.[7]

When one views the entire scope of Ladd's life and work, his career as a heretic becomes a meaningful expression of personal needs and interests that were brought into play, in one form or another, throughout his life. His heresy was not the dramatically impressive stand that some solitary religious thinkers have taken at various

[7] "Autobiography," p. 257.

points in history. He had the company of a growing number of theologians, and the liberal forces of his day were beginning to make themselves felt on the religious scene. But we should not underestimate the importance of the position which Ladd represented; considered within the context of Congregationalism at that time, his heresy was real enough and it required persistence and courage. His argument with orthodox theologians was personally significant for the precise reason that, at a crucial period in his life, it served as a test of his ability to express his own ideas with notable effect. Out of the long years of labor on his book *The Doctrine of Sacred Scripture*, Ladd developed a position that was at once liberal and intellectual. He knew from his elaborate studies that dogma which was held apart from the best available evidence was foredoomed, and he insisted on the right to decide for himself the character of the evidence that should be used.

The same needs and interests that led him to abandon the ministry for an academic career were expressed in his readiness to challenge the orthodox forces within the church. His strong interest in reading and research and his ability to write with ease—perhaps with too much ease—made him impatient with many of the duties of a busy ministry. He complained of the lack of time to dig deeply into issues and to present the results of his thinking for others who were able scholars. And this complaint would seem to have been directed at the unresponsiveness of Sunday-morning audiences.

Ladd's ten-year heresy, overlapping his ministerial and academic careers, was a period of personal transformation that was both intellectual and emotional. It grew out of the serious intellectual efforts that were required by his book on the origin of the Bible, but it reflected also the internal commitments and loyalties that were making an increasing claim upon his life. The intense feelings that he brought to the defense of his theological stand served to intensify his identification with those who sought scientific and rational answers to important questions. In many respects this period was the time of transformation from minister-theologian to philosopher-psychologist. The transformation probably would have occurred without the public heresy, but the controversy sharpened the focus upon his new role.

The years that followed Ladd's career as a heretic were to produce an irony that was as frustrating as it was bitter. He was to be criticized by scientists and philosophers for what they held to be an inability to accept the fruits of science and of modern scholarship. The scientists often dismissed him as a flaccid philosopher who could not let go of outmoded notions; his fellow philosophers considered him to be a Christian theologian who was inclined to prejudge important philosophical questions. The mediator was destined to be an alien caught between the two worlds that he sought to join.

Chapter · 7 ·

The "Speaking Teacher"

When Ladd arrived at Yale in 1881, American psychology was in a critical period of incubation, growing slowly from its philosophical and naturalistic seeds but awaiting still the nourishment that would be provided by the minds and pens of a small number of bold and forceful men. William James, G. Stanley Hall, James Mark Baldwin, James McKeen Cattell—these men, with Ladd and others, formed a suitably select nucleus of innovators who would launch a psychology strong enough to survive in the academic world and distinctive enough, by the turn of the century, to be considered something of a national product. The twenty-five years of Ladd's active association with Yale were the years of birth and bumptious infancy for American psychology, and while the new field was the product of historical and cultural forces that had been at play over a long period of time and on a broad front, the minds and pens of Ladd and his sturdy colleagues were the necessary agencies of development. In and through the life and work of each of these men, psychology became both a legitimate field of study and a hallmark of intellectual history.

The flowering of American psychology during the last two decades of the nineteenth century was an expression of a number of foreign and domestic developments. Among those abroad, two were of surmounting importance for Ladd and for his new field. The appearance of Darwin's *The Origin of Species* in 1859 intensified a concern with the naturalistic explanation of human nature and human potential. Evolutionary theory became a central problem for biology, but it produced as well a reassessment of philosophical and theological issues and provoked the controversy about man that was a necessary precursor of fresh psychological theory. The audacity and fertility of Darwin's thinking helped to create an atmosphere in which man could be approached as a fit subject for natural observation and study. Biological theory became a liberalizing force that opened more doors than it closed; peering through these doors one found, in various states of excitement and resentment, philosophers, theologians, scientists, and those intelligent laymen who were so important in the early development of scientific theory. Deeply impressed by Darwinian theory during his student years, Ladd realized that philosophy and theology would have to contend with Darwin in spite of their favorite preconceptions about man. The biological and theological theories were foremost in his mind when he decided to devote his life to a mediation between the old and the new learning.

At the same time that Darwin's evolutionary theory was helping to intensify the interest in human origins and potential, a new German experimental science was getting under way. In 1860 Gustav Fechner published *Elemente der Psychophysik*, holding that "psychophysics should be understood here as an exact theory of the functionally dependent relations of body and soul or, more generally, of the material and the mental, of the physical and the psychological worlds."[1] While Fechner spent a great share of his time writing philosophical treatises intended to defend idealism against materialism, his *Elemente* had the effect of helping to launch experimental psychology. Fechner, Helmholtz, and Wundt were the

---

[1] Gustav Fechner, *Elements of Psychophysics*, trans. Helmut E. Adler (New York: Holt, Rinehart, & Winston, 1966), vol. 1, p. 7.

principal agents of the new German experimental science, labeled physiological psychology by Wundt in 1874, and running through these pioneer efforts was an exciting new hope that sense physiology and some of the methods of experimental science could be usefully applied to the study of the soul.

The English and German developments were the necessary precursors of American psychology. The lines of influence are well summarized by Boring:

> The adult character of American psychology was formed in its youth, in the last quarter of the nineteenth century, when James and Hall and Baldwin and Cattell [Boring adds Ladd to the list elsewhere in his chapter] were building something new, based on what was going on in Germany and in England. The paternal ancestry of American psychology is German psychology, but the maternal ancestors are the biology and psychology of England. The child was, moreover, greatly influenced by the environment in which it grew up. Its nurture determined how its nature should realize itself.[2]

While American psychology has a history which extends beyond the year of Ladd's arrival at Yale, it was at this time that most of the academic, scientific, and personal history of the field began. Those interested in the new science were still going abroad to study with Wundt at Leipzig (G. Stanley Hall took the first American Ph.D. in psychology at Harvard in 1878), the psychological laboratories and journals were largely founded after this date, the important texts were yet to be written, and university professorships of psychology and separate academic departments were still to come. The necessary English and German influences were at work, American academic and cultural conditions were generally receptive, and, fortunately for the new field, Ladd, James, Hall, Baldwin, Cattell,

[2] E. G. Boring, "The Influence of Evolutionary Theory upon American Psychological Thought," in *Evolutionary Thought in America*, ed. S. Persons (New Haven: Yale University Press, 1950), pp. 291–292.

and others were worrying their highly individual ways into the exciting new problems and methods that were to characterize psychology. The last two decades of the nineteenth century saw a confluence of those factors that made American psychology possible, or perhaps even necessary. Ladd entered New Haven fully conscious of his own hope to ride on the crest of this new wave. Considering his lack of familiarity with the details of psychology, especially of the German variety, it is likely that he had only a vague notion of where the wave would carry him.

So, with ten years of preaching and two years of teaching behind him, Ladd went to Yale at the age of thirty-nine, a man in a hurry to get himself launched upon a new course of activity. He had some solid achievements to reinforce his already abundant self-confidence, but he began his work at Yale characteristically overburdened by lecture and writing commitments. His *Doctrine of Sacred Scripture* was as yet unfinished and he had agreed to give a course of lectures on systematic theology at Andover Theological Seminary. It would be two years before he was sufficiently free of these labors to devote himself to building up the philosophy (and psychology) department.

When Ladd left Bowdoin he carried with him the one hundred new books that he had purchased in an effort to gain a sudden exposure to the materials that a young professor of mental and moral philosophy ought to have readily at hand. His library went with him to Yale, but he took along also some rather serious reservations concerning his ability to teach college students. Apparently the abortive revolt of the "uncommonly manly and well-meaning fellows" at Bowdoin worried him a great deal and he was apprehensive about the response of the Yale undergraduates. There is both surprise and relief in a letter to his brother-in-law, dated October 16, 1881:

> I find my teaching—to my surprise—creating considerable positive enthusiasm. This news comes to me from so many quar-

ters that I suppose it to be true. It is very helpful to have a good
entrance into the men; they could make it very uncomfortable
and mar my work exceedingly if they got set against me.[3]

At least in the early stages of his teaching career at Yale things
seem to have gone well, but Ladd was not especially effective with
the undergraduates even though he worried about their attitudes
and tried hard to do a good job in the classroom.

Ladd's teaching schedule required one preparation each day, in
addition to which he offered two hours a week of optional study in
psychology for advanced students, based largely upon President
Noah Porter's *Human Intellect*. In his first year he gave many talks
to campus groups, speaking frequently in college chapel, and spent
most Sundays preaching as a guest in New England pulpits. The
teaching was going well, the work on his own unfinished manuscripts was progressing, and he and his family were being given a
cordial welcome to the community. In the fall of his first year at
Yale he was moved to write his brother-in-law, "Never before have
my days gone on with such a full stream of sweet content."[4]

Days of "sweet content," but nights of anxious probing. After
his evening meal and a brief period at the piano, Ladd would light
a professorial cigar and retire to his study for a six-hour period of
reading and wrestling with his one hundred new books. Night after night, for six long years, he read, compiled, and wrote with a
fervor born of one grand vision, "to know all that modern materialism has to offer" concerning "our demand for explanation of the
nature of that force which we call the human soul."[5] In those hours
after most reasonable professors had so reasonably gone to bed,
Ladd struggled with nagging physical symptoms and daily exhaustion in that quiet heroism which marks the great scholar. Boring
has written that "history is a part of nature where multiple causa-

[3] "Autobiography," p. 161.
[4] *Ibid.*, p. 163.
[5] *Ibid.*, p. 162.

tion rules and where single effective causes are the over-simplifications, devised to bring the incomprehensible complexity of reality within the narrow compass of man's understanding."[6] The history of American psychology must acknowledge the fervor of George Trumbull Ladd, who, ill-prepared by formal training but aglow with the nineteenth-century hope of applying the fruits of "modern materialism" to the illimitable human soul, produced *Elements of Physiological Psychology* at a crucial point in the early years of the new science. *Elements* became the timely handbook of the field, but the vision and human struggle from which it grew are, thus far, unacknowledged aspects of the multiple causation that rules the field.

The creation of *Elements* dominated Ladd's first six years at Yale. There was a growing family behind the arduous program of teaching and scholarship (a daughter, Elisabeth, had arrived on February 15, 1884), but Ladd's home life was tightly organized so as to serve his ambitious pursuit of the new mental science. He knew what he had to do and he did it. In his autobiography he wrote that he began early to specialize

> . . . in the field somewhat vaguely and incorrectly denominated "physiological psychology." This task was at that time, in spite of the vast increase in research, achievement, and publication, during the last thirty years, much more difficult than it would be at the present time (1910). The results of experimental work were to be found almost exclusively in German—with comparatively few French—monographs. The second edition of Wundt's *Grundzüge der Physiologischen Psychologie*, which appeared in 1880, was the only treatise in any language which attempted to deal with the entire subject in a summary way. Many of the words employed in these German monographs were not to be found in any dictionary. Not infrequently, the

[6] E. G. Boring, *A History of Experimental Psychology* (New York: Appleton-Century-Crofts, Inc., 1957), p. 744.

only way to determine their meaning was to translate the German roots into the corresponding Greek roots, our English technical terms in anatomy, physiology, psycho-physics, and the other allied particular sciences, being almost exclusively compounds of Greek roots. Indeed, had it not been for my knowledge of Greek, I do not know how I should have managed to read intelligently these scientific treatises. I had at that time no laboratory for experimental research, and only a very meagre equipment of apparatus for illustrating the results of the research of others. In the matter of the study of the brain and nervous system and of what was known as general physiology of the nerves, through the great kindness and active co-operation of my friend Professor Thatcher, I was somewhat better off. But for several years I worked very hard upon this course, —not infrequently as many as twenty-five or thirty hours a week, until it was expanded to two hours weekly running through the entire year, and still later took the form of the book, *Elements of Physiological Psychology.*[7]

It is clear that Ladd depended heavily upon Dr. J. K. Thatcher, professor of physiology in the Yale Medical School, for advice and friendly criticism of the materials concerning the nervous mechanism. Thatcher took a strong interest in Ladd's efforts to bring physiological evidence to bear upon psychological problems and it is questionable whether Ladd could have succeeded in his ambitious task if it had not been for Thatcher's aid. With no formal background in the field of physiology, his dependence upon Thatcher was an acknowledged and crucial part of the whole undertaking. In his preface to *Elements*, he wrote of Thatcher, "If I have escaped the mistake of assuming to teach more than is really known upon this subject, it has been in large measure due to his friendly and skillful guidance."[8]

[7] "Autobiography," pp. 179–180.
[8] *Elements of Physiological Psychology* (New York: Charles Scribner's Sons, 1887), p. v.

Over a period of several years, then, Ladd searched for "all that modern materialism had to offer" and drew it together in a form suitable for teaching a course in physiological psychology. His *Elements* was tried out on Yale students topic by topic and chapter by chapter until it was considered sufficiently complete for publication. In 1887 Scribner's published the huge work. It was recognized at once as a valuable source for the infant field.

Ladd's monumental *Elements of Physiological Psychology* was one of the most influential books in the early history of American psychology. The book was large, dry, scholarly, respectable, and, most important of all, timely. It was large, dry, scholarly, and respectable precisely because Ladd himself was thorough, serious, learned, and terribly proper; but it was timely because in 1887 American psychology had not been fully launched and the book helped to state the case for a discipline that was altogether ready to be born.

Elements of Physiological Psychology was an expression for American psychology of an increasingly abundant European, and particularly German, literature on a new science. It was a painstaking summarization of this literature, but it was more than a mere compilation of points of view. It expressed, through Ladd's scholarship, an American interpretation of psychological problems. It was a restrained and somewhat tentative statement of the functional perspective that was to infuse itself into American psychology. It was faculty psychology, the psychology of consciousness, and metaphysical disquisition; in addition, however, the book was unified and characterized by a pronounced faith in the relevance of science to the study of mental life. It advocated experimentation and controlled observation, though some of the procedures which were espoused in the name of science seem quaint from a distance of seventy-five years. *Elements* became an indispensable handbook for the new science, just as Hall had predicted in his long and favorable review in the first volume of the new *American Journal of*

Psychology.[9] It went through ten printings, was widely read by students of psychology both here and abroad, and was revised with the assistance of Woodworth and reissued in 1911 under the same title.[10]

There is reason to believe that the publication of Ladd's book came as a surprise to American psychologists. One indication of this is to be found in a congratulatory letter from William James quoted in Ladd's autobiography. The letter is unmistakably "Jamesian," both in literary style and in the attitude expressed toward certain aspects of the field.

Cambridge, April 4 (1888)

My dear Sir,

I have rarely experienced more delight than in turning over the leaves of your book, which arrived yesterday. I had no idea that you were interested in any such thorough way in that side of psychology. I am competent to judge of the immense amount of repellent labor required to digest that thorny mass of literature, and it fills me with admiration of your power of will and of body as well as of intelligence. As well as I can tell after so hasty an examination, it is well and judiciously done, too. What with Dewey's, Bowne's, and your books, all published within three months, and Hall's Journal announced, American

[9] G. S. Hall, review of G. T. Ladd's *Elements of Physiological Psychology*, in *American Journal of Psychology*, 1 (1887), 159–164.

[10] Apparently Woodworth accomplished most of the revision, Ladd then being involved in other matters. A psychologist who was aware of the day-to-day revision of the book, but who prefers to remain anonymous, has commented as follows: "It is my impression that joint authorship with Ladd was not originally planned, but that Professor Woodworth's contribution was of such magnitude that justice required his name on the title page. . . . I seem to have a recollection that the decision was not made without difficulty." (Personal communication to the writer, October 22, 1961). The publisher's record of correspondence with Ladd for that period reveals that the proofs were to be sent to Woodworth when they came from the press. (Personal communication to the writer from Charles Scribner's Sons, dated November 17, 1961.)

psychology need not hang its head, and may look, methinks, to a rather brilliant future. I am too loaded down with arrears of work of my own to sit down and read your book through at present. I shall begin, naturally, with the final theoretic chapters, and trust to do that soon. As for the time-measurements and things, my soul is a little weary of them and of their absolute sterility in the way of throwing light on any psychological question whatever. Still they are facts, and must some day serve a purpose. Your book will be of priceless convenience to all students. To myself it is especially a godsend, for I am with shameful slowness—*valetudine impeditus*—scribbling a "Psychology" toward completion, and a few references to your book will hereafter save me many tedious hours of rummaging in archives and of writing. In short, it is an honor to American scholarship, and I congratulate you most heartily on having brought it to so successful a completion.

Sincerely yours,

Wm James[11]

The book was, indeed, useful to James. He drew upon it in a number of ways, and, as students of his work know, the opening sentence of the abridged edition of *Principles of Psychology*, originally published in 1892, refers to Ladd's work: "The definition of Psychology may be best given in the words of Professor Ladd, as the *description and explanation of states of consciousness as such.*"[12]

[11] "Autobiography," p. 696. In a letter to Theodore Flournoy, dated December 31, 1893, James remarked: "Everyone seems to be publishing a Psychology in these days. Ebbinghaus, Külpe, Müller, Ladd, Stout, and who knows who besides. It seems as if some precipitation of truth ought to result from all this industry and I hope it will. Those who wait before emitting their own thunder till all this irrigating shower has passed by, and fertilized the ground will be in the best position to write something good." R. C. Le Clair (ed.), *The Letters of William James and Theodore Flournoy* (Madison: University of Wisconsin Press, 1966), p. 31.

[12] W. James, *Psychology* (Cleveland: The World Publishing Co., 1948), p. 1.

George Trumbull Ladd

Looking back across eighty years of the development of American psychology, *Elements of Physiological Psychology* stands as a classic example of the early efforts of scholars to create a new approach to the human soul. It is a bit difficult from this vantage point to appreciate the radical departure from established methods that physiological psychology represented, and to recognize also the book's importance as a comprehensive summary of the state of the science up to that time. Ladd was well aware of the fear and resentment that many would feel concerning his book; he was, after all, busily engaged in defending himself against charges resulting from the publication of his liberal *Doctrine of Sacred Scripture*. Writing as both mediator and heretic, he began his preface by commenting upon the importance of the new experimental and physiological methods in psychology and then, revealingly, stated:

> Some writers have certainly indulged in extravagant claims as to the past triumphs of so-called Physiological Psychology, and in equally extravagant expectations as to its future discoveries. On the other hand, a larger number, perhaps, have been inclined either to fear or to depreciate every attempt to mingle the methods, laws, and speculations of the physical sciences with the study of the human soul. These latter apparently anticipate that some discovery in the localization of cerebral function, or in psychometry, may jeopard the birthright of man as a spiritual and rational being. Or possibly they wish to regard the soul as separated, by nature and with respect to its modes of action, from the material body in such a way as to render it impossible to understand more of the one by learning more about the other.
>
> As a result of some years of study of the general subject, I express with considerable confidence the opinion that there is no ground for extravagant claims or expectations, and still less ground for any fear of consequences. In all cases of new and somewhat rankly growing scientific enterprises, it is the much better way to waive the discussion of actual or possible achieve-

ments, as well as of welcomed or dreaded revelations of new truth, and proceed at once to the business on hand.[13]

Discussing "the business on hand" for nearly seven hundred pages, Ladd concluded with the observation that physiological psychology cannot deal with the origin, destiny, mortality, or corruptibility of the mind—these "first and last things of the mind" must be entrusted to rational psychology, ethics, metaphysics, and theology. After six years of the most intense effort to discover what modern materialism had to offer, he was satisfied, and probably relieved, to find that it had nothing to offer concerning the first and last things of the mind. As a philosopher and theologian he believed that the first and last things of the mind were the most important and that psychology could not be helpful concerning these issues; as a psychologist he was ready to assist in any way possible in bringing modern materialism to bear upon all those things of the mind that fell in between.

Elements drew heavily upon Wundt's *Grundzüge der Physiologischen Psychologie,* but there was another source which did even more to set the basic theme of Ladd's approach to psychological problems. Between 1884 and 1887 he had translated and edited six small volumes of the lectures of the German philosopher-psychologist Hermann Lotze, and it is Lotze who shines through his treatment of many of the central issues of psychology. While Ladd was in no sense an uncritical disciple of Lotze, he did have a high regard for Lotze's work and took issue with him only after very careful thought about alternatives. In his preface to Lotze's *Outlines of Psychology* he spoke of Lotze as "almost incomparably well fitted to deal with the great science of Psychology," and held that "he may fitly be called a born psychologist." His preface to Lotze's work on psychology contains a statement which reveals part of the reason for the high esteem in which he held the philosopher: "But

[13] *Elements of Physiological Psychology,* p. iii.

Lotze was equally well equipped by nature and cultivation to discuss the metaphysical problems which enter into the study of psychology and which so largely impart to it its peculiar value and charm."[14] For Ladd, it was the metaphysical problems that gave psychology "its peculiar value and charm."

Ladd and Lotze shared a deep interest in metaphysics. Their common concern about the limits of science put them on the same side of many of the issues that confronted psychology as it began to go its own way, free of philosophy. In fact, neither Ladd nor Lotze wanted the field to slip away from philosophy, and each in his own way tried to mediate between the materialistic and spiritual tendencies in psychology. Ladd's philosophical and humanistic reservations about the new science of the soul were ably stated throughout his career as a psychologist, and he often seems to have taken heart when, in the midst of his battles with the materialists, he returned to Lotze's calm statement of the hoped-for reconciliation of rival claims. He was especially encouraged to find that Lotze could remain the idealistic mediator, even though he had received, as Ladd had not, a thorough training in physiology and medicine.

Ladd's most intense period of psychological writing spanned the years from 1881 to 1894. During this period he published, in addition to *Elements*, the following books: *Outlines of Physiological Psychology* (1891), *Primer of Psychology* (1894), and *Psychology: Descriptive and Explanatory* (1894). *Outlines of Physiological Psychology* was a reduced and revised edition of *Elements*, an adaptation intended for textbook purposes, and *Primer* was written as a beginning text. Each of these was a rather successful venture, thereby extending his reputation as a leading spokesman of modern psychology. But *Psychology: Descriptive and Explanatory* was a major new effort by Ladd to state his own case for the field. While acknowledging his indebtedness to others, his preface to this

[14] H. Lotze, *Outlines of Psychology*, ed. and trans. G. T. Ladd (Boston: Ginn & Co., 1886), p. vii.

large volume made a point of the fact that "I can truthfully acknowledge no special obligations to any individual," and that "it is
my belief that there is not a page, and scarcely a line, of this treatise
which does not show that all its material has been wrought anew
into a distinct and characteristic organism of truth."[15] Now this is
a rather robust claim for any author to make for each line of a 669-
page book; however, Ladd was eager to have others recognize
that he was writing new material. Once he had put his zealous
heart into his work, he always seemed to feel that it was imperish-
ably his own and that it was true. His self-assurance was not easily
appreciated by his psychological colleagues at Yale, and, as we will
see later, this personal characteristic was one reason for his premature and rather awkward retirement.

Though each line of *Psychology: Descriptive and Explanatory*
may have revealed a characteristic organism of truth, the book did
not have the success that Ladd had expected for it. There were some
important new facets to the work, especially in the arrangement of
chapters and in the treatment of topics, and the book was a good
statement of Ladd's functional and mediational approach to the
field; by 1894, however, there was a serious competitor in the text
market. The book suffered by comparison with William James's
Principles of Psychology, which had galvanized the field with its
appearance in 1890. Where Ladd was ponderous and dry, James
was light and incisive; also, it must be admitted, though Ladd
might not have done so, that James was the more original thinker
concerning psychological matters. *Psychology: Descriptive and Explanatory* was a solid and useful book and it enhanced Ladd's reputation, but it argued a fading cause in 1894, and, unfortunately
for Ladd, it was issued a half-dozen years too late for the best effect. Ladd was probably right in believing that the book did not receive the attention that it deserved. With James at the height of his

[15] *Psychology: Descriptive and Explanatory* (New York: Charles Scribner's Sons, 1894), p. viii.

nimble powers, writing psychology texts in the 1890's must have been a discouraging business.

Ladd's career in psychology reached its high point in 1894 with the publication of *Primer of Psychology* and *Psychology: Descriptive and Explanatory*, and with the conclusion of his presidency of the American Psychological Association. (Hall had served as the first president, to be followed by Ladd and then James.) His role as a scholarly leader in psychology, his growing reputation in philosophy, and a broadening influence in academic circles both at home and abroad represented a solid achievement for the man who only a decade and a half earlier had left the ministry to mediate between the old and the new learning.

Ladd's early years of teaching at Yale involved hearing recitations from Porter's *Human Intellect*, giving some rather informal instruction in psychology to a few advanced students, and lecturing occasionally to theological students. In 1884–1885 Ladd offered courses in physiological psychology and the history of philosophy. In physiological psychology he used his growing syllabus in the field; his philosophy course stressed the work of Kant. Placing Kant at the center of philosophy, Ladd insisted that students become familiar with the Kantian position on crucial issues. Ladd's teaching copy of *The Philosophy of Kant* by John Watson, published in 1884, has been preserved. The margins are crowded with notations and questions.[16] It is clear that he was a highly critical reader who brought to the material at hand the relevant items from other books and from his own experience.

During the academic year 1885–1886, Ladd began his work with graduate students, offering a small seminar on Lotze's *Microcosmus*, and in 1886–1887 he began a course for advanced philosophy students on Schopenhauer's *World as Will and Idea*. By 1889–1890 he was using *Microcosmus* in support of a study of "philosophical anthropology," and was offering a graduate seminar on

16 J. Watson, *The Philosophy of Kant* (New Haven: Tuttle, Morehouse & Taylor, 1884). Copy in the possession of Miss Cornelia T. Ladd of Cleveland Heights, Ohio.

Hartmann's *Philosophy of the Unconscious*. From approximately 1894 until his retirement, his teaching moved more exclusively into philosophy, and because of internal academic difficulties to be discussed in a later chapter, he abandoned most of his undergraduate teaching in favor of work in the graduate and theological departments. The catalogue for 1904–1905, the year before his retirement, lists four courses for graduate students, all in philosophy.

Deeply concerned about his teaching, Ladd maintained that it was his work as a "speaking teacher," rather than as a "writing teacher," that was the most precious in his own eyes. From the time of his early and painfully self-conscious ministry in Edinburg, he seemed to have a conviction that he would make himself into an unusually effective speaker and teacher. It was as if, fearing the worst in his efforts to speak in public and not quite trusting his own reticent ways, he was determined to excel in what was least natural to him. Whether "driving straight for the people" of Edinburg or Milwaukee, or lecturing to a group of school teachers in Japan, or leading a graduate seminar at Yale, he put enormous energy and concentration into his teaching efforts. He wanted desperately to be a great teacher. While he did not become a great teacher, he certainly was not a poor or shoddy workman. Ladd was most effective with the advanced students who were ready to exert some effort to stay with him in his dry and serious delivery. He taught with "moral earnestness"; there was no room in his delivery for wit and fancy, but apparently he found ample room for biting criticism and satire.

Ladd's difficulties as a teacher are reflected in the comments of former students. While stating that the students in his classes felt that they were being addressed by an expert in his field of study, a Yale student of the class of 1894 held that "he seemed to feel it was his duty to give his latest results of study and reflection without considering its adaptability to the student mind."[17] A student who had studied philosophy with Ladd later characterized him as "al-

[17] Personal communication to the writer, October 31, 1961.

ways friendly, but not intimate," and stressed his love of long and obscure words, his tendency to speak "over our heads," and his belief that the text should be followed "slavishly."[18] Another former student, referring to the required course in psychology that Ladd had taught with his own *Psychology: Descriptive and Explanatory* as the text, commented: "I think it is not unfair to state that both he and his book were thoroughly disliked by the undergraduates." The writer of the letter referred to Ladd's patronizing practice of dictating to his classes, during the closing five-minute period, the notes he wished each student to preserve.[19] Former Yale President Charles Seymour, a friend of the Ladd family, characterized the attitude of the undergraduates toward Ladd as one of "despairing resignation," adding that "it is easy to understand that he was not a popular or effective undergraduate teacher. His course was maintained by faculty fiat so that the students were compelled to attend it. The attitude of the graduate students was, I think, quite different."[20]

An ardent advocate of the required curriculum, Ladd held that undergraduate students were not capable of selecting the courses that they should have for a sound education. Until the reorganization of the curriculum in 1900, a course in psychology was required of all undergraduates, and the lack of choice probably contributed to their "despairing resignation." A man of great learning but little wit, formal in his relations with others and impatient with the carefree attitudes of youth, Ladd was not a colorful or compelling teacher of students who were forced to attend his classes. His effect upon graduate students, as President Seymour indicated, was an entirely different matter. When great learning and the implicit motivations of serious students come together, the formality, lack of humor, and impatience of the teacher may even become the fondly remembered personal traits of an impressive man.

18 Personal communication to the writer, November 11, 1961.
19 Personal communication to the writer, November 14, 1961.
20 Personal communication to the writer, November 13, 1961.

Ladd's influence upon graduate students is well illustrated in the remarks of Luther A. Weigle, who received one of the last Yale Ph.D.'s under his supervision. Weigle has stated: "My memories of Professor Ladd are very pleasant. He was unfailingly kind to his students . . . . He was fair and just in his criticisms of the judgments and positions of other men. He always impressed me as having a proper respect for the facts and for sound scientific method."[21] In an account of his personal education, Weigle gave Ladd credit for his own lifelong interest in Kant and eulogized Ladd as a great teacher and scholar. He commented that "undergraduates could not understand him, and scoffed at his definition of psychology as the science of 'states of consciousness *as such*'; but we graduate students found him a stimulating teacher and gained profound respect for his prodigious learning."[22] Weigle recalled that during his work under Ladd's direction, Ladd could be found in his office working on his *Philosophy of Religion*. "He sat as he wrote in an ample cane-seated rocking chair, one arm of which was enlarged to make a fairly good substitute for a desk. His detractors used to comment blithely that his books read as though they were composed in a rocking chair—a remark which we who were his friends would indignantly reject as slanderous and as evidence merely of their inability to understand him."[23] What scholar would not appreciate the understanding and support of young partisans? Rocking chair, indeed!

Ladd was especially effective as a graduate teacher of Kant, Schopenhauer, and, of course, Lotze. Many of his former students have recorded their appreciation of his courses on Kant and Schopenhauer, and there is reason to believe that he was at his best as a "speaking teacher" of these philosophical systems. William Lyon Phelps has written of his two years of hard labor with Ladd on

21 Personal communication to the writer, February 7, 1962.
22 L. A. Weigle, "The Religious Education of a Protestant," in *Contemporary American Theology*, 2nd series (New York: Round Table Press, 1933), p. 324.
23 *Ibid.*

George Trumbull Ladd

Kant's *Critique of Pure Reason,* commenting also that his study of
Schopenhauer under Ladd's direction was the greatest intellectual
stimulus of his first year of graduate study.[24] A similar tribute is recorded by Wilbur L. Cross concerning Ladd's graduate courses on
Kant, Lotze, and Schopenhauer.[25] Graduate students of philosophy
were deeply influenced by the combination in Ladd of sound classical scholarship, a knowledge of the new mental science, and a
teaching technique which ennobled learning through its sobriety
(the "despairing resignation" of undergraduates notwithstanding)
and moral earnestness. Ladd's classes may not have been fun, but
they were likely to be memorable.

The distinguished American psychologist Carl E. Seashore, who
was a graduate student at Yale during Ladd's most influential
years, has left an excellent statement recalling his work with Ladd
and others in the department. Seashore worked in the Psychological Laboratory under Edward Scripture, but he was enrolled in
Ladd's courses throughout his graduate career. Ladd was not fond
of laboratory work and, just as James found it necessary to bring
Münsterberg to Harvard to manage the lab, Scripture had been
brought to Yale, thereby relieving Ladd of the day-to-day supervision of this growing enterprise. Unfortunately, Ladd was not prepared to give Scripture the freedom that he needed to develop the
lab and there was some rivalry between the two men. This relationship was but one element of the complicated internal politics of
the department that contributed to Ladd's early retirement and
Scripture's removal from the faculty. Seashore profited from the
instruction and guidance of both men, even though he must have
found his position a bit difficult at times.

[24] W. L. Phelps, *Autobiography with Letters* (New York: Oxford University
Press, 1939), p. 203.
[25] W. L. Cross, *Connecticut Yankee* (New Haven: Yale University Press, 1943),
pp. 97–99.

In his autobiographical account Seashore commented:

> Much as I now see the shortcomings of Ladd's system, I still maintain that he was a great teacher. His "system" rang like a bell. In this respect I have not known his equal, unless it be Paulsen, in Berlin. He had his subject thought out. His lectures were clear, convincing, and fair. He was a man of great erudition and had digested it all into his own system. He had an extraordinary power for balancing evidences and organizing logical arrangements of facts. His submission of fundamental issues to a rigid critique is often lost sight of because not stated in controversial form, but in his constructive and tempered style of review. In my own case, entering philosophy and psychology from such a constructive point of view was wholesome and pedagogically good from the point of view of natural growth. Having one self-consistent view in mind, it was easy for me later to entertain and evaluate conflicting notions.[26]

In a brief necrological article published in 1921, Seashore characterized Ladd in appreciative terms and then stated: "His definitions were those of a logician; his scientific perspective was that of a philosopher; his power of appeal was that of the forceful teacher."[27] Ladd would have been greatly pleased by this statement.

The prolific writer and forceful teacher was also a campus politician and a peripatetic lecturer. The pressures of campus politics were a continuing part of Ladd's life at Yale, largely because he had strong opinions and usually wanted his own way in academic matters. It was in the political arena that he finally suffered defeat. The story of his downfall is an important one in an account of his life; it will be reserved for a later chapter.

[26] C. E. Seashore, in *History of Psychology in Autobiography*, ed. C. Murchison (Worcester, Mass.: Clark University Press, 1930), vol. 1, pp. 249–250.
[27] C. E. Seashore, "George Trumbull Ladd," obituary, *Science*, 54 (1921), 242.

George Trumbull Ladd

Ladd was irresistibly inclined toward the public platform and seldom turned down an offer to speak, whether in a single appearance or, as in the case of his trips to Japan, in a long series of addresses. The moral tone of his self-assumed mission in life urged him on; he felt that the refusal of a chance to speak before an audience was a violation of a sacred trust that he, as an educator and philosopher, held for mankind. He would speak his piece in life and he would do so whenever the opportunity presented itself. Opportunities were numerous. It is estimated that, during twenty-five years of active affiliation with Yale, he made more than 2,300 public addresses. When this figure is added to his regular teaching load it becomes clear that he was as addicted to speech as he was to writing.

He felt a special inclination to speak before religious, fraternal, and business associations. Ladd considered himself obligated to bring the fruits of his mediational scholarship to the general public, and he distrusted those university teachers who felt that the products of scholarship were too complex to offer the untrained mind. He early developed an interest in university-extension teaching.

> I have always regarded a certain large measure of work in the line of university extension as a sort of moral obligation. It is the people that build and equip the universities; and to the people, for their welfare and uplift, the devoted work of the teachers in them is justly due.[28]

In 1888, Ladd assisted in the formulation of a plan for extension teaching in Brooklyn. He was one of the original participants in a special program of extension courses offered in New York, lecturing on "The Elements of Human Mental Life" and "The Development of Human Mental Life" at Columbia College and at

[28] "Autobiography," p. 217.

the Pratt Institute in Brooklyn during the spring of 1891. Throughout the spring he lectured at Columbia in the afternoon and at Pratt in the evening, and then, following a midnight train ride to New Haven and a brief period of sleep, he rose early in the morning to prepare lectures for his classes at Yale.

As his reputation grew, Ladd was called away from Yale with increasing frequency. Though he worried about the disruption that it caused in his own scholarship and in the management of the Yale department, he seemed unable to turn down invitations to speak. He gave a course of lectures on "The Pastor as Student" at the Union Theological Seminary during the academic year 1893–1894 and added to his burdens at that time a special course at Columbia on the fundamental problems of philosophy. He lectured on hypnotism before the Brooklyn Institute of Arts and Sciences in 1895–1896. The study required by this engagement was the beginning of a continuing interest in the medical and legal implications of hypnotism. A flowering of this interest is seen in his address before the 1902 Albany meeting of the New York State Bar Association, subsequently published in the *Yale Law Journal*.[29]

In the 1895–1896 academic year Ladd journeyed to Harvard once a week to teach during G. H. Palmer's sabbatical. The experience was a pleasant one, characterized by Ladd as "the most happy experience of teaching abroad which has ever fallen to my lot this side of Japan and India."[30] Apparently the pleasure was increased by receiving an honorarium that was one hundred dollars more than had been promised! In the summer of 1896, Ladd lectured for six weeks at the University of Chicago on ethics and on the philosophy of religion. He also served as acting professor of philosophy at Western Reserve in the second semester of the 1905–1906 academic year and as a visiting professor in the 1906 summer session of the University of Iowa.

[29] "Legal Aspects of Hypnotism," *Yale Law Journal*, 11 (1902), 173–194.
[30] "Autobiography," p. 229.

George Trumbull Ladd

The "speaking teacher" was especially effective in his lectures away from the Yale campus. He devoted himself fully to his audiences, "driving straight for the people" with quiet fervor and a certainty born of great learning and moral conviction. Preceded by his reputation as a prodigious scholar, he rose before each audience without the handicaps that seemed always to beset him in his own neighborhood. In speaking abroad he was freed of the nagging bitterness and jealousy of his relations at Yale and freed also of the undergraduate attitude brought on by long exposure to his vanity and occasional pomposity. His teaching nemesis was the Yale undergraduate who was required to sit in his classes. But if there were troubles with the Yale men, there was at least the consolation of high success with Wellesley women:

> His method is one of marked moderation and well balanced consideration of all points of view. . . . The lectures of Dr. Ladd were not only extremely helpful to the students in course IX, but also most inspiring to those other members of the College who were privileged to attend. The clearness and reasonableness of the presentation of these rather abstruse and complicated teachings made the discussions especially valuable.[31]

[31] *Wellesley College News,* April 20, 1904.

Chapter · 8 ·

Psychology: The So-Called Natural Science

The first issue of the *Philosophical Review*, published in 1892, featured a long and critical article by Ladd entitled "Psychology as So-called 'Natural Science.'" The article was long because it was written by Ladd and it was critical because it dealt with the metaphysical impurities of William James's *Principles of Psychology*. For many years Ladd had marched, pen in hand, up and down the metaphysical byways of the new mental science until he knew by heart the snares and pitfalls of this confusing country. His mediational route was not an easy one; he had survived and advanced only by superior effort. By 1892 he realized that, though he was a philosopher-psychologist who was interested in the larger realm of mental science, the crux of his argument concerned the metaphysical assumptions that were necessary to the development of that field.

Ladd knew what he was for and by 1892 had identified what he was against. He was for sound metaphysics and he was dead set against cerebral psychology, especially when it was offered in the bright, deft style that graced the works of William James. With a mixture of respect, envy, and indignation, he attacked. The battle had two phases: first, the skirmish of 1892 featuring Ladd's article and a rejoinder by James; and, second, the effort to establish a solid theoretical basis for the inclusion of metaphysics in mental science, with the publication of *Philosophy of Mind* in 1895. Ladd lost the battle, but he lost with significance.

Using James's *Principles* as the text for his discussion, Ladd began the skirmish on a positive note by referring to the two volumes as "so learned, so full, so interesting, so frank, so 'pronounced' on doubtful issues, and—I may add—so provoking, that they are particularly well suited to such a purpose."[1] With the customary compliments out of the way, he began to express his reservations. It is not possible to know just why James discusses some issues in detail and wholly omits others, he complained. The author's own mental evolution in dealing with psychological issues is displayed in the book, but it is difficult to follow this evolution because the reader cannot be certain that it corresponds to the order of the chapters. Observing that the discussion is "intensely personal," Ladd concluded that "each reader's estimate will probably therefore depend upon whether he has, or has not, a personal acquaintance with the author."[2] He worried through three paragraphs about the book's occasional assaults upon Herbart, Kant, and Spencer, and then observed that the "somewhat too free, and even loose" regard for the opinions of others is to be understood as "a native exuberance of interest in all the possible phases of all psychological problems. At worst, it is the irresistible but kindly disposition to hit a head wherever one is visible."[3] On the question of James's style: "One is constantly tempted to exclaim: Brilliantly and captivatingly said; yet I am not sure whether you mean *exactly* this, and not rather something else which I must proceed to say for you!"[4] Ladd then de-

[1] "Psychology as So-called 'Natural Science,'" *Philosophical Review*, 1 (1892), 24.
[2] *Ibid.*, p. 25.
[3] *Ibid.*, p. 26.
[4] *Ibid.*, pp. 26–27.

voted the remaining twenty-six pages of his article to saying what he thought James said and what he did not say properly.

Ladd did not object to characterizing psychology as a natural science, but he did differ strenuously with those who were willing to buy their way into the scientific fraternity with counterfeit metaphysical coins. What bothered him most about James's book was the author's apparent readiness to strip the field of its metaphysical complications and then, having laid the issue to rest, to proceed to a facile consideration of topic after topic without acknowledging the metaphysical inconsistencies that were involved. There was no greater offense possible in a Laddian lexicon of crimes than that of dismissing metaphysics while proceeding to use it.

He believed that James's psychology, as a natural science stripped of irrelevant metaphysics, could only be a limited cerebral psychology. Aware of the importance of physiological processes, he was ready to admit the crucial involvement of cerebral processes in behavior, but he definitely could not go along with the view that extra-cerebral considerations were to be sacrificed in order to have a natural science. No matter how skillfully James might describe, classify, and explain the phenomena of human behavior, Ladd saw the treatment as an oversimplification that either masked or omitted those issues that were at the heart of Ladd's psychology. Ladd held that cerebral psychology reduced the states of consciousness to mere epiphenomena, thrown off by the cerebrum in a manner that defied scientific analysis. Introspective psychology was undermined, the self was laid to waste, and the ineluctable human soul was no longer necessary. For many years to come, Ladd would return in his writing and lecturing to the issues raised by a soulless, cerebral psychology in much the same manner as he had been unable to forget, a dozen years before, the "promise and potency of Professor Tyndall."

One statement in *Principles of Psychology* revealed to Ladd the metaphysical absurdity of James's argument. In his chapter on "The

Mind-Stuff Theory," James discussed the metaphysical problem of defining the connection between mind and brain and closed the chapter by considering "the soul-theory." He held that positing "a soul influenced in some mysterious way by the brain-states and responding to them by conscious affections of its own, seems to me the line of least logical resistance, so far as we have yet attained."[5] He pointed out that the immediately known thing is the states of consciousness, rather than the soul itself, and advocated an empirical parallelism with the statement that we should

> . . . ask ourselves whether, after all, the ascertainment of a blank unmediated correspondence term for term, of the succession of states of consciousness with the succession of total brain-processes, be not the simplest psycho-physic formula, and the last work of a psychology which contents itself with verifiable laws and seeks only to be clear, and to avoid unsafe hypotheses.[6]

By holding to this position, James felt that psychology could "remain positivistic and non-metaphysical."

Now, Ladd held that positing a soul in some form of reciprocal relation to brain states was not "the line of least logical resistance," but rather "the line of most logical momentum." It was the best kind of metaphysical postulate and the one which gave proper credence to the testimony of the entire personal and racial history of mankind. He did not feel that, once posited, the relation between the soul and brain states should be considered any more mysterious than any other kind of relationship. It remained for a psychology properly sensitive to philosophy and metaphysics to remove whatever mystery there might be, just as it might remove the mystery of relations between physiological processes.

Believing that James's psychology, as a natural science without metaphysics, was wholly cerebral, Ladd then considered the man-

[5] W. James, *Principles of Psychology* (New York: Henry Holt and Co., 1890), vol. 1, p. 181.
[6] *Ibid.*, p. 182.

ner in which James treated the relation between the soul and brain states in his argument. It was not at all to his satisfaction. He could see metaphysics hiding in the argument and, what was worse, it was offered as the "last word" of a psychology which was to content itself with verifiable laws and avoid unsafe hypotheses! He returned again and again to the culprit phrase, as if fascinated by the ring of it—"a blank unmediated correspondence, term for term, of the succession of states of consciousness with the succession of total brain-processes." James was trying to bring his theory position to a point where metaphysics could be put aside as admitting of no further immediate resolution, so that the field could go on about its proper business. Ladd would have none of this. He could see only an evasion of one of the most important issues facing the field, and this in the dubious service of a psychology that was to risk its fortunes on the human cerebrum. He held, quite properly, that the term "blank unmediated correspondence, term for term" conveyed no specific definition of the relationship between mind and body, and that it was offered in passing on to a psychology that was supposed to rival physics in its objectivity and scientific reduction. As for the reduction of psychology to the terms of molecular science, he commented, "Not all the physiologists in the world can say 'in terms of molecular science,' what is done by the sciatic nerve of a frog, with the gastrocnemius muscle attached, when it is stimulated by the electrical current. And as to a science of nerve-physiology, which shall apply with any accuracy of detail to the variety of cerebral processes concerned in human thoughts and feelings—well, it is hard to measure our present remoteness from such a science."[7] For Ladd, psychology as an explanatory science without metaphysics, based upon the cerebrum and held together by "blank unmediated correspondence," was simply no science at all.

Ladd closed his article with the affirmation that psychology was entitled to be considered a natural science. It had a well-defined field of phenomena for description and explanation, and sufficient

[7] "Psychology as So-called 'Natural Science,'" pp. 34–35.

data to serve for both purposes. Perhaps the field could be pursued effectively without postulating a soul and without metaphysical implications, but obviously Ladd doubted that such a course would bear fruit. He held that the metaphysical postulate of a soul "stands as a great light at the end of our pathway," illuminating every scientific step. Ladd quoted once more James's statement that positing a soul which was influenced by, and which responded to, brain states, was the line of least logical resistance, and then concluded:

> Beside this confession I will place my own, made and defended in another place: "The development of Mind can only be regarded as the progressive manifestation in consciousness of the life of a real being, which, although taking its start and direction from the action of the physical elements of the body, proceeds to unfold powers that are *sui generis*, according to laws of its own."[8]

Ladd's "confession" was a mentalistic gauntlet flung down before the charging knights of materialism. It was no empty or ill-considered comment; he meant what he said and he wanted everyone, but especially James, to know what they were up against. They were confronted by a clear-headed, unapologetic argument on behalf of Mind. The inveterate metaphysician would have Mind in psychology or he would take science out of the field.

Following the "noteworthy passage of arms"[9] in the *Philosophical Review*, Ladd decided that he would have to give his position a more extensive treatment, and of course this meant the writing of still another book. For three years he labored over a manuscript, sharpening his argument as he moved from topic to topic. In 1895 the book was published under the title *Philosophy of Mind: An Es-*

[8] *Ibid.*, p. 53.
[9] A. A. Roback used this term to characterize the Ladd-James dispute. See his *History of American Psychology* (New York: Library Publishers, 1952), p. 164.

say in the Metaphysics of Psychology. The book was a great satisfaction to its author, a minor irritation to its critics, and a commercial failure.[10]

In his preface to *Philosophy of Mind* Ladd worried about the tendency of modern psychology to deny the reality, unity, and possibility of a permanent existence of the human mind, and made clear that he was writing the book as an answer to those who, in the name of science, "are resolving its entire being into a stream of mechanically associated 'epiphenomena,' thrown off from the molecular machinery of the cerebral hemispheres."[11] The two opening chapters dealt with the necessary relation between psychology and metaphysics. Taken together, they provided an excellent eighty-page argument for the preservation of a philosophical perspective upon psychological issues; also, they provided an argument, which Ladd did not intend to offer, in favor of putting aside many of the philosopher's favorite quandaries while the psychological scientist gets on with the business at hand. Ladd was both right and wrong in his position concerning psychology and metaphysics. He was right in pointing out the metaphysical assumptions that underlie the scientist's day-to-day efforts, but he was wrong in his persistent tendency to flail science because it was unable to provide answers to all the problems of mind, life, reality, and the inscrutable realm of human spirit.

Ladd argued that the laudable desire of psychology to rival the older, well-established empirical sciences had had many beneficial results, but that the influence of the physical and natural sciences upon psychology had created some significant problems for the

[10] In his autobiography, Ladd quoted a letter from James, written at Chocorua, New Hampshire, August 28, 1895. While James complained that the book represented his views "rather unfairly," he did express his "admiration at the extraordinary spirit and go of the whole thing, and testify my belief that the book will be *most* effective in the way of *settling opinion* on the subject of the self and many other matters. In fact, I don't see how anything scholastic and abstractionist can hold up its head after it, at all." "Autobiography," p. 697.

[11] *Philosophy of Mind* (New York: Charles Scribner's Sons, 1895), p. x.

new field. As he saw it, the problems were largely the fault of psychologists. He noted in them "a certain half surrender, or too timid and deferential use, of their own peculiar psychological standpoint." Dazzled by the gleam of "scientific objectivity," the psychologist was prone to surrender the discriminating consciousness or introspection that was his peculiar strength.

> Only in representative self-consciousness can we ever know what the phenomena of consciousness really are. The piling up of experimental results, the enlarging of collections of statistics, the anthropological and other "objective" data, all assist the science of psychology only in so far as they help the more extensively, accurately, and profoundly to analyze this representative self-consciousness. For the world in which his science moves is ever mirrored in his own soul; and if he first goes outside to collect and arrange signs of the conscious processes of other minds, he must always come back to his own consciousness to interpret the meaning of these signs.
>
> When, then, any student of psychology, through fear of being considered too subjective or too metaphysical, neglects to cultivate or depreciates and denounces the analytic of a trained introspective observer, he is in a fair way soon to be found offering for sale his own peculiar birthright; and the chances are very largely in favor of his exchanging this birthright for some mess of half-cooked pottage.[12]

For Ladd, the "mess of half-cooked pottage" was composed of the refined, but barren, leavings of an objective, scientific psychology stripped of metaphysics. The experimental results of the statistical data were a welcome addition to psychological science, but Ladd shared James's impatience with the accumulation of "mere facts." What he wanted to make clear was that facts were fiction unless they were somehow made noble by the queen of sciences.

12 *Ibid.*, p. 17.

The trouble with objective science was that it made psychologists become poor philosophers.

Philosophy of Mind argued the case for the reality of psychic life. Ladd believed that a vital psychology rested upon an assumption of a mental being or spiritual agent at the center of all other processes, and he warned that the consistent champion of science, without metaphysics, could not even "draw his sword to slay the metaphysical ogre."[13] His advocacy of metaphysics in psychological science was really part of the larger case for man's spiritual life, and the urgency of his insistence upon keeping metaphysics in psychology increased as "cerebral prejudices" became more fashionable in the field. He had James to thank for the growing acceptance of "cerebral prejudices," or at least this was his belief, and he returned often to an attack upon James's cardinal semantic sin—"blank, unmediated correspondence." He did his best to make the phrase a lasting symbol of the bankrupt metaphysics of those who argued most vigorously for a psychology that was to be positivistic and non-metaphysical.

Having shown to his own satisfaction the relevance of metaphysics to psychological science, Ladd proceeded to discuss the various mind-body theories that had been for centuries the steady diet of philosophers and scientists. One by one he rejected parallelism (and its modern variant "empirical parallelism"), phenomenism and solipsism, monism, spiritualism and materialism. The essence of his argument against each of these was that, in its peculiar way, each failed to support the logic of his own argument for "uncritical dualism." Ladd's case for uncritical dualism was a metaphysical potion that was brewed in passion and distilled by reason. He would have been the first to admit that the potion's medicinal effects were greatly increased when accompanied by faith.

To understand Ladd's advocacy of uncritical dualism it is necessary to recall that he was trying as best he could to find a reasonable

13 *Ibid.*, p. 32.

metaphysical position that would support both the old and the new learning. He was functioning as philosopher and psychological scientist, seeking with all the power of his great learning to reconcile the apparently irreconcilable faiths of two worlds. As a psychologist he urged upon his colleagues the uncritical dualism which he believed to be the only position that could support the stringent requirements of science and at the same time preserve the choice fruits of philosophy and religion. Bound by character and temperament to overreact to the bold empiricism of his fellow psychologists, he clearly pushed his argument for dualism beyond the limits he might have established for himself in a less defensive situation. The highly critical psychologist was an uncritical dualist, but, ironically enough, the scholastic philosopher was a hopeful monist. Ladd the mediator was making a mighty effort to span the widening gulf between his own personal convictions.

Introduction to Philosophy, published in 1890, was an early expression of the painful conflict that Ladd felt concerning the dualism which he advocated and the monism for which he yearned. He wrote as a philosopher when he held that

> . . . all the instincts of the philosophical mind, all the tendencies of modern scientific discovery and modern speculative thinking, all the influences from the examples of the greatest thinkers (materialistic, idealistic, pantheistic, theistic), are committed to the cause of monistic philosophy. . . . In conflict with all dualistic systems, some form of a monistic system will ultimately maintain the supremacy.[14]

Ladd set before the reader his hope that a new monism which satisfied the facts and truths of both realism and idealism would someday prevail. It would be a monism which properly reflected the findings of the physical and psychological sciences, as well as the truths of ethics, aesthetics, and religion.

[14] *Introduction to Philosophy* (New York: Charles Scribner's Sons, 1890), p. 403.

The hopeful monist was especially revealing when he discussed dualism. It is apparent that the dualistic position represented a temporary accommodation to conflicting forces:

> Dualism may . . . be regarded as the guardian of the interests which are jeoparded by either a materialistic Realism or an Idealism that resolves the extra-mental reality of the world of things into merely a series of objectifying psychical processes. It has a certain use and value in defending the rights of scientific physics against an incomplete philosophical analysis. It may also defend the rights of psychology against unwarrantable encroachments of a materialistic view of nature.[15]

The frequency and fervor of Ladd's arguments for dualism, especially in the years following the publication of *Introduction to Philosophy*, revealed how unwarrantable he found the encroachments of materialism. Twenty-nine years later, at the age of seventy-seven, he was still publishing material that reflected his interest in the dual nature of man.[16]

Ladd's temporary metaphysical accommodations to science offered him a choice between parallelism and dualism. He rejected parallelism because of what he considered to be the incomparability of mental and material phenomena. The mental phenomena were reducible to thinking, feeling, and willing, while material phenomena were ultimately to be reduced to motion. He held that "the mystery of knowledge cannot be resolved into the mystery of an unknown being manifesting itself in two parallel and proportional series of utterly incomparable phenomena."[17] Convinced of the incomparability of the two sets of phenomena, he was compelled to believe that there were two kinds of entities that somehow worked together. "Body we know, and mind we know; and if we are compelled to assume any real being to furnish a metaphysi-

15 *Ibid.*, p. 406.
16 "A Case of Multiple Personality," *Yale Review*, 8 (1919), 318–333.
17 *Philosophy of Mind*, p. 344.

George Trumbull Ladd

cal ground for the phenomena, then we can afford one kind of being for each kind of phenomenon."[18] In the vagueness of his argument on this point, he drew perilously close to the dreaded Jamesian black box of "blank, unmediated correspondence."

Though Ladd considered dualism to be a metaphysical necessity in scientific work, his heart was drawn ever nearer the cause of monism as he suffered the defeats of his later years. In 1903 he published an article which stated once more the inadequacies of parallelism and the importance of recognizing the two sets of entities. The article closed on an optimistic note, expressing again the philosopher's faith that monism would prevail:

> As philosophy reflects upon the data of facts and laws which psycho-physical science hands over to it, philosophy sees ever more clearly that this bond must be found in the Being of the Cosmos itself. For in this Being man, both body and mind, has his being; and in the nature of the Cosmos must somehow be found the more ultimate explanation of the infinitely varied, complicated and subtle interrelations of the two.[19]

Philosophy and faith led to monism, science and reason to dualism. Ladd was willing to consider psychology a natural science on the condition that psychologists embrace a dualistic metaphysics which left the door open to a fervently desired, but still unformulated, grand cosmic scheme.

[18] *Ibid.*, p. 346.
[19] "Brief Critique of 'Psycho-physical Parallelism,'" *Mind*, 12 (1903), 379-380.

Chapter · 9 ·

Reflective Consciousness

As a rational dualist with a monistic faith, Ladd felt compelled to fashion a psychology that was scientific and at the same time consistent with his commitment to mentalism. It was a task of enormous, if not impossible, proportions. He realized that many scholars already had failed in the effort to unite science and spirit. With his characteristic blend of audacity, endless effort, and ego, he developed a position on basic psychological issues and published it with reckless frequency and detail. At the heart of his theoretical position was the concept of human consciousness. Consciousness was the beginning and the end of psychology, the arbiter of reality for the species, and the precious and vital core of personal identity. It was the irreducible subject matter of psychology and, through a process of reflective self-consciousness or introspection, the imperative method of psychological analysis.

Ladd defined psychology as "the science which describes and explains the phenomena of consciousness, as such." Facts of consciousness become objects of knowledge when studied scientifically, but he wanted it understood that these facts are always related to the development of the psychic life of individuals. Psychology investigates "the becoming of the soul, the genesis and growth of mind in individual man."[1]

While holding that facts of consciousness may become objects of knowledge, he was careful to point out that isolated and disconnected facts cannot be made into the data of science. He distrusted the analytic process that was necessary in the delineation of psychological data and stressed the totality of mental function as a basis for scientific inference. The psychologist had a fundamental obligation to hold inviolate, somewhere beyond his aseptic scientific labors, the rich, human qualities of mental life. To speak of isolated facts of consciousness was a contradiction in terms, and while the psychologist might need to consider these facts as separate data, he should not slip into the serious error of believing that they were separable in mental life. Consciousness was a living process; psychology was concerned with its morphology, but it was even more concerned with its unsullied function. Ladd held that "if neither question nor answer makes any reference to states of consciousness, directly known by the subject as such, then the experimental inquiry is not psychological at all."[2] The qualification that the states must be known by the subject assured that psychology would study consciousness as a living unity. It was a prescription for science that would cause Ladd some embarrassment, however, when he began a study of hypnosis, dreams, and multiple personality.

Ladd's definition of psychology as the science of the phenomena of the states of consciousness, as such, was treated in detail in the huge text *Psychology: Descriptive and Explanatory*, published in 1894. The text made abundantly clear that its author considered the states of consciousness to signify the life of a real mind, or as he was inclined to express it, a Real Mind. Given the intensity of his

[1] *Psychology: Descriptive and Explanatory* (New York: Charles Scribner's Sons, 1894), p. 8.
[2] *Ibid.*, p. 24.

concern for the living unity behind the phenomena of consciousness, it is strange that he did not make that concern evident in his
formal definition. This oddity of scholarship is even more pronounced when one considers the definition that was offered in his
unusually brief *Primer of Psychology*, published in the same year.
The *Primer* stated that "psychology is the science of the facts or
states of consciousness, as such, and thus of the life of that subject
of the states which is called the Self, or the Mind."[3] Perhaps Ladd
felt that the *Primer*'s brevity required a compression of his argument and that the formal definition should announce his larger
conviction at the beginning of the book. Whatever the reason may
have been, the definition in the *Primer* was a more apt characterization of his psychology than the definition in the larger text.[4]

In a basic sense, then, Ladd's psychology was a psychology of
consciousness and, as James put it in a review of *Psychology: Descriptive and Explanatory*, his "aim may be called the unravelling
of the fibres of consciousness. Consciousness, like a rope, has for
Prof. Ladd a fibrillated structure."[5] As Ladd expounded his theory
in this book, consciousness has an irreducible threefold complexity:
it is always composed of intellection, feeling, and conation.[6] While
a specific psychosis may involve an ascendance of one over the
other two, all are inextricably interlaced in the living unity that is
mental life. It is the business of psychology to depict the relative in-

[3] *Primer of Psychology* (New York and London: Longmans, Green & Co., 1894),
p. 7.

[4] Ladd was such a prodigious writer that the bulk of his argument overwhelms
the reader. Various critics complained about the quantity of his writing and it is
likely that many potential readers were offended by the length and detail of his books
and articles. A briefer and more disciplined presentation of his ideas would have
increased the number of friendly readers and might have assured a more incisive
theory. There is so much that he could have profitably left unsaid without impairing
his psychology.

[5] *Psychological Review*, 1 (1894), 287.

[6] Ladd used the terms "conation" and "will" interchangeably in describing the
three aspects of conscious life, but he seems to have preferred the term "will' when
describing the active involvement of the mind in behavior.

volvement of intellection, feeling, and conation in the states of consciousness, as such, and so to weave these aspects of mental life together that the peculiar richness and force of mind is retained as the primary datum of the field.

If it is the richness and force of human life, "the becoming of the soul, the genesis and growth of mind in individual man," that is the primary datum of the field, what, then, is the theoretical meaning for psychology of the three irreducible fibers of the rope of consciousness? Those who are familiar with the early development of American psychology will assume that intellection, feeling, and conation are faculties of the mind and that Ladd's tripartite arrangement was in the best tradition of post-Kantian philosophy. The assumption is correct, but as with so many features of Ladd's psychology the obvious soon becomes hidden in a confusing array of qualifications. The fact of the matter is that Ladd made constant, apologetic use of the concept of mental faculties. He preferred to call them "the so-called mental faculties," and it is apparent that he realized the sterility of faculty psychology when the psychologist faced the enormous task of analyzing mental function without impairing "the richness and force of mind."

In his valuable critique of Ladd's psychology, Titchener complained that "Ladd, in all literalness, both accepts and rejects the doctrine of faculties. He speaks, in formal reference, of the 'so-called' faculties; he explains that the term (faculty) is both futile and dangerous; and still he employs the concept, repeatedly and constructively, in his psychological exposition."[7] Titchener was correct in his assessment. Ladd did attempt to have things both ways in his discussion of the faculties. This is nowhere more evident than in the following passage:

[7] E. B. Titchener, *Systematic Psychology*: *Prolegomena* (New York: Macmillan Co., 1929), p. 173. Titchener appropriately added that "Ladd's use of 'so-called' is a mannerism, which began as a defensive reaction against the possible charge of looseness of language. Since it has come with him to mean anything from 'what is ordinarily called' to 'what is falsely called,' it does him little service."

By the so-called "faculties" of mind, therefore, scientific psychology can, at most, only mean to indicate the different modes of behavior, or forms of functioning, which discriminating consciousness assigns to the one subject of all psychical states. In so far as this word or other cognate terms (such as "capacity," "power," etc.) can be safely used in the clear light of this understanding, we need not greatly object to them. But they afford no explanation of psychic facts, whether in general or in special; they are rather themselves the result of imperfect classification and confused analysis. Moreover, they lend little help to improved classification. On the other hand, their use, however guarded, is likely to occasion the separation in theory of that which is indissolubly and necessarily related in fact, the substitution of mere classification for real explanation, and a generally inadequate and misleading account of the development of mental life. At the same time, after uttering proper warnings, the limitations and necessities of psychological language are such that we are obliged to employ the terms assigned customarily to the so-called "faculties."[8]

Intellection, feeling, and conation were the different modes of functioning which everywhere characterized conscious activity; but consciousness was to be considered as both function and content and Ladd's discussion moved back and forth between the active and the passive meanings of the term.[9] While his writings did not always make clear to the reader which sense of the term he had in mind, in his defence it should be stated that it was precisely this double aspect of consciousness that offered the psychologist his scientific challenge and his opportunity. Consciousness was an active, purposive expression of mental life and, when arrested through trained introspection, a proper content for scientific study. It is perhaps appropriate that Ladd was ambiguous in his use of the con-

[8] *Psychology: Descriptive and Explanatory*, p. 51.
[9] Titchener held that Ladd's facts of consciousness were both "ambiguous and instable." See E. B. Titchener, *Systematic Psychology: Prolegomena*, p. 173.

cept. His writings were inordinately long and involved, with frequent digressions into neighboring topics, but his psychology was characterized by an urgent attention to Mind as an indivisible reality. He believed that the problems of function and content were problems created by philosophers and psychologists. Beyond the problems that were occasioned by inquiry loomed the Mind as an ultimate fact, and he enjoyed the confusion and despair that he could so easily elicit from his scientific colleagues when he reminded them that "all scientific explanation ends in the unexplained."[10] It is not surprising that Titchener worried about Ladd's system.

In both history and content, Ladd's psychology of consciousness was distinctly pre-Freudian.[11] While he occasionally used the term "unconscious," he meant only to dramatize the theoretical contrast between the psychical and the non-psychical. "The unconscious" was used in contradistinction to consciousness; he held that it was synonymous with no psychic state, and therefore beyond the domain of psychology. His definition of consciousness was surprisingly vague. Considered in light of the requirements of contemporary operational research, the definition was useless. At best it was but a descriptive effort, signifying his concern that psychology concentrate upon the mind as a phenomenon that was open to awareness and reflective exploration.

> What we are when we are awake, as contrasted with what we
> are when we sink into a profound and perfectly dreamless sleep,
> or receive an overpowering blow upon the head—*that* it is to be

[10] *Psychology: Descriptive and Explanatory*, p. 635.

[11] While Ladd's writings contain a number of heavily veiled references to Freud's work, there are no direct comments upon the Freudian shock waves that were so generally felt at the turn of the century. Undoubtedly Ladd read Freud, but he was not personally or intellectually friendly to such departures from sound, rational theorizing. There is no evidence that he attended Freud's American debut at Clark University in 1909, arranged by G. Stanley Hall. Ladd's psychological system was relatively "sexless," though he did hold that, owing to a deficiency of will, women could not compose music as effectively as men. When he tackled the problem of sex differences, his effort usually amounted only to an admission that the sexes differed!

conscious. What we are less and less, as we sink gradually down into dreamless sleep, or as we swoon slowly away: and what we are more and more, as the noise of the crowd outside tardily arouses us from our after-dinner nap, or as we come out of the midnight darkness of the typhoid-fever crisis—*that* it is to become conscious.[12]

Consciousness was used to refer to "psychic facts in general." Ladd acknowledged but rejected the concept of consciousness that was urged in Noah Porter's *Human Intellect*—namely, "the power by which the soul knows its own acts and states." His enormous respect for Porter made it difficult for him to differ, especially since he found the general burden of Porter's argument so live and compelling. But he wanted to place consciousness at the heart of his system and realized that the term would have to be made inclusive of all psychic states. It may appear to be a matter of small progression, from Porter to Ladd, but, historically considered, Ladd's admittedly vague and general position concerning consciousness represented a trend of significance. His acquaintance with the physiological literature, some of a suggestive clinical nature, and his awareness of the gradual accretions of laboratory research provided a vision of the borderlands of the field and led to a conviction that the subject matter of psychology was something more than "the power by which the soul knows its own acts and states." It is an interesting fact that, having opened the subject matter to include all of psychic life, he proceeded to develop a position that rested upon the power that he rejected. The twin concepts of attention and introspection were featured in his psychology; considered together, they went a long way toward meeting the requirements of Porter's definition.

Consciousness as the totality of psychic life was not to be considered a product of the brain; as a metaphysician, Ladd stressed the distinction between the "nerve-commotion" of the central nerv-

[12] *Ibid.*, p. 30.

ous system and the changing states of the mind. He held that the material world was reducible to molecules in motion, and that psychic states were of a different order of reality.

> To speak of mental states and processes as the "product" of the nervous mass of the brain, in any sense of the words corresponding to that which we rightly apply to the various secretions of the body, involves us at once in the grossest absurdities. . . . In so crass a way of speaking it is difficult to distinguish what can properly be meant by comparing—under the term "product"—the relation of conscious sensation and thought to the brain with the relation of the gastric juice to the stomach or of the pancreatic juice to the pancreas.[13]

The issue may seem quaint or irrelevant from the vantage point of the mid-twentieth century, but to Ladd, the mediator, it was crucial to consider whether the brain was, as some claimed, the seat of the soul. Unalterably opposed to a mechanistic cerebral psychology, he frequently repeated in his books and articles that the mind was a progressive manifestation in consciousness of the life of a real being which took its start and direction from the body, but which proceeded to develop according to laws of its own. The mind had integrity and reality; and he was attentive to any physiological evidence that seemed to argue for its independence.[14]

The body was composed of molecules in motion, the mind was a real being of a totally different nature, and the two were implicitly related. But how could an immaterial real being (mind) have a necessary location with reference to a molecular unity in space

[13] *Elements of Physiological Psychology* (New York: Charles Scribner's Sons, 1887), pp. 590–591.

[14] Three articles by Ladd illustrate his effort to assemble physiological and clinical evidence for the reality of mind: "A Suggestive Case of Nerve-Anastomosis,"*Popular Science Monthly*, 67 (1905), 319–328; "Suggestions from Two Cases of Cerebral Surgery Without Anesthetics," *Popular Science Monthly*, 74 (1909), 562–567; and "A Case of Multiple Personality," *Yale Review*, 8 (1919), 318–333.

(body)? To admit that "nerve-commotions" were necessary pre-conditions to the functions of mind "according to laws of its own" was to risk locating in space a phenomenon that was immaterial. Ladd's position on this knotty problem was similar to that which was argued by Lotze, from whom he drew comfort on a number of occasions.

> An immaterial real being can have no *extension* in space: it may, however, have a position; and this we define as the point up to which all influences from without must be transplanted, in order to make an impression on this being, and from which alone outward this being exercises immediate effects upon its environment.[15]

The mind, then, acts upon the physical world through, and only through, the mediation of the body. While the body might not be the seat of the soul, Ladd's psychology insisted that consciousness be allowed to stand near the body so that it could sit when necessary.

Consciousness was characterized by discriminable states, each of which was a fact of intellection, a fact of feeling, and a fact of conation. The discrimination of states of consciousness was a process that rested upon two pillars of Laddian psychology: attention and introspection. The fact that Ladd employed attention and introspection is no cause for surprise; indeed, the concepts were an expected part of the early functionalist's theory construction.[16] It is Ladd's view of the unusual interdependence of attention and introspection that helps to set his psychology apart from other functional theories of his day.

[15] H. Lotze, *Outlines of Psychology*, ed. and trans. G. T. Ladd (Boston: Ginn & Co., 1886), p. 105.

[16] A good example of the importance of attention and introspection in an early functional psychology is found in the work of James Rowland Angell. Angell held that introspection was the basic psychological method and his treatment of attention highlighted an entire chapter of his book. See his *Psychology* (New York: Henry Holt & Co., 1904).

George Trumbull Ladd

In *Elements of Physiological Psychology*, Ladd had discussed attention as a feature of several other topics, but the concept was not employed with the telling effect that is evident in *Psychology: Descriptive and Explanatory*. For one thing, the earlier book was a treatise that covered systematically the existing evidence as seen from the experimental and physiological points of view; Ladd gave his synthesis of this widely scattered material, but it was not his own psychological theory. Not until he presented his own position in the later book did the peculiar importance of attention become apparent. In *Elements* he did consider the relation of attention to such topics as memory, reaction time, and perception, but the concept played an inferior role in his presentation. Some foretaste of the importance that the term was to play in his psychology was provided in *Elements*, however, when he sketched the relation of attention to will. He said that when the control of attention is deliberately exercised, it provides us with

> . . . the consciousness of "choice"—the activity of will in deciding the direction and amount of attention bestowed upon one object among several in the field of consciousness. Percepts and ideas do not move from the various obscurer parts of the field of consciousness into the focal point by virtue solely of a momentum belonging to them as such; they are placed and kept there by an act of will. This must be admitted as an indubitable fact of consciousness, whether or not the physiological correlate or so-called explanation of this fact can be discovered or even conjectured.[17]

The power of will to direct attention was one of the most important of several "indubitable facts" of Ladd's psychology. It was indubitable in 1887, but it was even less open to doubt by the time that he wrote *Psychology: Descriptive and Explanatory*.[18]

[17] *Elements of Physiological Psychology*, p. 539.
[18] In *Primer of Psychology*, issued in 1894, Ladd featured attention by combining

Ladd's psychology required a metaphysics that was spacious enough to accommodate mind as a separable and unified reality, and a subject matter that was focused upon psychic life as a personal, developing phenomenon; but the theory also required that man have the opportunity to exercise options—to conceptualize alternatives and to behave in direct response to a knowing will. The concept of attention was crucial to the theory because it served as the psychological device by which will, and thereby free choice, was infused into consciousness. By 1895, he was characterizing attention as "the necessary presupposition and unceasing accompaniment of all the life of consciousness."[19]

An act of will fixes attention and influences the rhythm and the distribution of attention. Involuntary attention is an aspect of all psychic processes and need not express the direct force of will, but voluntary attention is characteristic of the developed and trained mind. In making a case for the control of voluntary attention by the act of willing, Ladd held also that education provided the means by which the will was elicited. It was the informed will that offered the greatest degree of control over attention and, by this means, the largest hope for personal freedom. Willing implies some knowledge of means and ends, and he argued persuasively that it was man's attention to and deliberation about the means-ends issues of life that ennobled his mind and offered the best hope for personal satisfaction.

Attention, then, was an indispensable element of Ladd's general theory, and he devoted a great deal of effort to making the process scientifically respectable. As one who was well acquainted with physiological and experimental evidence, he worked hard to develop a convincing argument. Apparently it was his hope that a physiological justification could be established for attention; he

---

it with the subject of consciousness in a single chapter. His discussion of consciousness and attention stressed the fundamental interdependence of the two topics.

[19] *Psychology: Descriptive and Explanatory*, p. 33.

was certain that he could provide the psychological justification for the process.

A search of his published work reveals several efforts to highlight the role of attention in behavior. We find that he published in 1893 a brief and rather insubstantial article on the development of attention in infancy, an article which displayed his impatience with "old fashioned speculative psychology."[20] In 1898 he published an article on color illusion which suggested that "the illusion is somehow dependent upon the rhythm of attention, and, in a limited way, it is under the control of will exerted through some obscure modification of the point and manner of regard."[21] Though he abjured the old-fashioned speculative psychology, his efforts to establish a scientific basis for attention were not especially successful. He did succeed, particularly in *Psychology: Descriptive and Explanatory*, in demonstrating the importance of attention in his own theory.

It was Ladd's belief that attention is a focusing of psychic energy. He held that

> . . . the physiological conditions of all attention seem to involve the focusing of physiological function in some of the cerebral areas, or forms of nerve-energy, and the withdrawal of such function from other areas of the brain or forms of its energy.[22]

The process was considered to be synonymous with the rise, fall, and redistribution of psychic energy. This was one of the crucial steps in Laddian theory. Embedded as it is in the bulk of his descriptive writing, the truth slips by the reader with less stress than it de-

[20] "The Development of Attention in Infancy," *Childhood*, June, 1893, pp 197–200.

[21] "A Color Illusion," *Studies from the Yale Psychological Laboratory*, 6 (1898), 5.

[22] *Psychology: Descriptive and Explanatory*, p. 66.

serves. Ladd made attention equivalent to psychic energy. The consideration of this concept represented the only point of direct contact between psychic and physiological processes. A close reading of this discussion in light of the repeated but scattered use of the term throughout his works suggests that he accepted the correlation, if not the fusion, of psychic and physical energy, at least in a degree and manner necessary to the mind's function.[23]

Ladd's psychology of consciousness featured the problems of intellection, feeling, and conation, and it is clear that he regarded these as basic elements of mental life. What is not clear is his rationale for including sensation, which he defined as "those peculiar modifications of consciousness which are experienced in the use of the organs of sense,"[24] in many of his discussions of feeling and intellection. He held that each state of consciousness is a fact of intellection, a fact of feeling, and a fact of conation. His preoccupation with the problems of sensation, however, often seemed inconsistent with his discussion of the intellection-feeling-conation triumvirate that he put at the heart of consciousness. Perhaps he wanted to suggest that each state of consciousness also is a fact of sensation.

A major portion of *Psychology: Descriptive and Explanatory* was organized under the heading "The Development of Mental Life." The heading would appear to have been more a matter of editorial convenience than of theoretical conviction. An exhaustive discussion was offered concerning such varied topics as perception by the senses, memory, reasoning, knowledge of self, the emotions and passions, and space, time, and causation. Topic by topic the discussion revealed the breadth of Ladd's knowledge of philos-

---

[23] Though he may not have realized that he did it, at precisely this point Ladd backed himself into the theoretical corner in which previously he had found James hiding behind the phrase "blank unmediated correspondence, term for term, of the succession of states of consciousness with the succession of total brain-processes." The previous chapter describes Ladd's response to this phrase.

[24] *Primer of Psychology*, p. 33.

ophy and of the experimental and theoretical psychology of his day. Most issues were considered in what might be characterized as Ladd's own style—namely, that of "deep synthesis." In his review of the book, James expressed a particular liking for the discussion of conation, impulse, instinct, and desire, and pointed to the discussion of will as "an admirable performance." He held that the treatise was "independent from beginning to end," and added:

> But with all the concreteness, honesty, veracity, and shrewd humor that I find, I can, with the best will in the world, find no one idea or argument that abides with me as an unforgettable addition to the subject. What does strike me with the force of freshness is the amazing thoroughness with which Prof. Ladd realizes the intricacy of his facts. It seems to me little short of wonderful that a man should be able to make so many subdivisions, and find so many distinct things to say on the descriptive level. In this sense he *is* original, for no one has yet attained to writing up the subject in as fine-grained a way as this.[25]

The fine-grained and amazingly thorough discussion may not have contained an unforgettable addition to the subject, but considered as a whole it was an impressive piece of scholarship. Considered historically, the book is more impressive and memorable than it may have seemed to James three quarters of a century ago. It was a mighty effort to grapple with the entire literature of the field in a manner consistent with the best of the old learning and of the new modes of mental science. Ladd did a fine job of drawing together the burgeoning literature. On most issues it was a conventional and broadly integrative effort. But the important point is that he succeeded in writing a book that was perhaps the period's best representation of an informed and deliberate effort to develop a scientific psychology of man that preserved mind as a unitary and real phenomenon, and at the same time stressed man's capacity to control his own destiny.

[25] *Psychological Review*, 1 (1894), 291–292.

The principle of self-determination was a matter of supreme importance to Ladd. He felt that consciousness and the reality of mind would be hollow concepts unless it could be supposed that individual man was capable of purposeful and self-generated behavior. James's remark in his review, quoted above, conveyed a significant point—it was in the discussion of conation and will that Ladd seemed to come alive and write with a freshness and persuasion that hold the reader. In the many thousands of pages of Ladd's writing, there are two general subjects that are graced by a special vigor and conviction. He was eloquent in his disapproving discussion of a mechanistic, cerebral psychology and in his principled argument on behalf of man as a conscious being at work in the determination of his own destiny.

Man's capacity to direct his own fortunes was rooted in the principle of the independence of mind, operating according to laws of its own. The behavioral expression of this principle, however, required the process of reflective self-consciousness or introspection. It was the individual's capacity to turn consciousness back upon itself that provided him with the opportunity to make decisions in light of goals; and, of course, these goals were often the conceptualized ideals of ethics and of religion. The next chapter will discuss Ladd's view of the relevance of ideals to mental life, but here the important point to consider is the role of introspection, or "reflective self-consciousness," as he often called it, in Ladd's psychology. He saw reflective self-consciousness as the agency of man's ennoblement as a free being and also as the dominant method of scientific psychology.

Before the turn of the century, introspection was the method of psychological inquiry featured in the writings of most American psychologists. Ladd, James, Hall, and others stressed the importance of introspection, and of course the principal influence in this direction had come from German, and especially Wundtian, psychology. E. B. Titchener's Wundtian outpost at Cornell provided an on-the-scene force for preserving introspection as the respected method; furthermore, a number of early students of the subject had studied under Wundt at Leipzig and had returned with a strong bent toward introspective science. It would not be accurate, however, to say that American psychology became "introspective."[26] The rapid growth of interest in individual differences and the infusion into scientific psychology of new techniques for the measurement of human performance and human potential began to make the question of method a much more complex matter. The limitations of introspection were dramatized, of course, by the vigorous development of behaviorism, initiated with such telling effect by J. B. Watson.

When Ladd entered the field, American psychology was still in an embryonic condition, nourished and to some extent contained by philosophy. It had yet to move through the pangs and trials of a lively youth, discovering as it went that many new methods of study were fruitful, that objectivity rather than subjectivity was to be valued by the scientist, and that even the subject matter of the field would be radically changed. When Ladd began his study of the new mental science, James was a young assistant professor at Harvard in the beginning stages of the twelve-year project that would lead to his *Principles of Psychology*; Hall had just received the first American Ph.D. in psychology and was studying abroad in Berlin and Leipzig; Cattell, who would do so much to define the future of American psychology, was leaving Lafayette College for a two-year period of study under Lotze and Wundt; and J. B. Watson was an infant with no interest at all in the problems of psychological method.

Ladd entered the field at a time and in a manner that assured his commitment to introspection. He attempted to span the old and the new, but his classical and essentially non-scientific education fed a deep faith in the reality of consciousness. Try as he might to be-

26 See G. Murphy, *Historical Introduction to Modern Psychology* (New York: Harcourt, Brace and Company, 1949), pp. 437–438.

come a practicing scientist, he was not prepared to alter his conviction that the only dependable method of studying the mind was that of disciplined reflective thought. He defended introspection because he considered it the most appropriate and most informative method; but he defended it also because surrendering introspection would have undermined the basic structure of his theory of consciousness.

While varied and ingenious methods were welcome in scientific psychology, Ladd insisted that introspection or reflective self-consciousness[27] was the indispensable method for achieving true knowledge in the field. One should be objective in studying conscious phenomena, but no amount of objectivity could produce a disembodied consciousness. A natural observation or a laboratory datum could only become a "true fact of the psychic life of man" when it had withstood the test of reflective consciousness. He was explicit concerning the importance of introspection when, in his presidential address before the American Psychological Association, he stated:

> That no method can be developed in psychology which will enable us to dispense with introspection, or which will cease to be very largely dependent for its own value, upon the value of introspection which accompanies it, is too obvious to require discussion. Of course, the proposal wholly to get rid of self-consciousness as the medium of knowledge of the phenomena of consciousness is absurd. . . . For scientific psychology is the science of the phenomena of consciousness, as such. And no interpretation of consciousness is possible in any terms whatever without self-consciousness.[28]

[27] Ladd often used the term "reflective self-consciousness" in referring to the introspective process, but he seemed also to have been satisfied with the term "reflective consciousness." Apparently he was worried about the possibility that his readers would interpret "self-consciousness" as "embarrassment."

[28] *Psychological Review*, 1 (1894), 6.

George Trumbull Ladd

As a descriptive and explanatory science psychology offered a hard-headed and ingenious means for delineating the facts of individual conscious life. Natural observation, laboratory experiments, and statistical manipulations were useful methods for furthering the new science, and Ladd argued persuasively, if intermittently, in favor of a vigorous and controlled approach to the problems that faced the field.[29] It is clear, however, that he found the "external" methods of science useful only on the supposition that the data ultimately could be given meaning by an "internal" psychic process. The fundamental method remained that of introspection. Psychic facts, however isolated and enumerated, must be made immediate objects of knowledge if psychological science is to proceed with its work.

Ladd conceded that there were difficulties and dangers involved in the use of introspection. He traced these problems to the fact that psychic states are resistant to direct analysis under observation, being "subtle and complex in their composition, rapid and difficult to follow in their changes, alterable—swiftly and largely—by the very act of attention which makes them objects of knowledge, and characterized by a high degree of individuality."[30] The method was hazardous, but it offered the only means by which man could gain access to his own immediate experience. Indirect observation was necessary to the advance of psychological science, but Ladd held that "the soul of another is a darksome forest" and that it was only through direct introspective analysis and the disciplined pursuit of self-knowledge that meaning could be ascribed to mental life.

[29] While the basic methodology presented in *Elements of Physiological Psychology* was preserved in the revision of 1911, the revision did reflect the changes in the field that had taken place in the intervening years. A number of sections contain a de-emphasis of mentalism and a greater dependence upon empiricism. Probably much of the change in emphasis can be attributed to the fact that Woodworth was heavily involved in reorganizing the original text. One reviewer did complain, however, about the "common-sense" dualism that was maintained in the revision, and suggested that the discussion of the problem should have been relegated to philosophy. See V.A.C. Henmon, review of G. T. Ladd and R. S. Woodworth's *Elements of Physiological Psychology, Psychological Bulletin*, 9 (1912), 239–242.

[30] *Psychology: Descriptive and Explanatory*, p. 18.

Ladd made an important distinction between the methods of psychology and the sources of psychology. The sources of the field were to be found in the major forms of expression of human mental life. The one rule for the student of psychology was this:

> Seize upon every manifestation of the psychical life, try to make it an object of knowledge, and try to explain it in accord with other facts and known laws of psychical life. From the infant to the adult Kant, from the idiot or madman to Aristotle, from the meanest subject to the statesman or emperor—all things psychical are yours, and are to be converted if possible into integral parts of your psychological theory.[31]

He enumerated the chief sources of the field as follows: (1) study of all forms of the artistic delineation of life, (2) study of social phenomena, (3) study of abnormal and pathological phenomena, (4) observation of the phenomena of infant and child life, and (5) reading.

In considering the diverse methods and sources of the field Ladd made a special case, albeit rather briefly and late in his discussion, for induction as a method of psychological science. He recognized the importance of induction in bringing order to "what appears at first an indistinguishable mixture, a chaotic mass of psychic facts."[32] There is no doubt that he wished to incline the field toward the establishment of mental laws. He argued for both induction and deduction, and for analysis and synthesis "after the fashion of the science-making mind of man."[33]

"The science-making mind of man" was a fundamental model in Laddian theory. He considered the morphology of the mind to hold the key to science and to provide, through its customary forms of function, the necessary grounds for psychological inference. The science of the mind would have to be that science which expressed

[31] *Ibid.*, p. 21.
[32] *Ibid.*, p. 25.
[33] *Ibid.*

the mind as an immediately real entity. No science was feasible which did not express directly and appropriately the laws of mental life. The direct expression of the laws of mental life in science, and their most acute relation to mental science, was seen as justification for Noah Porter's claim that psychology was the mother of all sciences and man's best "discipline to method."[34] The reflective study of psychic states was at one and the same time the central psychological method and the most effective discipline to lucid thinking.

Ladd urged his fellow psychologists to treat the mind as a whole, to consider its genesis and development as a living unity. In doing so, he could not promise final solutions to all the riddles of mental life. Mind as a living unity contained the mystery of self-existence —a mystery which bred humility in the ardent methodologist and assured the permanent necessity for further psychological inquiry. The reflective consciousness of man contained an existential paradox. Through consciousness man could become aware of reality, of that which is; but the immediately real that is known by experience is somewhat remote and always partial. To the irritation and bewilderment of his scientific colleagues, Ladd insisted that psychology remain vital by accepting its role in a universe of permanent mystery.

> And now I am prepared to make a claim in behalf of the superior immediacy and certainty of the data available for the progress of the metaphysics of psychology, which many psychologists will perhaps consider extravagant. But, in my judgment, the claim is invincible. We do not need to search for a new door because the one we should like to open has no key; we do not need to try to tear asunder the veil which hangs before our eyes, because of its essentially impenetrable character. Every advance in the verifiable and true discoveries and consistent and

[34] *The Elements of Intellectual Science* (New York: Charles Scribner's Sons, 1883), p. 10.

tenable theory of psychological science opens the door a little more widely, draws the veil a little more to one side. The grandeur and beauty of this science are enhanced by the indisputable conviction that the door will never be open to its full extent; that the veil will never be drawn wholly aside. But what aspiring soul would wish to remain so small as completely to know itself? What ambitious psychologist would wish the end of the development of his science to come, although he should have succeeded in gathering its finished wisdom to himself, with a view to have his name go down in the history of scientific development as the last of his kind?[35]

It was the active, reflective consciousness of man that made possible a science of things as existent, measurable, and comparable. Man's mental life was locked in a system of infinite relations framed by a world of space and of time, and psychology, "the mother of all science," must not confound the universal mystery by seeking a simple answer to complicated problems.

[35] "The Ontological Problem of Psychology," *Philosophical Review*, 20 (1911), 378.

Chapter · 10 ·

Function and the Ideal-Real

In 1904 Ladd was invited to deliver the "leading first" paper in philosophy at the Congress of Arts and Sciences of the Universal Exposition in St. Louis. Throughout a summer of lecturing and preaching in the universities and churches of England he struggled with the text of the address. Returning in the autumn, he hurried to St. Louis to read his paper, which was entitled "The Development of Philosophy in the Nineteenth Century." The timeliness of the invitation and the choice of topic were matters of good fortune for Ladd's career. The new school year would produce the deterioration of his professional position at Yale, and a loss of status and morale from which he would never completely recover. But 1904 was a productive year and Ladd was eminently qualified to look back upon the century he had known by devoted scholarship and personal experience. The paper was one of his finest pieces of work. Satisfied with his performance in St. Louis and pleased by his reception as a leading figure in the field, he returned to New Haven to welcome as guests in his home the distinguished scholars Professors James Ward and Pierre Janet, both of whom had attended the congress.[1] A summer of lecturing in England, a featured paper at an in-

---

[1] "Autobiography," p. 496.

ternational congress, the entertaining of leading English and French scholars, the beginning of correspondence concerning a third trip to the Orient, and two more books nearing completion— all were unmistakable signs of Ladd's scholarly maturity and international reputation.

In "The Development of Philosophy in the Nineteenth Century," Ladd looked back across the years of ferment and change that had followed the death of Immanuel Kant in 1804. He viewed the death of the great philosopher of Königsberg as the end of eighteenth-century philosophy and the beginning of a period of critical reformulation of the epistemological, ontological, and ethico-religious problems that Kant had stated so forcefully. Ladd's discussion of philosophy in the light of Kantian criticism was an appropriate expression of his high regard for Kant's role in intellectual history; but it was also an expression of his own lifelong preoccupation with the particular philosophical and psychological issues that were placed in sharper focus by the positive sciences of the nineteenth century. The article reviewed one hundred years of the development of philosophy, and it served as a summary comment upon the position that Ladd had defended during his long career.

> The nineteenth century has left us with a vast widening of the horizon,—outward into space, backward in time, inward toward the secrets of life, and downward into the depths of Reality. With this there has been an increase in the profundity of the conviction of the spiritual unity of the race. In the consideration of all of its problems in the immediate future and in the coming century—so far as we can see forward into this century —philosophy will have to reckon with certain marked characteristics of the human spirit which form at the same time inspiring stimuli and limiting conditions of its endeavors and achievements. Chief among these are the greater and more firmly established principles of the positive sciences, and the prevalence of the historical spirit and method in the investiga-

tion of all manner of problems. These influences have given shape to the conception which, although it is as yet by no means in its final or even in thoroughly self-consistent form, is destined powerfully to affect our philosophical as well as our scientific theories. This conception is that of Development. But philosophy, considered as the product of critical and reflective thinking over the more ultimate problems of nature and of human life, is itself a development. And it is now, more than ever before, a development interdependently connected with all the other great developments.[2]

Ladd appealed to scientists and philosophers to work together in a spirit of reconcilement and reconstruction, and suggested that both may consider "the universe as a dynamical Unity, teleologically conceived, because in a process of evolution under the control of immanent ideas."[3] Nature was held to be "a real-ideal Unity," and science and philosophy were seen as assisting in the satisfactory explanation of the totality of racial experience. He argued that

. . . a summons of all helpers, in critical but fraternal spirit, to this work of reconstruction, for which two generations of enormous advance in the positive sciences has gathered new material, and for the better accomplishment of which both the successes and the failures of philosophy in the nineteenth century have prepared the men of the twentieth century, is the winsome and imperative voice of the hour.[4]

It had been nearly forty years since Ladd had first responded to that "winsome and imperative voice," and while the interven-

[2] "The Development of Philosophy in the Nineteenth Century," in *Congress of Arts and Sciences, Universal Exposition, St. Louis, 1904* (Boston: Houghton Mifflin Co., 1905), part 1, pp. 219–220.

[3] *Ibid.*, p. 217.

[4] *Ibid.*, p. 219. A similar theme was stressed in Ladd's presidential address at the fourth annual meeting of the American Philosophical Association, held in Philadelphia, December 29, 1904. See G. T. Ladd, "The Mission of Philosophy," *Philosophical Review*, 14 (1905), 113–137.

ing years may have made the voice less winsome, certainly it had become more imperative. The work of reconstruction called for establishing a framework of principles within which science and philosophy could seek all possible accord; and with the flowering of science, particularly during the last half of the century, the search for a principled common ground was a difficult and often thankless task. Ladd's self-assigned role as a reconciler of differences was complicated by the fact that he brought to the task certain strong convictions that he was unwilling to compromise. He was committed to the doctrine of final purpose in nature. The teleology that he defended placed man in the natural world, a living expression of ideals which could only be realized in and through his behavior.[5] Intimately associated with this belief was the conviction that the mind was an active and useful organ and that the rational process, integrally related to human will, was the ultimate test of truth. Problems of conduct and of morality must stand before the bar of human reason; and even formal religion must submit to the most refined and rigorous examination. Pervading all Ladd's work, and deeply involved in the original decision concerning his life's mission, was an optimistic faith that man possessed the capacity to understand and to improve his own condition.

Development, teleology, the mind as a useful organ, and optimism concerning the power of reason to benefit man and his society were familiar themes in American philosophy and psychology during the latter half of the nineteenth century. Ladd's position was his own creation, but the times and circumstances of his life dictated in large degree the peculiar web of beliefs by which he was so widely known. His work was accomplished during a period of American intellectual history in which philosophy advanced from a speculative, theological, and unprofessional status to a secular and professional position that became firmly established in academic circles. Orthodox theories concerning man were yielding to

[5] See our discussion of Ladd's "Final Purpose in Nature," pp. 75–76.

rigorous, empirical methods of study, and philosophy was beginning to feel the effect of critical studies in other disciplines. Across the years there was infused into intellectual life an idealism that was to assist in the birth of a unique American contribution to philosophy and psychology, and this was nowhere more apparent than in the collegiate institutions of the land.

In his excellent history of American philosophy, Herbert Schneider discussed the academic awakening that accompanied the transition from orthodoxy to idealism, and added that a faith

> . . . in a Kantian idealism as a power to reform American morals and religion was shared by a notable group of teachers, each with his own variant system, but each succeeding in kindling in his students a sense of the importance of philosophy and thus creating a source of "spiritual energy" independent of the churches. These idealists, without intending to set up rival pulpits to those in the churches, nevertheless emancipated academic faith and morals from clerical domination, as the literary transcendentalists had done outside academies. Almost all of them were theists, but they approached God through criticism rather than through prayer. . . .[6]

Schneider placed Ladd in this group of idealists, in the good company of George Herbert Palmer of Harvard, Nicholas Murray Butler of Columbia, and a dozen other stalwarts of the period.

In the last quarter of the nineteenth century the growth of American psychology was inseparably intertwined with the academic and general intellectual influences that have been mentioned above. In addition, the establishment of graduate education, largely along the lines of the German pattern, and the growing commitment to research in the universities of the country nourished the scientific and scholarly efforts which were under way. It was a time of reassessment and innovation as American colleges and uni-

[6] H. Schneider, *A History of American Philosophy* (New York: Columbia University Press, 1946), pp. 452–453.

versities moved away from the curricular restrictions that had been imposed by an educational theory primarily based upon faculty psychology and the supposed virtues of mental discipline. The required curriculum was challenged by the upstart notion of "free election." This yeasty period in higher education was an auspicious time for launching the new field of psychology.

In commenting on the relation between the changes in American higher education and the development of psychology, Watson noted:

> In these changes psychology occupied a favored and strategic position. It was one of the "new" subjects introduced into colleges and universities from the German system. Whereas psychology was still located in the departments of philosophy in German universities, the introduction of the subject in schools in the United States often meant the creation of an independent department. It also supplied a weapon to attack faculty psychology. No matter what the differences of opinion among the first American psychologists, they were united in their opposition to faculty psychology. Moreover, the economic and social conditions prevailing under the pioneer spirit made application of psychology almost a foregone conclusion.[7]

It can be assumed that the pioneer spirit which characterized the development of American society was also a vital force in the development of philosophy, science, and the institutions of higher education. America was still an open-ended country and its citizens were facing forward, preoccupied with the problems and the pro-

7 R. Watson, *The Great Psychologists—from Aristotle to Freud* (New York: J. B. Lippincott Co., 1968), pp. 345–346. While psychology enjoyed a favored and strategic position on many counts, an earlier assessment highlighted the relatively unfavorable conditions which psychology experienced, with particular respect to financial support and the allocation of space by universities. It is of interest that the introspective method was found to be a possible "hindrance to the ready acceptance of the discipline because of the false assumption that it requires either an abnormal gift of some sort or years of toilsome training." C. A. Ruckmich, "The History and Status of Psychology in the United States," *American Journal of Psychology*, 23 (1912), 531.

mise of frontiers yet to be exploited. The *Zeitgeist* elicited certain forms of institutional development and favored certain styles of practical and theoretical thinking. The mature, formal, and stratified German society gave us Wundt and structural psychology, but the young, dynamic, and often brash American society gave us functionalism.

In discussing American functional psychology, Boring acknowledged that the American temper fostered functionalism and stated that the functional viewpoint is "close to common sense." It is "the natural view." The functionalist is interested in the "why" of behavior. He added:

> It is as natural to be a functionalist as it is to want to predict, to be more interested in the future than in the past, to prefer to ride facing forward on the train. The future concerns you because you think you might change it if you had the ability. The past has gone by, lies there open to description but unalterable.[8]

Boring believed that there were four characteristics of Ladd's theory that made him a functional psychologist. First, Ladd postulates an active self. Second, consciousness, which is the activity of the self, has an adaptive function. Third, the mind has a purpose, thereby making psychology teleological. Fourth, the resulting psychology has a useful or practical value. He added that all of these points are "in Ladd at the level of theoretical systematization. The history of American psychology is little more than their working-out in reality."[9] Boring observed that from a historical standpoint Ladd's *Psychology: Descriptive and Explanatory* was "a systematic text that is really a functional psychology in the American sense."[10]

In his critical review of Ladd's psychology, Titchener held that the theory was "broadly typical" of functional systems. As a re-

[8] E. G. Boring, *A History of Experimental Psychology* (New York: Appleton-Century-Crofts, Inc., 1957), p. 551.
[9] *Ibid.*, pp. 526–527.
[10] *Ibid.*, p. 525.

doubtable structuralist, Titchener viewed functional psychology as "a plea in avoidance offered before the court of science on behalf of empiricism,"[11] and he did his best to reveal the weakness and confusion of Ladd's broadly typical theory. In doing so, he offered four major tenets or tendencies of functional psychology, some of which were similar to those enumerated by Boring. Titchener considered each tenet to be generally true of functional theories and specifically true of Ladd's psychology.

In the first place, functional theories distinguish between "activity" or "function" and "content" or "structure." Titchener properly observed that this distinction expresses the biological distinction between function and structure, and of course psychology was strongly influenced by the accelerating developments in biological science. Second, functional theories hold that conscious processes emerge from "hesitant" or "inadequate" activities of the nervous system. Clarity of awareness is related to the evenness of cortical function.[12] Third, functional theories are teleological. Titchener commented that "it is one of the ironies of the history of science that the great biological generalization which was to free us of teleology in our study of the phenomena of life should give rise, in post-Darwinian days, to an unbridled license of teleological 'interpretation.' "[13] Fourth, functional systems are transitional, "a halfway house on the journey to something else, and not . . . an abiding-place."[14] In discussing this point, Titchener took note of Ladd's belief that psychology was propaedeutic to philosophy, a science that carried certain of its problems forward to a point from which they could be offered to philosophy for final resolution.

Boring and Titchener were both right, even though they differed concerning some of the most important criteria for assessing

[11] E. B. Titchener, *Systematic Psychology: Prolegomena,* p. 180.

[12] Titchener's point is an appropriate expression of Ladd's concern for the relation of attention to the function of the nervous system. See our discussion of attention in the previous chapter.

[13] *Ibid.,* pp. 185–186.

[14] *Ibid.,* p. 190.

functionalism. Ladd was a functional psychologist and his work fell within the essentially American theory-building of his day. While this would appear to be a safe generalization concerning his psychology, it falls far short of being a satisfactory representation of the larger meaning that his writing conveyed. His psychology was functional, but he intended that it serve a broader purpose. It was, indeed, "propaedeutic to philosophy," and he would have argued strenuously with those who might wish to excise his psychology from the total mission of his life work.

As a functionalist, Ladd considered "activity to some end . . . the ruling principle of mental development. The self-conscious, intelligent adoption of a plan, and selection of means for its pursuit, is distinctive of the *acme* of man's development."[15] The mind is enlivened and directed by will, and man's character, that personal configuration of tendencies and beliefs by which the quality of behavior is maintained, is basically composed of "self-formed habits of will."[16] Mental life has solidarity and unity; it is more than a series of interconnected events. Ladd was impatient with those who stressed the elements of behavior—the sensations, stimuli, responses, or reflexes—failing thereby to capture the meaning of human life as it is expressed in the flow of conscious processes. He viewed the mind as active, adaptive, purposeful, and capable of self-direction. His position was compatible with that enunciated in Dewey's celebrated article, "The Reflex Arc Concept in Psychology,"[17] generally acknowledged as the historical beginning of a more formal functional theory.

The mind, characterized by its "activity to some end," is able to conceptualize ideals. For Ladd, ideals were not remote, ethereal concerns of the philosopher, but conditioners of man's everyday mental life. The development of mental life tends toward self-

[15] *A Theory of Reality* (New York: Charles Scribner's Sons, 1899), p. 535.
[16] *Primer of Psychology* (New York: Longman's, Green & Co., 1894), p. 208.
[17] *Psychological Review*, 111 (1896), 357–370.

organization or consolidation and "every activity, whether partial or more general, influences the entire development; . . . this development tends toward some unification of result."[18] The consolidation process is centered upon ideas; behavior is directed as much by the "living idea" as it is by the immediate physical and social conditions of life.

To appreciate the extent of Ladd's commitment to the directing power of ideas, and of ideals, it is necessary to recall that he considered the mind to be an extra-physical reality, capable of operating according to laws of its own. He believed that ideas gave the mind its essential structure and argued against the notion that they were mere epiphenomena, always passively resulting from other "real" events of the natural world. An interesting suggestion of his early attraction to the supremacy of ideas is seen in examining his personal copy of Alexander Winchell's *The Doctrine of Evolution*. He purchased the book during his years of ministry in Milwaukee and undoubtedly read it with the consuming interest that later inspired his decision to dedicate his professional life to mediation. In his signed and dated copy (1874) of the book, he marked this sentence: "The intelligence of which vital force is a function, subordinates even physiological processes to the attainment of premeditated consummations."[19]

Still sharing Winchell's belief, Ladd wrote in 1909 that "science . . . must recognize the truth that Spirit is the essence of Nature; and that the uniting force of the Universe is a Will guided by Ideas."[20] Now, this belief certainly was not a unique philosophical position. What was special about the belief was that, as late as 1909, it was held, and consistently and untiringly defended, by a professional psychologist who had tried to build a psychological theory

[18] *Primer of Psychology* p. 222.
[19] A. Winchell, *The Doctrine of Evolution.* (New York: Harper & Bros., 1874), p. 9. Copy in possession of Miss Cornelia T. Ladd of Cleveland Heights, Ohio.
[20] *Knowledge, Life and Reality.* (New York: Dodd, Mead and Company, 1909), p. 472.

George Trumbull Ladd

that embraced the new science without surrendering idealism. Ladd was not only a philosopher of idealism, but a philosopher who made a case for placing psychological science at the heart of philosophy. He often was accused of being a philosophical and hopelessly idealistic psychologist; less frequently was it appreciated by the scholars of his day that he was advocating a philosophy that not only accommodated but actually depended upon psychology. Advocating a dependent relationship between philosophy and psychology was an increasingly unpopular cause in a period that was producing an academic split between the two fields.

The interdependence of philosophy and all the particular sciences, including psychology, was argued forcefully in Ladd's 1904 address at the Universal Exposition. He believed that man's rational understanding of reality was a development with discernible phases, and that this understanding, at once so difficult to achieve and so devoutly to be sought, was a natural exercise of man's sentient being. Academic and social conventions might obscure the common purpose of the various fields of inquiry, but he held that ultimately each field would recognize its role in the larger effort. At the heart of his belief was the conviction that "there are no 'independent' sciences, because there are no isolated or independent realities."[21] The conviction underscored the idealistic monism that he pursued with increasing interest in the latter stages of his career.

The wedding between philosophy and psychology was arranged, presided over, and blessed by idealism. As a conscious being, man was a spiritual agent in a universe of spirit. Ladd believed that the nobility of man's spiritual life beckoned unremittingly toward the solution of his personal and social problems and that it contained the promise of an ever closer approximation to the Ideal. It was not enough to understand man's behavior; understanding was to be sought in the service of a greater spiritual unity of the race[22]

21 *Psychology: Descriptive and Explanatory*, p. 11.
22 In the frequent use of such terms as "the unity of the race," "racial intelligence,"

162

and a more perfect approximation of the Absolute. The active, adaptive, purposeful, and practical psychology that Ladd advocated was a psychology of idealism which was intended to affirm man's inseparable ties to an infinite Intelligence, both supra-human and personal.

In his most profound and self-conscious moments, sentient man reaches out toward an unseen reality, seeking always to identify himself with ideals of goodness and truth. While admitting that "that-which-is far outstretches man's feeble efforts to tell what-it-is and how-it-came-to-be,"[23] Ladd maintained with Lotze that the Absolute is "a self-conscious, rational, aesthetical and ethical Life,"[24] and that the rational basis for all ethical and religious life is found in the moral personality of the Absolute. For Ladd, the Absolute was a hypothesis made necessary by the logic of reflective reason, the evident unity and order of the universe, and the inner promptings of man's religious consciousness. Superstition and unreflective spiritism characterized man's early efforts to account for his relationship to the mystery of the universe; but with an increasingly reflective consideration of his position in the universe, and under the influence of a gradual social and political evolution, he began to develop a more anthropomorphic conception of God. Ladd found the purest and highest form of religious consciousness represented in "man's making of the Divine Being after the pattern of the constantly improving image of man."[25] The anthropomorphism did not mean that God was physically in human form; it did mean that God was viewed as "perfect Ethical Spirit, as well as the 'Ground' of the world and of human life."[26]

---

and "racial experience," he was referring to mankind as a whole rather than to any special group.

[23] *Knowledge, Life and Reality*, p. 36.

[24] "Lotze's Influence on Theology," *New World*, 4 (1895), 417.

[25] "The Religious Consciousness as Ontological," *Journal of Philosophy, Psychology, and Scientific Methods*, 1 (1904), 8.

[26] *Ibid.*

George Trumbull Ladd

Ladd used the terms "World-Ground," "Being of the World," and "Absolute" interchangeably and he was not always consistent in characterizing that "supreme but never perfectly attainable goal of human endeavor."[27] He believed that philosophy, religion, and the particular sciences shared a deep concern about the solution of this "ultimate problem of knowledge," but the difficulty of delineating the problem often forced him to fall back upon a justification by faith. Throughout his writings one finds a preoccupation with the problem of reality and a conviction, variously expressed, that reality "is essentially non-sensuous, intellectual, and self-like, in a far grander way than are the individual self-like things composing the physical system."[28]

A strong, if not always convincing, case was made for the spiritual identification of the self with the Absolute. Since Ladd considered the mind of man a necessary medium for development of a viable Absolute, he argued that self-consciousness is the only absolute form of knowing the Absolute. In the thousands upon thousands of pages that he published over the decades, one sentence summarized the central conviction from which arose his argument for the interdependence of philosophy and psychology, and his insatiable appetite for metaphysics. In a lengthy chapter on "The World-Ground as Absolute Person," and following numerous partial steps toward the enunciation of the principle, he drew himself together and wrote (in italics!), "*In a word: The perfecting of self-consciousness tends to raise the mind toward a more boundless and approximately absolute knowledge.*"[29] In a word: Ladd held that man is the measure of all things[30] and that the cultivation of self-consciousness is the road to spiritual salvation.

27 *Knowledge, Life and Reality*, p. 20.
28 *Ibid.*, p. 462.
29 *Ibid.*, p. 470.
30 Ladd's treatment of this theme is revealed in his 1913 address as vice-president and chairman of the section on anthropology and psychology of the American Association for the Advancement of Science. He acknowledged the limitations and dif-

By nature man is endowed with a capacity to experience the rewarding fullness of a reality that combines the perfection of ethics with the purity of aesthetics. It is in the natural order of occurrences that man should know intensely and personally that which is ultimate. Ladd always inclined his philosophy toward an "ideal reality" that could be known only through man's most active and self-conscious development. He believed that, from a psychological standpoint, man is positively motivated to seek the refinements of order, balance, and symmetry in his world view; moreover, orderly, balanced, and symmetrical ideals are positively sought by the educated man as he expresses in his life the perfection of an infinite and absolute personal life.

> The physical and chemical sciences, striving to discover and explain the phenomena of internal and external experience, reach forward toward the conception of the one Being of the World, the so-called Absolute and Infinite World-Ground, as a self-contained system of efficient forces operating under general laws. But the more definitely ethical and aesthetical factors in man's conscious life and development require for their satisfaction another sort of Ideal. Their goal is reached, or approached, only if they may successfully demand of imagination and thought that the reality of an ideally sublime and morally perfect Spirit shall be grounded in the facts of an actual and trustworthy experience. Their Ideal is the conception of an Infinite and Absolute Personal Life.[31]

In his effort to understand man's relation to reality, Ladd fell back upon the principles and the spirit of Christian religion. His

ficulties of the principle that "man is the measure of all things," but he seemed to accept the principle as long as proper weight was assigned to rational faith or "reason's own confidence in itself as the organon of truth." G. T. Ladd, "The Study of Man," *Science*, 37 (1913), 285.

[31] *The Philosophy of Religion* (2 vols.; New York: Charles Scribner's Sons, 1905), vol. 1, p. 331.

discussion of the religious consciousness of the race, however, was not confined to Christianity. He appreciated differences in religious perspective, but he was impatient with dogma. His major two-volume work on the philosophy of religion was sympathetic to Lotze's theories concerning the necessity for religion as an aesthetic and humanitarian force in the life of man, though he placed a somewhat greater stress upon Christian theism.[32]

Ladd believed that one could not logically consider the conception of God as a merely subjective development; he struggled to show the philosophical and psychological support for a sound theism. Throughout his life he remained faithful to the mission he had set for himself during seminary years; namely, the application of the principles of critical scholarship to the evaluation of all claims for religion. If he appeared to settle some important issues by an appeal to faith, he did so only after the most intense effort to understand the relevant evidence on the question. He argued that accepting a "proof from faith" required an even more exacting study of evidence than did the acceptance of a "proof by the trial of objective science."

Through the brambles of the new mental science and critical religious scholarship, Ladd carefully picked his way toward a definition of the ideal-real. His functional approach to psychology and his conviction that man may control his own behavior were joined in the effort to place man in a world of realism and idealism.[33] As we have seen, this effort required that man's religious consciousness be directed toward the "self-conscious rational, aesthetical and ethical Life" that is the Absolute. In his effort to characterize the pur-

---

[32] See G. Galloway, review of G. T. Ladd's *Philosophy of Religion, Mind,* 16 (1907), 133.

[33] Ladd argued that the *real Universe* is infused with "regnant human ideals." His persistent defense of idealism in the face of "mechanical and materialistic Realism" was in part an effort to build a framework which provided a reasonable metaphysical base for man as a spiritual being. He held that "the God of monism may be as closely identified with the mechanism of the material universe as the reality dubbed Nature by scientific materialism is identified with the perfect ethical Spirit of monotheistic religion." "A Defense of Idealism," *Mind,* 23 (1914), 473.

poseful life that inclined man toward this supreme goal, two concepts were of surmounting importance—individuality and moral freedom, the attributes that made possible man's ascendance toward the ideal-real.

The individuality of the human being is characterized by both uniqueness and development. Individual man is in possession of a never-to-be-duplicated self and "no individual is a momentary achievement or an original endowment; every individual Self is a growth."[34] The dynamics of self-conscious growth present each individual with a persistent but constantly changing awareness of his relation to supreme ideals. As the highest expression of this relation, religion is principally characterized by its individuality: "It is only in the reality of the living experience of the Individual Self that the Universal and Absolute becomes known and believed in or dimly apprehended as felt."[35]

The most noble aspect of man's functioning is his moral freedom. Through voluntary attention the intellect informs and orients the individual, providing him with the structure which supports the activity of a self-determining will. The active intellect enters the universe of values and the decision-making process is always an active interplay between the individual and moral alternatives.

> The religious feelings of the finer sort, depending as they do upon judgments of value, are always, so to say, suffused with a will that either accepts and cherishes, or else refuses and subdues them. It is preëminently in the construction of his religions, as of all his other Ideals, that man shows himself to be a self-determining Self, a morally free Will. Were he not active in thinking, imagining, feeling, he would not be free; but then neither would he be religious.[36]

[34] *Philosophy of Religion*, vol. 1, p. 594.
[35] *Ibid.*, p. 595.
[36] *Ibid.*, p. 335.

George Trumbull Ladd

A self-determining and morally free person is confronted, of course, by a life of puzzles and hard choices. Society places before him a bewildering mixture of opportunities and temptations. Gritty everyday problems, as well as issues of long-range importance, require solutions that express the individuality and test the ethical loyalties of each person. It is the mark of an educated and sensitive man that the solution of problems and the charting of courses of action are made matters of reflective thought.

> He who knows himself, who plans his own life, who takes himself in hand to carry out that plan, and who selects *such* a plan as will worthily dominate and control all the mental faculties—he it is who is most entitled to be called a true Soul, or Mind. A *planless* mental life is scarcely worthy to be called a genuine *mental* life.[37]

It is clear that he considered "a planless mental life" to be a contradiction in terms.

Ladd's psychological theories and his philosophical and religious convictions were brought together in one bright effort to illuminate the plight of man, as individually he faced the supreme challenge of making his life a testament. The self-determining and morally free person was of necessity concerned about social problems; moreover, he was incurably interested in his own problems of conduct. While Ladd had discussed the relation of ethics to moral life and moral development in a number of books, by the turn of the century he realized the increasingly vital role that the subject played in his general approach to mental life; he decided, probably without great hesitation, to write another book. The restless pen was ready, the topic was compelling, and the author was productively worried about the influence upon morality of three "mischievous" aspects of society. It would be a long book.

[37] *Primer of Psychology*, p. 224.

Ladd prefaced his book by stating that the theory of biological evolution had been intruded into ethics and that the practical effect of this intrusion was "exceedingly mischievous to the moral life of the people, and to the current opinions regarding the right and wrong of conduct."[38] He held that the theory was producing "a brutish point of view" and was lending credence to "the doctrine of the right of might." A second source of antagonism to a sound philosophy of conduct was "the reigning spirit of commercialism." He held a jaundiced view of "the ethics of economics" and frequently expressed in his writings and speeches a disdain for the self-justifying ethics of business. The third obstruction to a proper ethics was "the relatively low and nerveless ethical condition of the current Christianity." Ladd resented the silent acquiescence and bewildered conformity of organized Christianity. The outspoken foe of the Milwaukee political machine was impatient with those who enjoyed the comforts, but spurned the lofty battles, of Christianity. The problems of ethics were too important to be entrusted to men of comfort and repose.

Philosophy of Conduct was a revealing portrait of Ladd, the omnific theory-builder and social critic. Psychology, epistemology, and metaphysics were placed in the service of ethics and he gave free rein to his lifelong tendency to mix sermons with science.[39] He was keenly interested in many aspects of the improvement of human welfare. The "life of conduct" was the topic that expressed most directly the central point of his scholarship.

Ladd's philosophy of conduct involved three major issues: (1) the moral self, (2) the virtuous life, and (3) the nature of the right. His discussion of these issues affirmed his belief that man

[38] *Philosophy of Conduct* (New York: Charles Scribner's Sons, 1902), p. xi.
[39] One reviewer said of the book that "the 'practical' mind will award it unqualified praise; the scientific temper will incline to rate it much below its true merit. For, indeed, the greater portion is of the nature of a sermon rather than of a science." S. H. Fairbrother, review of G. T. Ladd's *Philosophy of Conduct, Mind*, 12 (1903), 259.

was a religious being whose mental life both rested upon and expressed a reality that was created and sustained by God. Morality was identified with the "World-Ground," a perfect ethical ideal most appropriately visualized and experienced as a personal God. The moral man was not a concoction of the philosopher, but a living symbol of a spiritual reality.

For two hundred fifty pages Ladd wrestled with the problem of living virtuously. He characterized the virtues of the will, of judgment, and of feeling; argued for a psychological analysis of duty, moral law, moral tact, and the conflict of duties; and brought the section to a close by courageously describing "The Good Man." The final third of the book was focused upon the social, ethical, and "ultimate metaphysical implications" of the concept of moral man.

While much of the book was a recasting of familiar themes, the work was an excellent illustration of Ladd's functional theory, in this case driven deeply and workably into the practical business of life.[40] The author obviously believed that sentient man was placed within the universe with the potentiality for freedom and the hope of approaching, through a deepened awareness of himself, ideals that were real. In the name of morality he issued a call to faith—"to faith in the permanence and triumph of the unseen; to faith in the overcoming of the powers of evil by the power of righteousness."[41] In the name of duty he warned the Yale undergraduate of the doom of an unillumined life and exhorted him to submit "to the supremacy of duty which opens the gates of light."[42] But in the

[40] In a review of the book, one writer commented favorably upon the psychological basis for the discussion of the moral self and added that "there are few accounts in English of the moral self psychologically as accurate and as exhaustive as Professor Ladd here offers." S. E. Mezes, review of G. T. Ladd's *Philosophy of Conduct, Psychological Review*, 1 (1904), 18.

[41] "The Present Crisis in Morals in the Churches," *Addresses Before the New York State Conference of Religion*, series 1 (1903), 8.

[42] Sermon preached in Battell Chapel, September 25, 1891, *New Englander and Yale Review*, 55 (1891), 473.

fullness of his belief in "the ideality of moral facts and the reality of the Moral Ideal," he advised: "Hold to the Ideal and ever lift it up; be sensible and wise in practical affairs, patient with yourself, and with all men, and with God,—also, courageous, and full of faith and hope."[43]

Ever the idealist, and always pointing to the ultimate triumph of the unseen, Ladd tried to make his functional psychology serve the good life, here and now. Through the perfection of self-conscious-ness man might approach the Absolute, but he was careful to warn against an assumption that the individual could expect to achieve a steady state of bliss. In one of his books he cautioned that "as a rule, the richer the life of the mind becomes, the more imperfect are its satisfactions."[44] This observation characterized his attitude toward man's ultimate fate in the world. Walk upright and be full of faith and hope, but do not expect an easy and pleasant reconcili-ation of divergent tendencies and goals. Life is a development made sweet by struggles and by the realization that it is purposeful, but the life of the mind invites man to walk beyond the limit of his own frail power.

[43] *Philosophy of Conduct,* p. 653.
[44] *Psychology: Descriptive and Explanatory,* p. 606.

Chapter · 11 ·

First Trip to Japan

At the top of a hill within the famous Sojiji Temple grounds near Yokohama stands a tall stone marker, deeply etched with the following tribute:

IN MEMORY OF
GEORGE TRUMBULL LADD
1842–1921
AMERICAN
GENTLEMAN, SCHOLAR
EDUCATOR, FRIEND OF JAPAN
"I HAVE LIVED, AND LOVED,
AND LABORED, ALL IS WELL."
ERECTED BY HIS
FRIENDS AND ADMIRERS

A more modest gravestone bearing the same quotation and featuring a rising sun is to be found in the old Grove Street Cemetery adjacent to the Yale campus in New Haven. These two widely separated graves symbolize well the extent to which Ladd's interests and loyalties were divided in his later years. The uncommon fact that there are two graves is traceable to a stipulation in his will that his body be cremated and that "a handful of the ashes be sent to Japan, to be buried, if the friends there so arrange, near the camphor tree which I planted in the grounds of the School of Commerce at Nagasaki, in March of 1907."[1] Faithful to the spirit of the will, Mrs. Ladd bravely returned to Japan in the spring of 1922, carrying with her on that long and lonely trip a can containing one half of her husband's ashes. The ceremony of commemoration at Sojiji was an occasion of great dignity as friends and admirers in academic and governmental circles gathered to pay tribute to an old "friend of Japan."

Ladd's "long, requited, love affair with the people of Japan"[2] was one of the dominant passions of his life. For thirty years he maintained a personal relationship with Japanese students, scholars, and government officials, followed avidly the national affairs of Japan, and worked with energy and intelligence to explain his adopted country to the American people. Japan was truly his second home.

The long love affair began in 1892 with an invitation to lecture on philosophy and religion at Doshisha, a Christian school in Kyoto. Though the invitation arrived late in the spring and no provision was made for financial assistance, Ladd was excited by the prospect of a summer in the Orient and decided that, one way or another, he would make the trip. Upon learning of his problem, President Dwight of Yale privately raised funds to cover the cost of traveling. Ladd cabled the date and the name of the ship on which he proposed to sail, concluded his work at the university, and left

[1] Document in the possession of Miss Cornelia T. Ladd of Cleveland Heights, Ohio. Japanese friends decided on the Sojiji location after careful study of various proposed sites.
[2] Ladd's own characterization of his deep interest in Japan, as reported by his daughter, Mrs. Walter A. Barrett of Fort Wayne, Indiana, during an interview with the writer on April 1, 1962.

New Haven on May 6. A week later he sailed from Vancouver on the *Empress of China*, bound for Yokohama and a world of new experiences that would crowd his dreams for decades still to come.

"The night of Friday, May 27, 1892, was pitchy dark," Ladd recalled,

> . . . and the rain fell in such torrents as the Captain said he had seldom or never seen outside the tropics. This officer did not think it safe to leave the bridge during the entire night, and was several times on the point of stopping the ship. But the downpour of the night left everything absolutely clear; and when the day dawned, Fujiyama, the "incomparable mountain," could be seen from the bridge at the distance of more than one-hundred and thirty miles. In many views which I have since had of Fuji, from many different points of view, I have never seen the head and entire bulk of the sacred mountain stand out as it did for us on that first vision, now nearly twenty years ago.[3]

Ladd emerged from the "pitchy darkness" of an exceedingly rough crossing to find before him the dream and the reality of a country that was also a civilization. From the first vision there flowed a parade of people, activities, and ideas that excited and invigorated him as, day upon crowded day, he stretched his mind and tested his philosophy. The quiet scholar from New Haven would become a seasoned traveler in Japan, but he would never forget the exotic impact of his first arrival when "I had to talk to myself, almost to pinch myself, to make sure that I was indeed I."[4]

The Japan of 1892 was made to order for Ladd. Here was a country with an ancient and colorful history, an enlightened aristocratic ruling class, and a national devotion to graciousness and manners. It was a society in which the peasant and the nobleman honored the man of learning and sat quietly and respectfully while the "sensei"

[3] *Rare Days in Japan* (New York: Longmans, Green, and Co., 1910), pp. 2–3.
[4] "Autobiography," p. 271.

spoke. The virtues of honor and duty were supremely important, and if loyalty was sometimes so inflexibly held as to be totally blind, at least the society was cemented by a known and predictable trait. While Ladd admired the national heritage and the personal virtues of the people, there was one further factor of surmounting importance that inclined him irresistibly toward Japan—the country was struggling through a period of fundamental transition, desperately seeking a proper balance between the old ways and the compelling new modes of life. Japan would be a social laboratory for the mediation that he had tried to achieve in the world of ideas.

With the reign of Emperor Meiji, extending across the entire last third of the nineteenth century, Japan began a concerted effort to reform her educational system and to promote the selective assimilation of Western learning. During this period the involvement of the national government in education brought about a unification of plans, where before there had been only the highly varied and often conflicting sub-systems that operated under feudal powers. Centralized educational control supplanted the old feudal divisions, new public schools and new universities were established, a foreign-language school was reopened, schools for girls were inaugurated, and a bureau of translation was organized to facilitate the use of foreign textbooks.

In 1872 new educational laws were proclaimed and stress was placed upon two principles within the new code—first, the educational system was to be utilitarian, assisting each student in his future goal of earning a living, and, second, the system was to promote individual and national morality. Since the appearance of Commodore Perry at mid-century, Japan had become involved in world commerce and the nation that had held so resolutely to its own resources and scruples was rapidly feeling the effect of new demands. The educational system was to be supportive of the larger national role, but it also was to foster the internal dynamics of a morality that would preserve the Japanese way of life.[5]

[5] See R. S. Anderson, *Japan: Three Epochs of Modern Education* (Washington:

George Trumbull Ladd

Doshisha had been established in 1875 as a private Christian school committed to the quiet transformation of society through education. Its Japanese founder, Joseph Hardy Neesima, had spent ten years in the United States, studying at Amherst and Andover Theological Seminary, and had returned with a conviction that education patterned after the Western tradition was essential to the creation of a new Japanese society. The school was successfully launched in the ancient capital of Kyoto and, at the time of Ladd's arrival, was playing an increasingly vital role in the education of those who would help to lead the nation out of its feudalism.[6] In urging Ladd to come to Japan, the president of Doshisha had spoken of the great political, social, and religious changes that were sweeping across his country, adding that "all our thoughts are in utter chaos; and the worst of all, there are very few competent scholars to lead our benighted countrymen into the way of the light."[7] It was an appeal that was perfectly constructed to challenge Ladd's restless spirit.

Under the deferential escort of a small group of scholars, and doubtless still unable to believe "that I was indeed I," Ladd arrived in Kyoto to begin a much advertised course of public lectures at Doshisha. The muggy summer weather had preceded him and he was ushered onto the platform in a state of near collapse. The weather, the excitement of his arrival in Japan, and the uncertain-

U.S. Department of Health, Education, and Welfare, 1959), bulletin no. 11; also H. L. Keenleyside and A. F. Thomas, *History of Japanese Education* (Tokyo: The Hokuseido Press, 1937).

[6] Doshisha has become an important Japanese institution. In its eighty-fifth year this great school corporation had a student body in excess of 23,000 and included a women's college, three senior high schools, three junior high schools, a commercial high school, a kindergarten, and a university with faculties of theology, letters, law, economics, and commerce and technology. During a conference on the Doshisha campus in July, 1964, a high university official told the writer that "we consider Professor Ladd to be one of the important figures in the early history of our institution." See J. H. Neesima, *The Founding of the Doshisha and Doshisha University* (Kyoto: Doshisha University, 1960), p. 1.

[7] Letter from H. Kozaki to G. T. Ladd, May, 1892, "Autobiography," pp. 260–261.

ties of lecturing with the aid of an interpreter would have been reason enough for his poor condition; but the most distressing development had been an immediate confrontation with Japanese students "as respects their rather embarrassing willingness (although this is undoubtedly chiefly due to an honorable eagerness to learn) to instruct their teachers as to the matters in respect of which, and the way in which, they desire to be taught."[8] These were not Yale undergraduates, and of course he was a guest in a foreign country, but Ladd was not going to let anyone alter his prepared lectures. He mounted the platform, a weak and shaken man, and began the first of some four hundred speeches to the people of Japan. It was an unsteady beginning, but Japanese audiences were famous for their patience; by the time that he last bid farewell to his second home in 1907, his four hundred speeches had reached 65,000 people.[9]

With the start of his lecture series on "The Philosophy of Religion," Ladd became the center of attention for a large body of Doshisha teachers and students. His work was extremely demanding, and, as the successs of his lectures became apparent, he began to receive a number of requests to appear in other cities. In a letter to his wife written on June 8, he observed:

> I am being driven very hard just now. I breakfast at seven, rising at a quarter past six; then to my room and prepare for the lecture at ten, which lasts (with the interpretation) till noon; then at one I meet the students for inquiry, and in the evening I am working on a prospectus for my course in Tokyo. Part of the afternoon I get for sight-seeing, which has been, thus far, no end of wonderful temples. I am likely to become, like Spinoza, a Göttervertrunkener Mensch.

[8] "Autobiography," p. 274.

[9] An estimate based upon data that has been obtained from the "Autobiography," *Rare Days in Japan, In Korea with Marquis Ito,* Japanese journal and newspaper reports, and an inspection of university, school, and civic records in those areas of Japan which Ladd visited.

> After this week some of the work will stop; but there seems
> no end to requests for more, and it is hard to say No! and stick
> to it, to any of them.[10]

It was Ladd's good fortune to have the assistance of an unusually sensitive and skilled interpreter. Professor Kazutami Ukita of Doshisha, who later became professor of sociology at Waseda University, provided the essential link between the speaker and his audiences. Though it was customary to break an address into ten-minute periods with alternating performances by the lecturer and his interpreter, Ukita was able to listen to the full lecture and then "render it entire into fluent and elegant Japanese, preserving as far as the great differences in the structure and genius of the two languages make possible, the exact turns of speech and the illustrations of the original."[11] Ladd considered Ukita "the most skillful interpreter I have ever known," and gave him much of the credit for the success of his lectures. Ukita served as Ladd's interpreter on a number of occasions during his subsequent visits to Japan and also assisted in transcribing the lecture notes for publication.[12]

Day by day, the Ladd-Ukita combination struggled through the early weeks of the hot summer, informing and admonishing the people of Kyoto on weighty religious and philosophical issues. The audiences were polite, receptive, and large. As Ladd began to feel more confidence in his work, and as the invitations to speak mounted, he slipped steadily and noticeably into an exciting new role. He began to function as a teacher-statesman, discussing philosophy, religion, and psychology from the personal vantage point of an experienced scholar, but directing all these efforts toward the problems of an emerging Japan. He believed that he had something of great importance to contribute to the political, social, and

[10] "Autobiography," pp. 275–276.
[11] *Rare Days in Japan*, p. 105.
[12] See "Dr. Ladd's Lectures on Religious Philosophy," *Dōshisha-Bungaku*, 55 (1892), 21–40.

educational transformation of this ancient land, and with the compelling restlessness of the young parson who had urged Kant and Lotze upon the farmers of the Western Reserve he began to advise and counsel a nation. It was a large and perhaps presumptuous undertaking, but like his frontier forebears Ladd had "convictions," and he was not afraid to be seen with them in public.

They were convictions tempered by great and sober learning, but they were infused with the spirit of Puritanism. In the words of a Japanese scholar who studied under Ladd at Yale and knew intimately the work which he undertook in Japan:

> He detested superficiality and injustice like so many snakes or wolves and to the last firmly adhered to his beliefs, in defiance of neutrality and compromise, never retracting from his determination, however much others might do to persuade him. It did in fact resemble the disposition of the old Puritan Fathers. In my opinion, this Puritan-like quality, when combined with the doctor's piousness, made his scholastic system complete and unique.[13]

Ladd did not find many snakes or wolves in Japan. What he did find was a society that was increasingly vulnerable to a whole menagerie of unsavory creatures that were lurking undetected in the hinterlands of world commerce. He believed that while Japan faced serious social and political problems that required immediate attention, the country was peculiarly idealistic and spiritual and there was still a chance to help shape it in the direction of right principles. Above all, he feared that opening the doors of Japanese society would bring about a ruinous mixture of commercial greed and philosophical materialism.

In Milwaukee Ladd had fought the crass interests of the political machine; as a theologian he had been branded a heretic be-

[13] N. Oshima, "My Recollections of Dr. Ladd," *Shinri-Kenkyū*, 20 (1921), 353.

cause his own critical scholarship put him at odds with orthodoxy; as a psychologist he had argued against impure metaphysics and cerebral psychology; and now, in Japan, he had discovered a society that daily impressed him more favorably—a society that was so critically poised between the old and the new that he found himself drawn, heart and head, into a consuming new partisanship. It was a partisanship that drew together many of his old commitments and rekindled many of his old passions. As if running for public office, he set out upon a campaign of lectures and public appearances that did not end until his exhausted retreat to the mountains of Nikko prior to his departure for home.

In the two-week period following his lectureship at Doshisha, Ladd made twenty-five speeches before a variety of audiences. He lectured at the Imperial universities of Tokyo and Kyoto, the government colleges of trade and commerce, and the Imperial Educational Association. In Osaka he lectured on ethics before one thousand businessmen, teachers, and government officials, and in Yokohama he appeared before the local literary society. In each presentation he attempted to make his remarks helpfully relevant to the problems and the promise of a new Japan.

Two themes characterized Ladd's addresses to Japanese audiences. First, he dwelled upon the relation of philosophy to science and religion, advocating a reconciliation of differences wherever common ground could be found among the disciplines.[14] Second, he urged the cultivation of a personal and national morality that would assure the supremacy of ideals over material and commercial necessities. He believed that financial greed and commercial rivalry were the major causes of war between nations and that the commercial spirit posed a serious threat to the most worthy virtues of national life.[15] In his later visits to Japan he lectured before

[14] See G. T. Ladd, "The Nature, Origin, Essence and Method of Philosophy," trans. M. Matsumoto, *Rikugōzassi*, 139 (1892), 340-345; and G. T. Ladd, "Philosophy of Religion," trans. M. Matsumoto, *Rikugōzassi*, 140 (1892), 366–383.
[15] See *Rare Days in Japan*, pp. 279, 313.

a number of business and civic groups, stressing the intimate relation between morality and business affairs. Finally, in 1907, he gave a course of ten lectures on commercial ethics before the Tokyo Higher Commercial School. These were published in their entirety.[16] It is perhaps appropriate to add that Ladd believed social classes should be arranged so that the scholar was at the head of the list and the money-maker at the bottom.[17]

During the third week of July Ladd went to the mountain region of Hakone to take part in the Christian Summer School. He was a featured speaker in the general sessions of the school and a leader of informal discussions on a variety of topics. The earnestness and humility of the students greatly impressed him. Their commitment to learning and concern for matters of moral and religious truth were "most encouraging to the teacher, and even astonishing to one acquainted only with the indifference to such discussions which was then beginning to pervade the Western mind."[18] Here in Hakone he found a reciprocation of his own lifelong interest in ultimate questions. It must have been a refreshing contrast to his experiences with the sophisticated Yale undergraduate who seemed to have so little of that knightly spirit of commitment.

At the conclusion of his work at Hakone, the school held a farewell convocation that featured complimentary addresses, gifts, and traditional Japanese songs. It was a "tender and touching exercise," and Ladd was deeply moved by the friendly but restrained concern for his welfare. The next morning, in a heavy rain, he was borne away on a chair carried by four strong men under the escort of a hundred students, the president of the school, and other dignitaries.

> Think of having a college president and a pastor of the
> wealthiest city church head such a procession in your honor! It

[16] *The Doctrine of the Virtues as Applied to Business Life*, (Tokyo: The Tokyo Higher Commercial School, 1907).
[17] See *Rare Days in Japan*, p. 101.
[18] "Autobiography," p. 292.

made me fairly ashamed, and was rather hard to submit to; but there appeared no help for it. The path was simply horrible the last mile and a half of the way. It rained steadily. In places we went down over slippery stones, and wading through a shallow mountain brook, by such a steep descent that I was obliged to cling to the chair with all my strength to keep my seat; I was even somewhat fearful lest the coolies might slip on the stones and send me headlong down the mountain. In other places it was a wading through mud more than ankle-deep and sticky as such mud can be. Yet the escort kept cheerfully on. When we reached the village on the other side, they gathered in the court-yard of the inn, and cheered me with their national cheer: *Bandai, bandai, bandai-dai* (ten thousand years, ten thousand years, ten times ten thousand years). Some half-dozen un-daunted admirers kept on to Yumoto, which is about nine miles, by that road, from Hakoné.

As nearly as I can learn I have succeeded where I most feared failure. I have won—they say—the respect and affection of the young men; and some of them are likely to remember and be influenced by my coming for a long time. I think also that my visit has done Yale good here.[19]

It was a triumphant departure for a teacher of philosophy and psychology, and one that would not be repeated in New Haven.

[19] Letter from Ladd to his wife, dated August 2, 1892, and quoted in his "Auto-biography," p. 294.

Chapter · 12 ·

A Scholar's Holiday

The glorious adventures of the summer of 1892 left Ladd a bit dazzled and wanting more. He had reached out and given himself fully, and in return the people of Japan had borne him on their shoulders down the rainy mountainside in a memorable farewell. That fall the old house on Prospect Street echoed with the cry, *"Bandai, bandai, bandai-dai!"* as the professor saluted his family from the door of the study.[1] But it was from the study that Ladd sang of his new love; despite his recent return, he was already engrossed in a psychological manuscript that he had started as he sailed home on the *Empress of China.*

The unexpected success of the journey might have wrecked the scholarly career of a less committed man. As a result of his efforts in Japan, Ladd was drawn into a heavy correspondence with American missionaries and Japanese scholars and government officials; even more demanding were the requests for speeches and articles of comment that came from within the United States. He be-

[1] In an interview with the writer on April 1, 1962, Mrs. Walter A. Barrett of Fort Wayne, Indiana, spoke of her father's unusual excitement about his trips to the Orient: "It was as if he had found there something very important that he had been searching for."

came a figure closely identified with the Orient and his home a port of call for those who shared his interests. Japanese students at Yale, and many who were attending other colleges and universities, looked to him for understanding and friendly counsel.[2] In reflecting upon these years, one former student recalled the hospitality of the Ladd home and added:

> While I stayed at Yale there were several professors deeply interested in Japanese students, other than Prof. Ladd. One of them even showed so great an interest as to climb up to my dormitory room on the fifth story, to take me to his evening table. . . . However, none understood us so well as Prof. Ladd.[3]

The demands were heavy and Ladd responded with characteristic thoroughness and devotion; but not even Japan would deter him from scholarly pursuits. The seven-year interval between the first and second trips was the busy, productive period of mid-career, during which he tangled with James, served as president of the A.P.A., conducted a seminar in ethics at Harvard, delivered hundreds of speeches throughout the East, received two honorary degrees,[4] and spawned six books and twenty articles.

The interval was marred by the sudden death of his wife in the autumn of 1893. Ladd made arrangements for the care of his nine-year-old daughter, Elisabeth, and then, though deeply depressed, drove himself furiously into his work. Two years later he married Frances Virginia Stevens of New York City. Writing in his autobiography in 1912, Ladd commented:

[2] Influenced by his lectures, several students returned with him on the *Empress of China* to begin studies at Yale in the fall of 1892. See *Dōshisha-Bungaku*, 56 (1892), 38.

[3] I. Miyake, "Remembrances of Professor Ladd," *Shinri-Kenkyū*, 20 (1921), 263.

[4] His alma mater conferred the degree of Doctor of Laws in 1895, and the following year he and Professors James Seth of Edinburgh and William James of Harvard received the same degree from Princeton. Ladd had received an honorary D.D. from Western Reserve in 1879.

The seventeen years which have elapsed since then have not dulled, but have deepened my convictions as to the priceless value for a man of the power imparted to him by a good woman's love. For a man trying to be good, to receive from Heaven the loyalty and affection of one really good woman is to receive a fair measure of Heaven's best gifts. But to receive such a gift twice over, is to have laid upon one a blessed obligation to gratitude of the most excellent sort.[5]

In 1899, Ladd decided that the time had come to return to Japan. There was tension in the department and faculty discussion of the need for curricular revision, but his involvement with Japanese people and problems was becoming insistent. He had received repeated invitations to lecture in Japan and in India, and he had been appointed a delegate of the A.P.A. to the World's Congress of Psychologists to be held in Paris in the summer of 1900. The more he thought about it, the more ambitious his plans became. Finally he put together an itinerary that involved traveling 35,000 miles, with speaking engagements in dozens of cities, occasional stops for periods of intensive writing, and, capping it all, attendance at a professional meeting. It was Ladd's idea of the perfect holiday.

When the "speaking teacher" and his wife arrived in Tokyo in early September, 1899, they were immediately provided with a large, attentive escort, a furnished house, and a staff of servants. Ladd was given a three-hundred-year-old saddle inlaid with silver. A reception and dinner had been arranged by Yale men. Japan was just as he had remembered it, and his response was peculiarly his own—he began to mount platforms and speak to the condition of "this great and honorable empire." To an audience of four hundred guests of the Imperial Educational Society he gave a series of lectures on the relevance of psychology to education,[6] and before three hundred professors, teachers, pastors, and missionaries at the

5 "Autobiography," pp. 308–309.
6 *Psychology Applied to Education*, trans. K. Ukita (Tokyo: Bungakusha, 1900).

George Trumbull Ladd

Imperial University he offered a course of ten lectures on "The Philosophy of Mind." There followed a crowded schedule of lectures at Waseda University, Keio Gijiku University, the School for Peers and Peeresses, the Higher Normal School, the Peers' Club, and the Nobles' Club.

On this second visit to Japan, Ladd spent a great deal of time conferring with those who were using his books in the schools and universities and making arrangements for further publication of his books and lectures. *Primer of Psychology* had been published in Japanese in 1897, *Outlines of Descriptive Psychology* in 1898, and *Philosophy of Knowledge* the same year. Following this visit, *Outlines of Physiological Psychology* appeared in 1901. His books were helping to launch psychology in Japan, as were his lectures and his work with Japanese students at Yale.

In contrast to his lecture trip of 1892, this visit drew more heavily upon his contributions to psychology. It is significant that his opening series of formal lectures featured a psychological topic; there was a growing interest in the new science and Ladd was regarded as one of the men whose views on the subject would be most highly prized.[7] He was a philosopher and psychologist with an international reputation, but, equally important, he was considered by the Japanese to have a sympathetic understanding of their special problems. This is evident in the remarks by President Shinji Tsuji of the Imperial Educational Society when he observed in a preface to the published version of Ladd's lectures, "Among so many philosophers and psychologists living both in Europe as well as in the

[7] William James was another. A former Yale student and one of the leading early figures in Japanese psychology referred to Ladd's *Elements* and James's *Principles* as "epoch-making works." He reported that during a visit at Harvard in 1897, he asked whether James might come to Japan: "He responded that if he did it would be useless since he could not understand Japanese, thus being destitute of a means for discussion. Prof. Ladd differed greatly on this point, and though he did not know Japanese at first, still he came to Japan as often as three times. I could not think of Prof. Ladd, but reflect on the relation between him and Japanese men." M. Matsumoto, "Memories of Professor Ladd," *Shinri-Kenkyū*, 20 (1921), 250.

186

U.S., none would maintain such a thorough understanding toward we Japanese as he."[8]

Ladd was deeply concerned about the development of psychology in Japan. His concern was not born of a quest for personal glory, though certainly he enjoyed the responsiveness of the people. Behind his tireless efforts there was a "conviction": he believed that psychology as he knew it was peculiarly suited to the mind and spirit of a Japan in transition. Psychology could serve as a unifying discipline, illuminating the precious traditions that deserved understanding and preservation and at the same time humanizing the practical affairs of an increasingly commercial nation. But psychology could not serve this noble purpose if it was viewed as an importation from abroad; it would have to develop as an indigenous discipline, rooted in the grammar and the temper of the nation and its leaders. In short, without fully realizing it, Ladd was encouraging the development of a Japanese functional psychology.

The future of psychology was one concern and the future of private, particularly Christian, education was another. The private missionary schools were having trouble complying with government demands. Japanese education was in a process of unsteady evolution as the government continued its efforts to establish a system that would be appropriate to its needs. The Sino-Japanese War of 1894–1895 had complicated matters a great deal; there had been an enormous drain upon resources and an intensification of nationalism. In some educational circles the opinion had grown that the government should not grant favors to educational institutions that were promoting an alien religion. Doshisha was one of the institutions that experienced difficulty in compromising the conflicts between government policy and missionary zeal.

While Ladd believed that government restriction of private education was unwise, he was even more worried about the conserva-

[8] *Psychology Applied to Education*, p. 3.

tive and parochial attitudes that were so abundant and troublesome in the missionary schools. He supported the missionary effort in Japan, but he most emphatically did not support those who were obsessed with the conversion of souls. The missionary zealot wanted to save souls for Christ; but Ladd was not interested in converting good Buddhists into poor Christians. Bringing to the missionary effort in Japan the informed, liberal beliefs about religion that had made him a heretic earlier in his career, he urged that the work be inspirited by love and compassion rather than by flaming righteousness. No doubt the reaction was mixed when he stated from the platform:

> No particular detailed creed, no one form of church organization, no special type of experience or manner of ordering one's life, can be said to belong to the essentials of Christianity.[9]

If this seemed to strip missionary work of its purpose, then it could only mean that the missionaries needed to reconsider the ends they were to serve as guests in a foreign country.[10]

Admonishing the missionaries was not enough. Ladd wanted to help create a government policy that would allow private education to continue with a minimum of restrictions. To this end he arranged interviews with Count Kabayama, then Minister of Education, and Marquis Ito, a national figure considered liberal in his attitude toward the development of Japan. With each of these men he urged the adoption of policies that would stimulate freedom and provide diversity of educational opportunities. There is no way to determine the precise effect of these interviews, though on later occasions both Kabayama and Ito acknowledged Ladd's helpful-

[9] *The Essentials of Christianity* (Tokyo: The Student YMCA Union of Japan, 1901), p. 7.

[10] Writing from the journal that he kept during his work in Japan, Ladd reflected in his autobiography that "there was no graver mistake made by the missionaries from this country . . . than the effort to *Americanize* their converts." "Autobiography," p. 283.

ness and sought additional opportunities for discussion of educational problems. The interview with Marquis Ito was the beginning of a long, eventful friendship that would end only with Ito's assassination in Korea.

Toward the conclusion of Ladd's stay in Japan two matters of importance, about which there had been doubt for several weeks, suddenly became perfectly clear—first, after hearing many conflicting rumors, he learned that he was to be honored by the receipt of the Third Degree of the Order of the Rising Sun, and to have a personal audience with the Emperor; and second, it was apparent that he was seriously ill.[11] The two were peculiarly related. The illness was brought on by weeks of furious activity in which each day and night was filled with speeches, official visitations, court and garden parties, and informal discussions; but it was this same untiring commitment that had won the Emperor's gratitude. In his journal for Thursday, October 12, he wrote:

> Dressed with no small difficulty on account of continued pain, soreness, and weakness, and went with F—— to the Legation in Colonel Buck's carriage. Learning there that the audience with the Empress had been countermanded by a note received only at two o'clock that morning, the sorely disappointed wife was left to be condoled with by Madam Buck. . . . In the carriage, on our way to the Palace, Colonel Buck and I spoke of the value of a better acquaintance of the educational circles of the two countries; and he was good enough to say that he considered such work as I had been doing worth more for cementing friendly relations between the two nations than much diplomacy. Arrived at the palace, we were ushered by the persons in waiting through long corridors into an elegant

[11] There had been troublesome symptoms for a number of weeks, the most distressing of which had occurred without warning during his interview with Marquis Ito. On that occasion he had fallen at Ito's feet and had remained unconscious for some time. Ito summoned four doctors and Ladd was sent home to rest, but he refused to stay down.

drawing-room, where Counts Toda and Nagasaki were, with other gentlemen, gathered to receive us. Here we were kept waiting perhaps ten or fifteen minutes before being taken to the audience room. Before its doors were thrown open, Count Toda informed me that "His Majesty was very gracious this morning and wished to shake hands with Professor Ladd" (a custom then far more infrequent than it is now). Colonel Buck and I then entered in the prescribed form. The Emperor, who was standing at the other end of the room addressed him a few questions first,—inquiring after his health, whether the Legation was injured by the storm of the previous day, etc. I was then introduced,—the Emperor extending his hand,—and was asked about my coming to Japan, the proposed time of leaving Tokyo, and several other questions. His Majesty also expressed pleasure at having seen me; and finally the hope that he might sometime see me again. This was understood as a polite sort of dismissal. We then backed out, bowing; and when I had signed my name in the Emperor's book, and mine and F——'s in the book of the Empress, I was driven to the Legation again, assured that all my *devoirs* had been suitably discharged.[12]

Sick with what was now diagnosed as a malarial fever compounded by exhaustion, Ladd lectured his way to Kobe, delivered a final "informal talk" to five hundred teachers from missionary and government schools, boarded the *Kawachi Maru* bound for Bombay, and "shivered with malarial chill all the way through the charming scenery of the Inland Sea."[13]

The winter in India was a mixture of pleasure and pain. The pain came from the malarial condition, and later influenza, that stayed with Ladd for many strenuous weeks, and from the deep distress and anxiety that would accompany any traveler as he made

[12] "Autobiography," pp. 341–342. "F——" refers to Mrs. Ladd, whom he called Fanny.
[13] "Autobiography," p. 344.

his way through a country sick with plague and famine.[14] Seeing the India of 1900 was a sobering experience, and he was both astonished and fascinated by the enormity of the human problem that lay before him. The extremes of wealth and squalor, refined culture and illiteracy, religious sensitivity and the social insensitivity of the caste system came to haunt him more and more as he moved through the country, until it seemed that they were merged as one great conspiracy to challenge his own world view. In one who was so addicted to writing books about his ideas and experiences, it is perhaps significant that he did not publish his book about the winter in India until nineteen years later.[15] It was the last book that he would write.

He had two reasons for going to India. As a lifelong student of religion, Ladd wanted to see firsthand the country that he acknowledged as a seedbed of living world religions. Both his autobiography and his book about India express in detail the careful study that he made of the varieties of Indian religion.[16] The main reason for the trip, however, was a direct outgrowth of his writings in psychology and philosophy. The story behind the invitation reveals the special meaning that his work had in one area of the world at the

[14] It was a chronic condition. Three years before, in publishing a firsthand account of the plague, complete with appalling pictures of sick and dying people, the editors of *The Cosmopolitan* had asked: "What is this sham of a Christianity [the government of England] which knows of these horrors and yet fails to raise its hand in protest?" J. Hawthorne, "The Horrors of the Plague in India," *The Cosmopolitan*, 23 (1897), 232. It was a question that deeply troubled Ladd, though he tried valiantly to appreciate the efforts that were being made by the British government's officials in India.

[15] *Intimate Glimpses of Life in India* (Boston: R. G. Badger, 1919). In marked contrast to this lapse of time, Ladd's book about his experiences in Korea was nearly completed by the time that he arrived home from that country.

[16] He drew upon this study of religion in writing some of his later books. One interesting by-product of the work was an article concerning "A Death Ceremonial of the 'Kapola Bania' Caste" (*Journal of the American Oriental Society*, 22 (1901), 227–236). Ladd joined the American Oriental Society in 1898 and remained a member of the Section for the Historical Study of Religions until 1912. (Personal communication from Ferris J. Stephens, Secretary-Treasurer of the Society, August 22, 1962.)

time that the new mental science was making its bid for academic respectability.

In the early spring of 1899, Ladd had received a letter from Professor M. Maher, a teacher of psychology and philosophy at Stonyhurst College in England. Professor Maher had written:

> A friend of mine on the Committee of the Bombay University wrote to me some time ago for advice with reference to getting some works in harmony with Theism on the University Philosophical Programme. I recommended your works and I have just heard from him that he has succeeded in getting a couple of your volumes, along with a little book of mine on Psychology down on the programme for one examination as an alternative to Sully and James. . . . There seems to have been considerable opposition and a stiff fight, as the present professors and examiners are apparently of the Empiricist school. However, my friend, though beaten in committee, triumphed in appeal to the Senate. But he tells me he expects a bit of a war in the press, especially as he expects to get the programme for one or two other examinations in the University similarly changed; and he therefore asks me for any review notices or criticisms that I can furnish in favour especially of your Physiological Psychology and Philosophy of the Human Mind. The latter book and the "Outlines" for the volumes he has succeeded in introducing. . . . The "conspiracy of silence" and the effort on the part of the agnostic and positivist sect to sneer down and suppress every work, no matter how able, that appears on the Theistic side, seems to be worldwide; but I should not have imagined, till I got my friend's letter, that even in Cathay a "professor of philosophy" could have ventured to profess his ignorance of your writings,—as one of them actually did before the Senate.[17]

[17] Letter from M. Maher to G. T. Ladd, dated April 2, 1899, and in the possession of Miss Cornelia T. Ladd of Cleveland Heights, Ohio.

The friend to whom Maher referred was Father Bochum, professor of philosophy at St. Francis Xavier College in Bombay. This Jesuit institution was an important one as a representative of Catholicism in India. It also was influential quite apart from Catholicism, since many of the wealthy and public-spirited Parsees sent their sons there as a way of preparing them for government examinations. Father Bochum had placed the college in an embarrassing position in its relation to the University by refusing to teach courses in philosophy and psychology on the ground that

> . . . he and his colleagues came to India in behalf of Christian truth, and could not reconcile it with their mission to inoculate their pupils with what they regarded as the poisonous doctrines of Spencerian agnosticism and infidelity.[18]

Father Bochum sought a way out of his predicament by proposing to the committee on curriculum that certain of Ladd's books be substituted for the "atheistic" books by Spencer. It was at this point that Bochum wrote to Maher, who wrote to Ladd, for support and ammunition to be used in his battle to have Ladd's works adopted. The committee on curriculum turned down the proposal to include Ladd's books on the approved list, but Bochum took the matter to the University Senate, and with the support of Chief Justice Candy, the Vice Chancellor, approval was obtained.

In his autobiography Ladd made a point of his belief that Father Bochum's interest in using his books stemmed from a desire to support the possibility of theism, rather than "Jesuitism," *per se*. He acknowledged that the Catholic interest was closely identified with a theistic position, but he held that in this case the support of his books was a justifiable and liberal educational effort.[19] Ladd had for

[18] G. T. Ladd, *Intimate Glimpses of Life in India*, pp. 14–15.
[19] See "Autobiography," p. 366.

many years argued against Spencerian doctrine,[20] and of course his own position was one that deliberately provided a framework for theism. He considered "the unknown God of Herbert Spencer" to be an illogical extension of a materialistic monism, in which both the monism and the extension were based upon an erring metaphysics. The Ladd-Spencer struggle, therefore, was a matter that concerned him deeply and he was greatly pleased when his books were approved. He may have been to one side of the mainstream of American psychology, but in the winter of 1900 he felt close to the center of the new psychology in India.

The Catholic attitude was held to be friendly in its "recognition of the importance and usefulness of empirical Psychology, if only it were kept within its own limits, and if it followed closely the scientific methods proper to an empirical science,"[21] but it also pointed to "the unsettled methods and doctrines" of the new psychology and eschewed the "materialistic tendencies" that were revealed in Spencer's work. A similar position was taken by Protestant missionary educators, though apparently they were reluctant to become too closely identified with the move that had been made by Father Bochum. Ladd reported that he was in great and rather surprising favor with the Catholics during his visit, but that it all "served to 'queer' me with some of the Protestant missionaries."[22] He was distressed by this missionary response because he felt that it stemmed from a competitive fear concerning the race for converts and did not express a proper concern about mutual interests in the "defence and spread of the fundamental truths of morals and religion."[23] He was consistently interested in "fundamental truths" and consistently impatient with those who were most worried about narrow doctrinal and denominational questions.[24]

[20] See our discussion of his position concerning "The Unknown God of Herbert Spencer," p. 63.
[21] *Bombay Catholic Examiner*, April 18, 1899.
[22] *Intimate Glimpses of Life in India*, p. 17.
[23] *Ibid.*
[24] The doctrinal questions were duly noted in faraway London. See "Christian or Anti-Christian Philosophy for India?" *The Weekly Register*, June 3, 1900.

Ladd's course of ten lectures at Bombay University was launched with a grand reception at which more than one thousand representatives of education, government, and the professions were in attendance. Welcoming speeches were delivered and reference was made to the controversy that had preceded his arrival. Justice Ranade, of the Supreme Bench of the Bombay Presidency, concluded his remarks with the observation, "I have glanced through the Professor's *Outlines of Physiological Psychology*, and find that he takes a conservative position, and while seeking for a physiological basis, yet he retains a true spiritual psychology."[25]

The lectures were pure Ladd. A syllabus that has been preserved reveals a concern with his favorite topics—psychology as a science, psychology as the philosophy of mind, the relations of the body and mind, psychological monism and dualism, and the place of man's mind in nature.[26] While it is difficult to know precisely what Justice Ranade meant by "a true spiritual psychology," it is evident that Ladd's psychology was friendly to those, Christian and non-Christian, who were primarily concerned with the spiritual and non-material realm. As a psychologist he may not have shared all of their beliefs about man, but at least he understood their problems and could talk their language. At a time when psychology was only beginning to seem relevant to the larger purposes of university education in India, Ladd's sincere and moderate arguments were easily translated into the familiar modes of philosophy, thereby helping to make psychology both relevant and unthreatening. It was no small contribution.[27]

[25] *The Times of India* (Bombay), November 30, 1899. In referring to this reception in his book about India, Ladd makes clear that he considered the final outcome of the controversy and the lecture series to be a major step forward in the development of a liberal position for Indian psychology. See *Intimate Glimpses of Life in India*, pp. 31–32.

[26] "Syllabus of Lectures on Psychology to be Delivered in the Sir Cowasji Jehangier Hall of the Bombay University, November 30 to December 15, 1899," *Essays*, vol. 3 (Sterling Library, Yale University, New Haven, Conn.).

[27] During his visit in Indian colleges and universities, Ladd discussed psychology and philosophy with many teachers, some of whom later used his texts in their classes. A good example of the delayed effect of his visit is seen in a special 93-page

George Trumbull Ladd

Following the work in Bombay, Ladd resumed his familiar routine of travel, lectures, public visitations, writing, and sightseeing. He was often sick and dispirited, but he pushed on, addressing thousands of educators, government officials, students, and missionaries in Calcutta, Benares, Ahmadnagar, Madras, and Colombo, Ceylon. His subjects included "The Reality of Mind," "The Conception of God Most in Accordance with Science and Philosophy," "The Essentials of Christianity," "The American University," and "Immortality in the Light of Modern Science." He argued for tolerance and understanding among the religions of the world and expressed clearly his own conviction that an enlightened religion that was freed of rigid doctrinal prescriptions had nothing to fear from the rise of science.

While it cannot be said that Ladd's work in India had a major impact upon the troubled nation, the effect of his lectures and public appearances upon certain individuals would seem incontestable. Students, college and university teachers, and missionaries received the most attention and for many years there were expressions of gratitude for his lectures and books. His personal reputation was enhanced by the trip and the use of his books increased accordingly. Students came to know and to appreciate his work,[28] though apparently many of them also continued to read Spencer.

Two months in Japan, a winter in India, and the spring spent in travel through countries of the Near East and southern Europe brought Ladd to Paris and the last major commitment of his working holiday. He was a delegate of the A.P.A. to the World's Congress of Psychologists and had been asked to preside over one of

annotated summary of his *Primer* that was published in 1903, for use by students who were preparing for university examinations. See P. B. Adhikari, *An Analysis of Ladd's "Primer of Psychology"* (Lahore: The Tribune Press, 1903).

[28] As one teacher from the south of India wrote after his visit, "It is no exaggeration to say wherever the English tongue is spoken your name is familiar and the students of philosophy here read your interesting and instructive works with delight and profit." Letter from S. K. Aiyar to G. T. Ladd, April 15, 1900; original copy in possession of Miss Cornelia T. Ladd of Cleveland Heights, Ohio.

the sessions. From August 20 to 24 he devoted all of his time to the congress; apparently it was something less than a complete success.

> In spite of two efforts made,—one some six weeks and the other three days in advance,—to obtain information as to the exact date of the opening of the Congress, by correspondence with the Secretary, I was at last obliged to go in ignorance of the matter. But on reaching the *Palais du Congres* at ten A.M., Monday, I found myself in good time. The conduct of the meetings showed the same lack of business quality which was displayed during the Exposition by its managers. The rules limiting the papers and the discussions were good; but they were very imperfectly enforced, and none of the French writers or speakers seemed to expect that they would be enforced. The attendance of French was, of course, very large; the attendance of Russians noteworthy; that of the Germans only fair; Professor Meyers was the only one put down from England; a Professor Brough from Wales; and from Holland, Scandinavia, Italy, and Switzerland, only a very few. Professors Bryan, Seashore, Munsterberg, and Munroe were the only members of the American Association whom I saw. Several others, not members of our National Association, were however present and seemed to receive equal recognition in every way from the Congress. This failure to distinguish did not contribute to the success scientifically of the Congress or to the reputation of American psychologists. The papers were nearly all read in French, and read so poorly that I had great difficulty—aside from my slowness of ear to catch the language—in understanding them. But I am satisfied that the average was scarcely up to —and was certainly not above—the grade of the papers presented at one of our annual meetings. Fully half of them were indeed rather weak; they were presented by young and relatively unknown men. It was especially instructive to see how the interest grew in the discussion of the burning questions, espe-

cially when the attempt to present experimental evidence was brought forward. Hypnotism, telepathy, the claims of spiritism as to externalization of the body, etc. were most plainly considered worthy of respectful attention and scientific investigation. And as in the case of some of the phenomena of physics, very extraordinary and formerly incredible alleged psychological facts are now quite generally coming to be admitted, although a wide difference of opinion prevails as to how these facts shall be explained; or as to whether they admit of any explanation at present. But the interest in the ordinary problems of psycho-physics and experimental psychology, as such subjects are treated in the laboratory, seemed to be waning rather than increasing, if one might judge by the attendance and interest shown at the Congress. On the whole, perhaps, the students of psychiatry were more satisfactorily represented than any other Section.

The meeting with men whom I had hitherto known by name only, and seeing how they looked and how they conducted themselves, was for me far the greatest privilege of the Congress. For example, at one of the earliest meetings, a man seated just behind me, who looked and spoke much like our Professor Brewer, leaned over and handed me his card; in return I handed mine, and a look of pleased surprise came over his face, for M. Flournoy and his, I fear, too sarcastic critic (I, in the "Philosophy of Mind") had met. At a dinner at Pierre Janet's on Tuesday evening, there were ten gentlemen and the hostess at table; and nine different nationalities were represented. They were—so far as I can recall them—Janet, Ebbinghaus, Sergi, Flournoy, Ichorowitz, Schrank-Notting, Demoor, and myself. Professor Meyers' card was at the plate just beside mine, but he did not appear. Professor Sergi seemed much pleased to see me and complimented the number and clearness (!) of my books. To my surprise he contrasted their quality of clearness with the obscurity of ———, whom he said he found very obscure and could not understand at all.[29]

[29] "Autobiography," pp. 483–485.

Ladd observed in his autobiography that "it is my experience, in general, that for the older and better equipped men such gatherings as this World's Congress are chiefly useful in a social way."[30] Of the social pleasures that he experienced, the most memorable one resulted from an invitation to visit Professor Bergson in his home. They talked for two hours and found a number of areas of agreement. Ladd was especially impressed by Bergson's belief that "the psychologists of France were almost all agreed that a merely empirical psychology—without metaphysics—could not be maintained; and that a purely experimental method would yield only scanty and unsatisfactory results."[31] This comment alone would have been enough to make Ladd's visit with Bergson a pleasant memory. It was a reassuring note on which to end his sixteen-month visit abroad.

[30] "Autobiography," p. 486. In a letter to James, who did not attend the Congress, one "older and better equipped" man observed: "I returned to Geneva on Saturday, happy to have finished with Paris and the Congress and almost regretting that I had not instead spent ten more days at the seashore. It is true also that if I had freed myself from this obligation I should regret it now! In any case, congresses are a thorn in the flesh and a source of painful impressions for natures such as mine, in which inhibitions and the tendency to stop dead in one's tracks predominate. I am incapable, therefore of telling you whether or not this Congress was a success. . . . It was obvious that all the French were bored to death playing host to the Congress." R. C. Le Clair (ed.), *The Letters of William James and Theodore Flournoy* (Madison: University of Wisconsin Press, 1966), pp. 102–103.

[31] *Ibid.*, p. 487.

Chapter · 13 ·

An Exercise of Rights

Late on the spring afternoon of May 17, 1904, Ladd locked the door of his office in Lawrence Hall and walked across the Yale campus toward his home. For nearly a quarter of a century he had concluded each working day with a quiet, reflective walk up Prospect Street. To a man of disciplined habits, the familiar ritual was a reassuring break between the public struggles of campus life and the scholarly adventures of the evening hours. He was well known to members of the campus community and to the citizens of New Haven. They knew Professor Ladd as a man of prodigious scholarship who was honored both at home and abroad. Reserved and stiff in manner, he was not able to indulge in the casual conversations that could have graced the many thousands of trips between home and campus. He preferred to walk alone, and those who fell within his orbit came to know and to respect that preference. They would see him striding with quiet dignity up and down Prospect Street—alone, lost in thought, and on time.

> Ladd was a man of regular habits, extremely restricted in his social contacts, a New England Puritan. He was regular in his attendance at recitations, never missed one while he was in

active service, equally regular in his attendance at Sunday College chapel, and frequently would appear at weekday morning prayers. It was characteristic of him that, in my memory, he wore the same straw hat for twenty years from 1893 until 1913, always breaking it forth regardless of the weather on May 15 of each year.[1]

Wearing his ancient straw hat, Ladd left the Yale campus on that spring afternoon in 1904 more alone and lost in thought than he had ever been before. In his pocket he carried a stunning letter from President Arthur T. Hadley which read, in part;

> In a conversation a few weeks ago arising out of the suggestion that your field of work might be so restricted as to avoid certain conflicts with your colleagues, you expressed the intention of falling back upon the exercise of your rights in this matter. Under the circumstances, the Corporation has felt compelled to take steps toward the exercise of its own rights as conferred and prescribed in the charter of 1745, for the well ordering and managing [of] the affairs of the College.
>
> At a full meeting of the Corporation on May 16, 1904, it was unanimously resolved that, in view of the unsatisfactory condition of the Department of Philosophy in recent years, the President be authorized and instructed, in behalf of the Corporation, to advise you that after July 31, 1905, your services as professor will no longer be required.[2]

Ladd was shocked by this development. Only two years before the time when he expected to retire with honor, he was confronted with the most distressing circumstance of his professional life. His career as a "speaking teacher," the role which he most cherished, though perhaps not the one in which he was most effective, was

[1] Personal communication from Charles Seymour, formerly president of Yale University, November 13, 1961.

[2] Letter from A. T. Hadley to G. T. Ladd, May 17, 1904, in G. T. Ladd, "Private Paper," Appendix, Letter No. 4, Henry P. Wright Collection of Letters and Papers, 1898–1911 (Yale University Library).

brought to a sudden and sad conclusion. In the legitimate exercise of conflicting rights the Corporation held the upper hand and once more Ladd was forced, as a matter of principle, to fight what he knew would be a losing battle. He was armed with a courageous tongue and a facile pen, but the Corporation held the charter of 1745.

The Corporation's resolution was not a request that Ladd resign. He was dismissed, with one year's notice, and there was no indication that he was to be granted emeritus status or retirement pay. Firing a renowned professor two years before his retirement, and after a quarter-century of service to the university, was serious business which obviously required strong provocation. The letter implied that the crucial matter was Ladd's recalcitrance in the face of efforts to restrict his field of work as a means of avoiding conflict with his colleagues. President Hadley spoke of troubles in the Department of Philosophy that "have gone so far and the attempts to remedy them have proved so fruitless that . . . radical measures are necessary to conserve the interests of the students and the reputation of the University." He held that the situation had become "so grave as to make its termination imperative."

> To this communication I made no reply; indeed there seemed to be no reply appropriate or necessary. I found myself accused, tried, and convicted and sentenced to extreme punishment; and beyond the fact that . . . "troubles had arisen in the Department," I was quite unable to conjecture any reason, so far as my own conduct was concerned, for the action of the Corporation. To the present time I know of no reason. Inquiry made by friends, of nearly all the members of that body, has utterly failed to develop any explanation beyond the bare fact that they acted on the recommendation of the President.[3]

The letter of dismissal came at a particularly bad time. Ladd was physically exhausted from the work of the academic year, deeply

[3] "Autobiography," p. 514.

committed to editors and publishers, concerned about his wife's frail health, and immersed in final plans for a summer trip to Europe. He placed his case in the hands of his old friend Professor Thomas Day Seymour. After a period of confusion and intense negotiation he was allowed to resign at the end of the next academic year, and was appointed professor emeritus, receiving the retirement pay that he normally would have received two years later.

The dismissal was embarrassing to Ladd and to the university. On both sides of the controversy there was evidence of pique and principle, and while it may not have been one of the most glorious moments in Yale's long academic history, certainly it was an occasion of notable transformation in the life of the institution. Ladd's dismissal was a personal tragedy; for President Hadley and the Corporation it was a legal but probably unwise exercise of their rights under the charter of 1745. But as in so many circumstances of Ladd's life, the events that precipitated this difficult situation were complex; in part, it must be added, because he made them so.

In his excellent educational history of Yale College during the period from 1871 to 1921, Pierson vividly described the attitudes and prerogatives of the professors in running the programs of the college. In large measure the professors *were* the college and they zealously guarded their rights and responsibilities. In earlier times the professors were assisted by tutors, but with the increasing complexity of the curriculum and the institution, and in response to a desire to improve the stability and quality of personnel, the transitory tutors gradually were replaced by men who were granted the rank of assistant professor. The all-or-none principle in granting professorships was being replaced by the now familiar academic ladder. Junior personnel were increasingly important in the educational work of the college.

> Yet the full professors still considered themselves apart, kept hold of their prerogatives, treated the younger men distantly or even stiffly, and acted on occasion as if a little disci-

pline and hardship were good for instructors. Each professor was still a free agent, the master of his own teaching domain, and without effective superior. In groups they ran the departments of study. In other small groups they dominated the important committees. All told they constituted a chamber of peers of enormous power and no little dignity and pride. Despite the filling of the middle ranks and the emergence of departments of study, the professors still ruled. The first decade under Hadley was the age of the barons in Yale College.[4]

In an age of barons, no Yale professor could have been more baronial than George Trumbull Ladd. He not only believed in the rights and essential nobility of the college professor; he lived his professorship. To be a professor was to commit a life—all of it—to the high purposes of teaching and of scholarship. It was not a matter of fits and spurts of reading and lecturing and writing; rather, it was a total priesthood in the service of God and fellow man. The fullness of conviction concerning his own high calling left no room for doubt about his prerogatives. Clearly, the professors should run the college.[5]

With baronial assurance and priestly commitment, Ladd exerted a strong, if not always decisive, influence upon the teaching of philosophy and psychology at Yale. He was interested in the development of the Department of Philosophy and encouraged the college to increase its offerings in psychology. The Yale Laboratory of Psychology, founded in 1892,[6] was in part an offspring of his efforts

[4] G. W. Pierson, *Yale College—an Educational History, 1871–1921* (New Haven: Yale University Press, 1952), p. 147.

[5] Ladd apparently felt that college administrators should be menial servants of the professors, and he was especially hard on presidents. He considered their influence to be largely mischievous and this attitude was greatly reinforced by his losing battle with President Hadley. Ultimately he was led to ask publicly why a university should have a president at all. See G. T. Ladd, "The Need of Administrative Changes in the American University," *Popular Science Monthly*, 80 (1912), 313–325.

[6] Ladd did undertake some early experimental studies in Professor James K. Thatcher's physiological laboratory in the Yale Medical School prior to the publica-

to create a flourishing center for teaching and research in the field, although of course he was not himself principally concerned with laboratory work. Dr. Edward B. Scripture had been added to the department in 1892, and for a number of years took responsibility for the direction of the laboratory. Also sharing in the work of the Department of Philosophy in the 1890's were Professors George M. Duncan, E. Hershey Sneath, and later Charles H. Judd. These men, junior to Ladd in length of service to the university, were deeply involved in the day-to-day affairs of the department, and, as Ladd was to realize later, in growing disagreement with many of his ideas about the department.

In the two decades of Ladd's service before the turn of the century, the department had developed into a significant center of philosophical and psychological study.[7] While this certainly was not an achievement to be credited to Ladd alone, he had been a primary force in the growing influence of the department. It is clear that he felt his own role had been the principal one in the department and that the destiny of philosophy and psychology at Yale was attached to his own professional success. When one adds to his strong personal identification with the history and fate of the department a rather superior attitude toward men who were his academic juniors, it becomes obvious that he would not take kindly to the intrigues within the department that were encouraged by Dun-

tion of his *Elements of Physiological Psychology* in 1887. It was in the autumn of 1892, however, that the Yale laboratory was "founded" in rooms in the Old Gymnasium or Commons on Library Street. See C. R. Garvey, "List of American Psychology Laboratories," *Psychological Bulletin*, 26 (1929), 652-660; also, "Early Psychology at Yale," *Yale Alumni Weekly*, January 31, 1936, p. 4.

[7] In 1901 Buchner listed 38 men and women actively engaged in philosophical or psychological instruction who had received all or part of their education in the Department of Philosophy since the time of Ladd's arrival in 1881. Twenty-five of this group had received the Ph.D. An additional twelve Ph.D.'s had been awarded to men who became ministers but had not "performed academical offices at the altar of reason." Three of the teaching Ph.D.'s held positions in Japanese universities. E. F. Buchner, "Teachers of Philosophy Among Yale Graduates," *Education*, 21 (1901), 549–556, 618–627.

can and Sneath. These two colleagues were restless under Ladd's severe and knowing tutelage, and when conditions were otherwise made ripe, they encouraged the restriction of his influence in the department. Scripture also contributed to his downfall, though not, it would seem, by any direct maneuvering. He disagreed with Ladd on a number of matters, but his principal contribution was indirect—a general resentment and unrest which added to the confusion within the department that was to be the major excuse for Ladd's dismissal.

Ladd's personal relations with his colleagues were never warm and intimate. He was impatient, rather arrogant, and incapable of the small talk that might have made for easier relations with others. He cannot be characterized as a likeable person. His abrupt and dominating ways made others resentful and undoubtedly made his position a much more difficult one when the question of personal roles and prerogatives finally was confronted by the university administration. In his autobiographical essay, Seashore commented upon the intimate relation between Ladd's personal characteristics and the break-up of the department. Seashore had a high regard for Ladd, both as a graduate instructor and as a scholar and theoretician, but he was by no means blind to the traits that aggravated the situation at Yale.

> Ladd had a profound confidence in himself, his philosophy and his mission. This "Lording" attitude he probably carried over from his earlier training and experience in the church both as a preacher and as a theological writer. It proved his downfall. He tried to impose his philosophy as science of sciences upon the sciences, history and religion. He regarded himself as Chaplain of the University and as spiritual advisor of the students, not realizing how few he reached. He had many supporters in the Faculty, but he overreached in his ambition to dominate. However, these weaknesses were very much like the

weaknesses in men opposing him. The struggle grew into a pitched battle in which neither side got justice. The smash-up of the Department was an internal war, in which he and his supporters and associates lost. There was no compromise and many of the rights and merits in the Department were overlooked. Innocent parties suffered and the Department was cleaned out.

It took philosophy and psychology a long time to rehabilitate themselves at Yale. Scripture was swept out with Ladd, although they had practically nothing in common. Indeed, Ladd had never given a hearty support to Scripture, certainly no free hand. This cataclysmic fall of the Ladd stronghold had an unfortunate effect upon his influence with students and philosophies. His works should stand as classics in American philosophy, but his influence was broken by the loss of his graduate student constituency and the administrative collapse. Everybody was discouraged.[8]

In "the palmy days of Ladd"[9] there was no doubt that one forceful figure was in control of philosophy and psychology at Yale. The prodigious scholar wrote and taught with a confidence that upset the more tentative theoreticians on the faculty. He "loved the long words, and even the obscure ones,"[10] and he pushed his long-worded views into every nook and cranny of the university. He enjoyed watching his ideas play upon the deeper issues of mental science and he welcomed combat on problems of university policy as an opportunity to test the merit of his own position. He "drove straight for the people" at Yale much as he had done with the congregations of Edinburg and Milwaukee. The baron professor must have been a figure to reckon with in classes and in faculty

[8] C. E. Seashore, in *History of Psychology in Autobiography*, ed. C. Murchison (Worcester, Mass.: Clark University Press, 1930), p. 250.
[9] *Ibid.*, p. 253.
[10] Personal communication from a former student, dated November 11, 1961.

meetings. When he told his classes, "Gentlemen, it has always been a pleasure to me to watch the workings of my own mind,"[11] he may have displayed a conceit that would be remembered for sixty years, but undoubtedly he meant what he said.

It is important to note the scholarly and professional interests that Ladd developed during his years at Yale. Upon joining the faculty in 1881, he was charged with direct responsibility for the teaching of philosophy and related courses in mental science. His interests in philosophy, however, were more abiding than was his concern with the formal study of psychology, and he continued to write on philosophical topics. Throughout these two decades he taught courses in philosophy; it is evident from a study of his autobiography that the teaching of philosophy was the function that he considered himself best suited to perform. He recorded his teaching preferences in the academic year 1900–1901 as follows:

> During the year 1900–01 Mr. Duncan continued in his place on the committee of revision of the curriculum; and, finally, by a majority vote all required work in the Department was abolished by the Faculty, and—though with no little reluctance— by subsequent vote of the Corporation. At the same time— namely, in the Spring of 1901—I was at my own request transferred to a University professorship. On making this change of relation toward undergraduate work of the Department, I assured my colleagues, Professors Duncan and Sneath, that I should trust them to take the more immediate charge there; that I desired still to assist in the instruction of undergraduates; and that I particularly wished to specialize, in the future, in ethics and in the philosophy of religion. I did not think it necessary to make specific terms with them; or to warn them against mistakes of Judgment to which I knew them to be especially liable.[12]

[11] Personal communication from a former student, dated October 31, 1961.
[12] "Autobiography," pp. 506–507.

Thus, by the turn of the century, Ladd was transferred, at his own request, to a university professorship; also, it should be noted that he expressed his preference for teaching ethics and the philosophy of religion. These two points are significantly involved in his later troubles.

During the period 1881–1900 American psychology developed at a rapid pace. Though Ladd played a notable role in the growth of psychology during its early years, by the turn of the century he was no longer in the mainstream of that academic and scientific effort. By inclination and by the force of his own scholarly work, he was cast to one side of the drama that was unfolding. His entry into psychology had come as a commendable and understandable extension of his efforts to mediate between the old and the new by familiarizing himself with what was new in mental science; but he did not, indeed he could not, abandon the old. The cherished preference for philosophy prevailed and this preference, coupled with his distaste for serious experimental work, left him out of touch with the rapidly expanding and increasingly experimental science.

Ladd's preferences were not lost on his colleagues at Yale. Scripture, Judd, Duncan, and Sneath were well aware of his interests and biases, and part of the resistance to him was a reflection of his increasing isolation from the mainstream of the young science. Apparently Ladd was unwilling to admit that he was losing touch with psychology, but this denial was usually based upon the fact that in the past he had made significant contributions to the field and had been the person most responsible for the growth of the department. In his private summary of the developments that led up to his dismissal by the university, he reported that in a conference in the Psychology Laboratory in the spring of 1904, Judd "frankly told me that I had not learned anything in Psychology during the last five years."[13] While this accusation, made in the heat of a se-

[13] "Private Paper," Henry P. Wright Collection of Letters and Papers, 1898–1911 (Yale University Library), p. 24.

rious argument between the two men, may have been an overstatement of the case, it expressed a sentiment that was held within the department and signified one of the factors contributing to Ladd's diminished status in the eyes of his colleagues.

In 1899, Arthur Twining Hadley was installed as president, succeeding Timothy Dwight, who had retired the preceding year. Shortly after his inauguration the new president brought to the attention of the professors the need for a thorough study of the college curriculum. It was made quite clear that he felt curricular change was in order, and with the steadfast support of the dean of the college and certain members of the faculty he proceeded to urge the professors along a circuitous and often rocky path toward

> . . . a program of reform that with amendments, additions, subtractions, and unforeseen extension was to be the main business of Yale College for the first four years of the new presidency. Small wonder time would be needed. For here was no inconsiderable milestone in American Collegiate history. Under a disarmingly modest title a revolution was being projected.[14]

Working in the time-honored academic fashion, the Yale faculty discussed and argued its way through a maze of proposals and counter-proposals in the general direction of a more "modern" and, as it happened, "liberal" curriculum. There was a strong sentiment to toughen as well as broaden the student's studies, provide more opportunity for a natural progression through pre-professional studies, and at the same time increase the student's freedom to choose his own courses. As the various proposals began to take shape and to move slowly through the faculty voting process, the revolutionary nature of the whole business became increasingly apparent.

[14] Pierson, *Yale College—an Educational History, 1871–1921,* p. 169.

> Nearly all of Yale's famous requirements were to be abandoned; for one after the other of these proposals attacked philosophy, classics, and the Freshman curriculum—the last strongholds of the old system. As a result, every department in the College would be affected, and one or two might be threatened with extinction.[15]

The "old disciplinary and foundation studies" were under attack and the curriculum was to be altered so as to increase the importance of science and the modern languages. After numerous meetings and a considerable dose of faculty politics, a "modernized" curriculum was adopted that included the elimination of the philosophy requirement.

To Ladd, the philosopher-psychologist-classicist who was an unregenerate believer in required studies, the new curriculum was a mistake compounded by what he considered to be a too direct presidential intervention in the prerogatives of the faculty. While acknowledging the need for some changes in the curriculum, he could not agree with either the spirit or the detail of the sweeping revision; therefore, he fought against the revisionists and resisted the president's moves in every reasonable way. It is not difficult to imagine President Hadley's attitude concerning Ladd's "reasonable" approach to individual members of the Yale Corporation.[16]

In response to the revision of the curriculum, Ladd asked to be transferred to a university professorship. The transfer was approved. With the change in status, however, an increasingly unpleasant rift in the ranks of the departmental staff soon developed. The truth of the matter is that Ladd had second thoughts about the consequences of this act of principle and passion, and tried to re-

---

[15] *Ibid.*, p. 172.

[16] There is evidence that Ladd attempted to extract promises of support for the welfare of philosophy and psychology from "prominent members of the Corporation." He hoped to forestall Corporation approval of all or part of the revision. The scholar was by no means above direct political action! "Autobiography," p. 505.

establish his claim to some of the undergraduate functions. The internal politics of the department were becoming hopelessly complicated and morale was rapidly ebbing. Then, with some courage and some bitterness, Ladd published a series of four articles in *The Forum*, broadcasting the new Yale curriculum, warts and all, to a national audience. The series was pungent and provocative, and it complicated even more his tender relations with the president and the members of the Corporation.

The series opened with a statement concerning the true functions of a great university: the highest mental and moral culture of its students; the advance by research and discovery of science, philosophy, and scholarship; and the diffusion of culture to all mankind. He held that the university serves through the pursuit of an ideal and that its function "so far as its own students are concerned, is to train an 'aristocracy.' "[17] Ladd believed in an "aristocracy of learning," not as a conceited and snobbish class, but as a committed grouping of trained leaders for society.

In the second article he argued for "truly disciplinary studies," holding that while the old curriculum did need to be modernized, there was a great difference between a modern curriculum and an elective curriculum. He proposed a shortening of the curriculum and protested against the intensity and superficiality of university studies: "For an increasing multitude, it is cram, cram, to get into college, and sham, sham, to get through."[18] Entrance requirements should be reduced, the curriculum shortened to three years, disciplinary courses required in language, mathematics, and the sciences of mental and moral activities, and the professional schools improved without jeopardy to non-professional studies.

The third article[19] worried about the erosion of professorial initiative and responsibility in governing the life of academic institu-

17 "The True Functions of a Great University," *Forum*, 33 (1902), 36.
18 "The Disintegration and Reconstruction of the Curriculum," *Forum*, 33 (1902), 174.
19 "The Degradation of the Professorial Office," *Forum*, 33 (1902), 270-282.

tions. This was a matter of deep and current concern to Ladd, and it was evident that the painful experiences at Yale had sharpened his opinions about professors and presidents. Finally, a year later, there appeared an article on the reconstruction of the college curriculum. It was a noble effort. He argued for a disciplinary, comprehensive, and progressive curriculum, and against an overextension of the elective system. He held that

> . . . the American college curriculum of today offers the only deliberately planned and respectable environment which habitually tempts the man who does not wish to do honest and thorough work, and which actually cultivates his facility in escaping from such work. It affords largely, in fact, a training-school for shamming and shirking.[20]

The answer to "shamming and shirking" was more discipline, more symmetry or balance in the program of studies (to be assured by requirement), and an honest and unapologetic advocacy of liberal education. Language competence, both ancient and modern, was to be insisted upon. While he stressed the importance of breadth of study and made strong claims for the psychological sciences and philosophy, his insistence upon language competence as the basis of scholarship revealed his own lifelong classical preference. He wanted learning as practiced by classical scholars like himself and he was impatient with vocational and professional training. Though he predicted that it was a passing phase in the development of American education, one can feel the despair in his words when he asked:

> Being bakers of bread, and often wanting to get the largest price for the smallest loaf, how can we prize highly that which confessedly "bakes no bread?" Believing that reflection upon the problems of "God, freedom, and immortality" is of rela-

[20] "How Shall the College Curriculum be Reconstructed?" *Forum*, 35 (1903), 132.

> tively little concern for the practical man, or else that the solu-
> tion of these problems can be had without clear and high think-
> ing, why should we wish to cultivate the discipline which pro-
> fesses to inform us about these priceless realities?[21]

He concluded the article by bravely charting a recommended mixture of required and elective courses that was designed to produce
a liberally educated student in three years.[22]

It was a hard time for Ladd and his supporters on the Yale faculty. A modified free elective system was to be given a try (after
all, Harvard was deeply involved in an elective experiment), philosophy and Greek were no longer required subjects, and more options were opened for satisfaction of those areas that still were demanded of the student. It was a very large step to take and some
felt that it was even a sudden and radical step. The administration
must have taken some comfort from a student editorial that announced reassuringly:

> It has clearly been shown that the Corporation is by no means
> a radical body, nor, on the other hand, a purely conservative
> one. The Yale Corporation has been neither radical nor con-
> servative, but has been wisely progressive. No sudden breaking
> away from tradition has come, but there has been a slow and
> natural development.[23]

The students were right. It *had* been a slow and natural development, and the "neither radical nor conservative" Corporation had
approved faculty action that was long in coming, hard won, and
consistent with academic changes that were liberalizing college

[21] *Ibid.*, p. 143.
[22] One critic anonymously complained about Ladd's "complaining tone" and characterized his position as "pessimistic." Ladd was complaining, of course, though his
articles were substantial and not to be dismissed on such a note. See "The American
University," *Popular Science Monthly*, 61 (1903), 90–91.
[23] "Curriculum Changes," *Yale Daily News*, May 13, 1903, p. 2.

studies throughout the land. The twentieth century began convulsively, but the adjustments were necessary if Yale was to maintain a role in the front ranks of American education.[24]

In his two principal comments upon his dismissal, the autobiography and the private statement in the Yale Archives, Ladd put much of the blame for his troubles on President Hadley. In the private statement, written shortly after he was dismissed, he suggested that Hadley had encouraged the intrigues within the department, but he seemed more resentful toward his colleagues Duncan and Sneath. The autobiographical account, written seven years after the final action by the Yale Corporation, focused upon Hadley as the chief instrument of his downfall. The later account is keynoted by the following statement:

> The way the affair terminated opened the eyes of the Faculty and the Corporation of the University to the risk involved in making the President the sole means of communicating between the two bodies. It also put an end—it is to be hoped for all time—to the tendency to put the Faculty at the mercy of their chief officer; it inaugurated a return of the tradition which from the beginning had given to the full professors at Yale a larger than hitherto customary (in our American college system) measure of self-respect and the honorable feeling of a reasonable security in the work of their profession.[25]

The extent of President Hadley's involvement in the affair is difficult to assess, but it seems reasonably certain that he was unsympathetic to much of the work of the Department of Philosophy, unconvinced as to the importance of the new field of psychology, and

[24] For an excellent portrayal of changing academic themes at Yale, see R. H. Gabriel, *Religion and Learning at Yale* (New Haven: Yale University Press, 1958). An indication of the problems that President Hadley faced in his attempt to enunciate and interpret these changing university policies is provided by the Papers of Henry Walcott Farnam on Yale Affairs (Manuscript Room, Yale University Library).
[25] "Autobiography," p. 504.

unenthusiastic about the case that Ladd made on his own behalf. Whatever they may have been, Hadley's attitudes would not have been sufficient ground for dismissing a senior member of his faculty, and it is likely that Ladd placed more blame upon the president than he deserved. More is required to dismiss an established and productive scholar two years before his normal retirement than a president's attitudes toward the academic field in question. Probably Hadley played a significant role in the whole affair, but this was possible only as a final step in a situation that had been developing its own sufficient reasons for a number of years.

Several factors, then, were involved in Ladd's involuntary early retirement from the position that he loved so well—the development of interests that were outside the main currents of the new psychology, the restlessness and resentment of colleagues, a personally contentious manner, the attitudes and beliefs of a new president, and a major curricular revision that was contrary to his own convictions. All of these factors were involved in the dismissal, but even these were insufficient. The one remaining and apparently necessary ingredient was that of his frequent and prolonged absences from the Yale campus. By leaving the campus he removed himself from the time and place in which he might have successfully counteracted the forces that were threatening his position as a senior faculty member. After he had lost the initiative in departmental affairs, all his arguments and maneuverings in later years seemed only to compound his troubles.

Ladd believed that a college or university professor was obligated to assume a position of leadership in his society. The intellectual should not hold himself aloof from the institutions of his society, but should make an effort, through direct counsel and personal example, to encourage the wise development of those institutions. Faithful to his belief that a professor should not be isolated within the campus, and in fulfillment of his appetite for travel and variety of experience, he sallied forth at the slightest excuse and played the role of teacher-statesman. These activities added to his own reputation and to Yale's influence in the affairs of the day, but they did diminish his control over the daily life of the department.

In 1892 Ladd had made the first of his three journeys to the Far East. There is reason to believe that his absence during the summer of 1892 began the attenuation of his leadership of the Department of Philosophy. He remained in a dominant position at this time, however, and his activities within the department and his scholarly contributions to philosophy and psychology continued at a high level. It was during his second trip to the Far East in the academic year 1899–1900 that his connections with Yale, especially in and through the department, became seriously complicated. With gradually mounting dissension within the department, a new president whose ideas on academic matters were still to be tested, and a major effort under way to revise the curriculum, Ladd left the campus for a long year abroad. It is little wonder that the department had changed by the time of his return.[26]

Before his return to New Haven, he received some hint of the direction that matters in the department had been taking during his absence. At a dinner in New York to which he and his wife had been invited, a former student reported his surprise at having heard from New Haven that it was planned to relieve Ladd of his work and "give the younger men a chance."[27] The significance of this report is difficult to establish, but it is consistent with the sentiment that had been growing among his colleagues. Perhaps the "younger men" had mixed feelings about his return.

Personal relations within the department became more strained with the passing of each year during the period from 1900 to 1904. The troubles were centered upon Ladd and were most often ex-

[26] Ladd complained that, in spite of previous agreements with Duncan and Sneath, he received only one or two letters from Duncan during his year abroad. Certainly, he was out of touch with the department during a particularly yeasty period. G. T. Ladd, "Private Paper," Henry P. Wright Collection of Letters and Papers, 1898–1911 (Yale University Library), p. 2.
[27] "Autobiography," p. 506.

pressed in conflicts concerning teaching responsibilities and departmental prerogatives. One issue of importance was that of the establishment of "parallel courses" within the department. Ladd argued that staff members should not duplicate the work that was being done by others, especially at the undergraduate level. Having expressed his interest in concentrating on the teaching of ethics and the philosophy of religion, he was distressed to find that Professor Sneath intended to increase his offerings in ethics. (It should be noted that Ladd launched a duplicate course himself at a later time, giving the rather weak justification that he did not expect it to have a large enrollment.) Sneath and Ladd were in conflict concerning the teaching of ethics, but this was not the limit of their difficulties. They argued as well over the administration of the Psychology Laboratory, although neither was involved directly in the work of the laboratory.

The Psychology Laboratory at Yale was a matter of great importance to Ladd. In some respects this is surprising, for he was not seriously interested in laboratory work, and except for some early efforts that did not make any lasting contribution to the field he made no attempt to establish himself in that part of the science.[28] It is true that he had helped to develop the laboratory and that he used it occasionally in his teaching; but, like his contemporary William James, Ladd believed in the importance of the laboratory for the field of psychology as a science and as a place of work for others. The principal reasons for his lasting concern about the laboratory were the following: (1) He had a proprietary interest in it because it was something he had personally helped to establish. (2) Since it was of importance to the field, an admission that he was not interested in it would have been to admit that he really was not inter-

---

[28] Seashore remarked that "so far as I know Ladd performed but one experiment, and that by proxy. I performed the experiment for him. The hypothesis was wrong, the technique inadequate, and the conclusion was unwarranted." C. E. Seashore, in *History of Psychology in Autobiography*, ed. Murchison, p. 248.

ested in the core of the new field as it was developing. (3) He needed access to the laboratory as a place of work for some of his graduate students. To be denied access to it would have seriously curtailed his relations with the graduate work of the department. (4) As a matter of academic principle he felt that, as a senior professor in the department, he had an indisputable right to all areas and agencies of the department of which he was a member. Suffice it to say that Ladd insisted upon his right to work in the laboratory without, in later years, an intention actually to work there.

At this time, shortly after the turn of the century, Scripture was still directing the laboratory. It is clear from Ladd's autobiography that he advised and counseled Scripture concerning the operation of the laboratory, but it certainly is not clear that Scripture asked for this advice. Probably he did not. At any rate, Ladd admitted that the running of the laboratory was a matter of disagreement among the members of the staff, and there is little reason to doubt his statement that Duncan, Sneath, Scripture, and Judd quarreled with him and among themselves about the role of the laboratory in the general work of the department.

> As things went on from bad to worse, it became more obvious that, on some theory or other, it was the intention of the President and the younger men to keep me as much as possible from any share in the management of the Psychological Laboratory. So far as its use was concerned for the instruction of the undergraduate students, I had never desired to interfere, and I had never even volunteered advice. But that I should have no clearly defined rights there as the head, at least, of the Graduate Department—its teaching and its research work—never had entered my mind. During the latter part of the academical year 1902–03 I repeatedly tried to have my colleagues take me into their councils and give weight to my judgment as to arranging the difficulties arising out of Dr. Scripture's position and action. Dr. Scripture and Prof. Duncan were in constant communica-

tion, it plainly appeared, with the President, both by letter and by way of visits to his office. I was forced to remain powerless while I saw the Laboratory which I had founded, and with which my name and reputation were very peculiarly connected, going to pieces as an effective branch of the Department service. Dr. Scripture was boasting openly that he had "a pull" upon the President. Professors Duncan and Sneath informed me that they had the President committed to all that they were doing. The Department was being disintegrated and disgraced.[29]

Finally, in 1903, Scripture was given a year's leave of absence and was informed that his appointment would not be continued. At least in retrospect, Ladd seems to have been generally friendly in his attitude toward Scripture. Perhaps he felt a certain amount of comradeship with him owing to the fact that they were suffering the same fate as a by-product of these difficult years. In any case, Scripture's leaving did not mend the problems of the department and Ladd's embattled position remained unchanged. The department was indeed disintegrating.

It is apparent that Ladd felt increasingly squeezed out of the affairs of the department and that, as he saw the situation, a basic issue continued to be that of his right of access to the laboratory.

It was late in May, 1903, that I first learned by letter in a perfectly definite way what the view of the President and of Professors Duncan and Sneath was as to my permanent and official relations toward the work of the Psychological Laboratory. Even for graduate work of teaching and research I was wholly dependent on these Academical Professors. I was afterwards to be there, and to have influence there, only by courtesy of my junior colleagues—one of whom had never made any serious study of Experimental Psychology, and the other of whom had studied it only under my instruction, and to no considerable extent. It came some months later to my knowledge that Dr. Judd, when the next Autumn he was given temporarily

[29] G. T. Ladd, "Private Paper," pp. 10–11.

the more immediate charge of the Laboratory apparatus and instruction, had, without consulting me, been informed to the same effect. That is to say, this young "Instructor" (such was Dr. Judd's title at that time), who had been only a single year on the ground, and who had no voice or vote in the conduct of the Graduate Department, was informed that, even for graduate teaching and research work the use of the Laboratory was for me *only by courtesy.*[30]

Ladd decided immediately "that such an arrangement was inconsistent with my dignity and with the proper and efficient discharge of my duties as a Professor in the Graduate School."[31] He resolved to do something about this violation of his academic freedom and he recorded in his reflections on this time that he consulted a member of the Yale Corporation about his rights and privileges as a university professor. Apparently the consultation led to no satisfactory adjustment of the situation.

As matters did not improve, Ladd requested that the Prudential Committee be asked to define his rights, particularly with respect to the Psychology Laboratory. Ladd, Duncan, and Sneath testified before the committee, but Ladd did his cause little good by what he had to say. He tried to make the committee appreciate what he had done in building up the department and in establishing the laboratory, to show them that he had had little to do with the troubles concerning Scripture, and, finally, to convince them that his work in the graduate department and his training of students could not be done effectively without access to, and some standing in, the Psychology Laboratory. He overplayed his testimony, for afterwards he was informed that the committee had considered his remarks "vainglorious."[32]

It was decided that a committee consisting of Ladd, Duncan, and Sneath should be appointed to advise Judd concerning the operation of the laboratory.[33] While it was intended that this advisory

[30] *Ibid.*, p. 13.
[31] *Ibid.*
[32] *Ibid.*, p. 20.
[33] In a letter to President Hadley, Ladd said that he saw "no reason why it [the

committee be a continuing means for directing the laboratory, it did not function with any noticeable effect, even temporarily. In his autobiography, Ladd claimed that the committee held but one meeting and that the direction of the laboratory and his role therein remained "cloudy and painful."

The life of the department was slipping away. Scripture was gone, Dr. Churchill, who had been working in the laboratory, was forced to resign under confused circumstances, it was erroneously but widely published that Ladd had resigned, and graduate students who had cast their lot with the Yale department were demoralized.

The final stage of this difficult period was ushered in by a skirmish over teaching responsibilities. It had been arranged that some "general-culture" courses be included in the curriculum, and Ladd was given an opportunity to offer an appropriate course. When he chose to offer a psychology course, Judd's response was critical, leading to his remark, cited earlier, that Ladd had learned no psychology during the last five years.

In the spring of 1904, upon returning from a lecture trip to Wellesley and Columbia, Ladd received a letter from Judd informing him that he had been offered a position at the University of California and that he knew Ladd would be interested in the three conditions that he had made for remaining at Yale. As Ladd cites them, they were: "(1) the abolition of the 'advisory committee,' (2) no paralleling of A courses [reference to a group of courses in which Ladd was offering a course similar to Judd's], (3) a reduction of his term of appointment as Assistant Professor."[34] With Judd's letter in hand, Ladd went to see President Hadley in order to express his position on these matters. He explained that, in spite

new arrangement] should not work with satin smoothness." G. T. Ladd to A. T. Hadley, November 26, 1903, Letters and Papers of President A. T. Hadley (Yale University Library).

[34] "Private Paper," p. 24.

of a move to a university professorship, he had always expected to do some teaching of undergraduates and did not wish to surrender this right. The president told him he had already promised Judd that the advisory committee would be abolished. Ladd informed the president that "I was coming to a point where I felt it would be necessary to have a clear understanding as to my rights as a Yale Professor."[35] Reference to this remark was contained in the president's letter of dismissal.

On May 10 a letter arrived from Duncan stating that Ladd should confine his work, graduate as well as undergraduate, to ethics and ontology, and that psychology would be taught by Duncan and Judd. Mincing no words, Ladd wrote Duncan:

> In view of the uncertain future—alas! of what was once the strong, united and respected Department of Philosophy in Yale University, I am unable to form any very definite plan.
>
> On two points, however, I can give you perfectly definite and final information.
>
> I. I shall never relinquish one iota of my rights to offer to graduate students such courses in the department as they may seem to demand, or as I may think for their best interests; and I shall diligently safeguard their *Academische Freiheit* in all their courses.
>
> II. If I continue to teach at all in the undergraduate department, I shall continue in the future as I have in the past to offer courses under the regulations of the Academical Faculty, which is the only safe, legal, and effective authority in this matter.[36]

---

[35] "Private Paper," p. 25. A few months earlier Ladd had begun to take a more inflexible stand concerning his rights. He informed the president that with respect to the operation of the department, "Twenty-five years experience in these matters I quite naturally feel entitles me to some corresponding confidence in the soundness of my judgment." G. T. Ladd to A. T. Hadley, October 4, 1903, Letters and Papers of President A. T. Hadley (Yale University Library).

[36] "Private Paper," Appendix, Letter No. 3.

A few days later, on May 17, Ladd received the letter from President Hadley informing him that the Yale Corporation had exercised its rights under the charter of 1745. Duncan also was fired, though later he was reinstated as professor of logic and metaphysics, and Sneath was given a professorship in the theory and practice of education.

A once flourishing department had died. The demoralizing effect upon students and faculty and the loss of continuity in teaching and research were serious matters for the university, as well as for individuals. It would be a long time before psychology and philosophy could be properly revived at Yale. With the revival, however, there would be a new style and a new spirit in these academic disciplines. The tattered department of 1905 was more a symbol of the pain of birth than of the agony of death.

Chapter · 14 ·
Mission in Korea

On the afternoon of March 25, 1907, Ladd sat in a hotel room in the port city of Shimonoseki in western Japan, carefully composing what he expected to be "a conspicuous and enduring message to the nation." He had been asked to provide a comment that would be copied in a facsimile of his handwriting on a bronze tablet to be placed near a camphor tree that he had planted at the School of Commerce in Nagasaki. It was an opportunity that appealed to him and he worked his way through a number of trial copies before settling upon one that was appropriate. With the completion of this task, he and his wife boarded the night boat to Fusan (Pusan), Korea, and immediately began intensive preparations for a mission that would test even Ladd's capacity for endurance.

His message to the Japanese nation was both an observation and a firm hope. It is one of the ironies of history that this particular statement by the American "friend of Japan" was placed in Nagasaki.

> By a happy union of modern education and the spirit of Bushido, inherited from countless generations of ancestors, Japan has triumphed in war. By ceaseless improvement of the

one, combined with enlargement and elevation of the other, she must win in the future the no less noble and difficult victories of peace. In industry and art, in science, morals, and religion, may Dai Nippon secure and maintain a well merited place among the foremost nations of the civilized world—thus enjoying prosperity at home, and contributing her full share toward the blessing of mankind.

The invitation to go to Korea had been unexpected, and the proposed mission was both vague and risky, but Ladd's decision was never in doubt. With the spirit of devotion to honor and duty that he so greatly admired in the Japanese, he announced his readiness to go to Korea to assist in any way that he could in the uplifting of that unhappy land. In doing so, he would serve also the difficult mission of Japan in Korea and the personal mission of his good friend Marquis Ito, the Japanese Resident-General.

As he crossed the Korean Strait, Ladd sat musing in his cabin about the mysterious ways in which his life had moved from one challenge to the next. He was supremely happy to know that he was heading toward an assignment that would require the fullest commitment of body and mind. Though he did not know how it would end, he had a boundless faith in the power of moral earnestness. Come what may, he was content to serve mankind, Japan, and Ito in one great effort. As he sat in his cabin, he recalled a similar wakeful night several crowded months before, when, arriving in his beloved country for the third time, "I lay awake most of that first night, listening to the dripping of the rain and the chirping of the cicadas, but quite content to be again in Japan."[1]

He had undertaken this third trip to the Far East as a way of dispelling the gloom that had been brought on by his premature dismissal from Yale. The letters he wrote to his wife during a semester of teaching at Western Reserve University in the spring of 1906

[1] "Autobiography," p. 524.

and a summer appointment at the University of Iowa show his sadness and anger over the affair. As the months passed, however, he assumed a more detached attitude. Alone in his single room at night, he would light an after-dinner cigar and write to his wife with a warmth and compassion that are not to be found in any other documents that have been preserved.

In working his way through bitterness and despair, Ladd found returning strength in responding once more to a request for a lecture trip to Japan. He discussed plans for the trip in each letter and it is obvious that the prospect of a new mission abroad was a major stimulus toward recovery. In June he observed that his class at Iowa was much larger than expected and added:

> I have a glow of satisfaction when I see how the chances for usefulness have not been impaired, but rather increased by the iniquitous treatment Yale gave me. It may make me, if no longer one of her teachers, a teacher of the world in a wider way than would otherwise have been possible.[2]

In the autumn of 1906, the Yale emeritus professor, now a teacher of the world, arrived in Tokyo. Still nursing his wounded pride, he was about to secure a massive dose of the only medicine that could restore his professional dignity. It was a therapy of total immersion in work and Ladd began the treatment on the morning of his first day in Japan. Under a commission by the editors of the *Encyclopedia Americana,* he opened negotiations for a series of articles on Japan by Japanese diplomats, scholars, and members of the press.[3] His lecture commitments began with a series on the phi-

[2] Letter from G. T. Ladd to F. S. Ladd, dated June 21, 1906, and in possession of Miss Cornelia T. Ladd of Cleveland Heights, Ohio.

[3] Through the years Ladd made a number of contributions to editorial work on the *Encyclopedia Americana,* particularly in soliciting materials concerning Japan and philosophy. The edition published shortly before his death contained two signed articles: G. T. Ladd, "Mental Characteristics of the Japanese," *Encyclopedia Americana* (1920 ed.), vol. 15, pp. 635–640; G. T. Ladd, "Philosophy," *ibid.*, pp. 768–777.

losophy of education at the Imperial University. On alternate days, he spoke before audiences at the Tokyo Girls Higher Normal School, the Tokyo Commercial College, and the Imperial Educational Society.[4] As he reached out from Tokyo that fall his speaking trips brought him into contact with churches, schools, village clubs, the Y.M.C.A., and the boys of the Imperial Fisheries Institute. It was all a vigorous re-enactment of his previous visits, complete with nagging physical symptoms, garden parties, and an audience with the Emperor.

Shortly after his arrival in Japan, Ladd was informed by a friend that the Japanese Resident-General in Korea wanted to invite him to visit Seoul. He was very much interested in the confidential news, but gave the matter little consideration until, at a garden party in early December, Marquis Ito personally requested his help. Ladd had enormous respect for Ito's enlightened attitude toward human problems, and over the years the two had developed a mutually satisfying and rather intimate friendship. Ito had been a guest in Ladd's home when, at Ladd's suggestion, he had been honored with a Doctor of Laws degree on the occasion of the 1901 Yale Bicentennial. His friendship with Ito and a keen interest in the Japanese presence in Korea made him certain that he would accept the invitation if his schedule and the conditions of the assignment were favorable. But a garden party was no place for formal arrangements, and the preliminary invitation was left hanging with Ito's return to Seoul.

A week later, however, a representative of Marquis Ito called upon Ladd to sketch the background for the invitation and to arrange for an extended discussion of the proposed visit at a time when Ito was back in Japan. Ladd was told that the Japanese administration was having extreme difficulty in developing a work-

4 Following this series of addresses, Ladd was presented with the Gold Medal of the Imperial Educational Society. It was a significant honor and a testimony to his untiring efforts on behalf of Japanese education.

able relation with the Koreans, and that one of the principal problems involved the widespread circulation of rumors and complaints that only subsequently could be shown to have been unfounded. It was felt that American missionaries were often unwittingly propagating "exaggerations and falsehoods" and that the dissemination of these reports abroad ultimately would injure the Korean people.

> In the office of Resident-General the Marquis greatly desired to be absolutely just and fair, and to prevent the mistakes, so harmful both to Korea and to Japan, which followed the Japanese occupation of Korea at the close of the Chino-Japan war. But it was difficult, and in most cases impossible, for him even to find out what the complaints were; they came to the public ear in America and England before he was able to get any indication of their existence even. And when his attention was called to them in this roundabout fashion, further difficulties, almost insuperable, intervened between him and the authors of these complaints; for in most cases it turned out that the foreign plaintiffs had no first-hand information regarding the truth of the Korean stories. They would not themselves take the pains to investigate the complaints, much less would they go to the trouble to bring the attention of the Resident-General to the matters complained of in order that he might use his magisterial authority to remedy them. In respect to these, and certain other difficulties, Marquis Ito thought that I might assist his administration if I would spend some time upon the ground as his guest.[5]

In many respects it was a classic case of the difficulties encountered by an occupation government in an unfriendly country. Ladd realized that the internal conditions in Korea under the Japanese protectorate were almost hopelessly complex from a political

[5] *In Korea with Marquis Ito* (New York: Charles Scribner's Sons, 1908), p. 5.

George Trumbull Ladd

standpoint, and that he was not qualified to serve as a diplomat.
Also, he knew that his appearance would be linked with the Japanese government and that the Korean people, as well as the missionaries, would view his presence as an effort to aid that government.
His faith in Marquis Ito's character and in the bonds of their
friendship convinced him that he would not be used in an under-
handed manner, but he was perfectly willing to have accrue to the
Japanese government any benefit that derived from his open effort
to promote understanding and public morality. With only a vague
sense of the means by which he might be useful, Ladd accepted the
invitation. His later conference with Ito made clear that he would
be an independent agent during his stay in Korea.

> I hoped through the agencies of the missionaries and the
> Y.M.C.A., to speak to the Koreans with respect to the de-
> pendence of their welfare on the improvement of educational,
> moral and religious forces and institutions; by these, and more
> private means to assure the missionaries and other foreigners
> of his [Ito's] benevolent plans toward the Koreans—especially,
> toward common people; and, finally in all these ways to strive
> to bring about a better understanding between him and all
> those who sincerely desired the welfare of Korea. This was our
> understanding; this was our "conspiracy"; in this way did I
> become the "cat's paw of Japan." And I put it on record for
> all time that never in a single instance did Marquis Ito con-
> ceal anything from me, much less misrepresent anything to
> me. Never in a single instance did he suggest or advise, or in
> any way influence my conduct.[6]

In early January Ladd's base of operations was moved to Kyoto.
Arrangements had been made by his former Yale student, Professor Matataro Matsumoto, for a three-month series of lectures on religious philosophy at Kyoto University. Matsumoto spent an enor-

6 "Autobiography," p. 585.

230

mous amount of time working behind the scenes to assure that the series would be a success. He wrote the daily summaries of the lectures for publication in the Kyoto morning newspaper,[7] printed an English outline of the lectures for daily distribution, and maintained a close watch on the size and behavior of the audiences. There was no limit to his attention to detail.

> Mrs. Ladd attended the lecture every time; this apparently followed the habit they exercised at Yale where Mrs. Ladd used to attend the lecture her husband gave for the post-graduates. As it appeared rather odd to have only one woman in the class, I made my wife attend also; moreover, I encouraged some feminine members of Doshisha Women's College to come too, all of which contributed much to give the scene a look as if it had been the American school.[8]

In his autobiography, Ladd referred to the Kyoto audiences as "unflagging in attention and undiminished in numbers, to the end."[9] Under the watchful eye of his former student, they could not have been otherwise.

By the middle of March, Ladd had worked his way to Nagasaki, planted the camphor tree, and was preparing a trip to Fukuoka for still another series of lectures when the call came to go at once to Seoul. He canceled the remaining engagements and made his way to Shimonoseki for the passage to Fusan.

The Korea that Ladd came to know firsthand in the spring of 1907 presented a shocking contrast to Japan. Crossing the Korea Strait had taken him from a revered civilization to a sick and form-

---

[7] The lectures, as well as reports of Ladd's intricate comings and goings, are faithfully detailed in the *Kyoto Hinode Shimbun* for the period of January–March, 1907. A report in the February 27 issue states: "The doctor, though old, proved very eloquent, as his speech, while elaborate in its minute logic, was backed by a fervent inner belief."

[8] M. Matsumoto, "Memories of Professor Ladd," *Shinri-Kenkyū*, 20 (1921), 254.

[9] "Autobiography," p. 560.

less society characterized by instability and corruption. India had at least offered the fascination of religious variety and a culture linked to antiquity. In Korea there seemed to be only a weak and immoral native government resting unsteadily upon an uneducated, despairing, and restless populace:

> It would be impossible to convey any impression, at the same time both brief and adequate, of the deplorable condition which prevailed in Korea during the Spring of 1907. To any outsider or superficial observer on the spot, the most moderate exhibit of the facts would seem exaggerated; the fairest defense of the Government of the Resident General would seem prejudiced. From the Korean Emperor downward to the lowest of his people, lawlessness, superstition, corruption, private vengeancefulness [sic], filthiness of body, of habitations and of streets, and loathsome crimes, were almost universally prevalent.[10]

The "Korean problem" was real enough, and certainly Ladd was duly impressed by its magnitude. The country was in a wretched condition. Poorly run by a vacillating and unpredictable emperor who was surrounded by a jumble of ministers and hangers-on, the internal affairs of the country made exceedingly dim any hope of progress. The country's finances were inadequate, the judicial system was weak and frequently arbitrary, the educational opportunities were extremely limited, and technological development was sporadic. Korea did not possess the strength that comes from national coherence and a sense of corporate identity and purpose; it was weak and it was vulnerable.

The vulnerability was an expression of Korea's internal misery, but it was also a product of a peculiarly important location with respect to the national ambitions of other countries. The "Hermit Kingdom" was a victim, though not always a passive one, of the struggles between Japan, China, and Russia. The first phase of

[10] *Ibid.*, p. 586.

this triangular struggle had been concluded with Japan's victory over China in 1895, by which independence was assured Korea, and the second phase had ended with a Japanese victory over Russia in 1905. From this war came the Japanese protectorate and, in 1910, the full annexation of the country. In a historical introduction to the edited papers of the British diplomat Sir Ernest Satow, who played such an important role in Far Eastern affairs at the turn of the century, Lensen observed:

> International rivalry over Korea has been due in part to the strategic importance of the peninsula. It is a bridge between the continent and Japan; it borders unto China and Russia by land and unto Japan by sea; it possesses ice-free ports and by this and its location can facilitate or hinder Russian outlet to the Pacific. To a large extent international rivalry in Korea was encouraged, if not invited, by the weakness, corruption and division of the Korean government. Korean disunity provided an opportunity for foreign interference, and the various Powers deemed it necessary to forestall each other's control of the region. Moreover, the Chinese and the Koreans sought to strengthen their own hands by playing the foreigners against each other.[11]

The internal affairs of Korea were supposed to be handled by the indigenous government, while the external affairs were managed by Japan. But it was not a simple matter to separate the two, and communication between the Japanese and the Korean government officials became almost comically confused. In an atmosphere of intrigue, suspicion, and wild rumor, the processes of government were highly personal and capricious. Day-to-day affairs were pushed and pulled along, distorted first in one direction, and then another, by the many vested interests which a government of men

[11] G. A. Lensen (ed.), *Korea and Manchuria Between Russia and Japan, 1895–1904* (Tallahassee: The Diplomatic Press, 1966), p. 2.

rather than law is expected to serve. There were the corrupt local government; the ambitious Japanese empire; the continuing undercover efforts by Russia and China; the foreign businessmen; the renegade Japanese who had landed in Korea in the wake of the war with Russia and were trying to exploit the situation for personal gain; the Christian missionaries; the men of the press, many of whom were American or English; and, of course, last and least in his pitiful plight, the common man of Korea.

Ladd defined his mission in an interview with Marquis Ito, who, offering no advice, accepted the definition on the spot. He was in Korea as Ito's guest

> . . . to speak to the Koreans in a sincerely friendly way, on matters of education, morals, and religion, especially as these matters concerned their national welfare . . . to discover what I could which might assist the Resident-General in dealing with his difficult problem and to assure all, whom I could reach, that he sincerely wished to serve the real interests of the Koreans and to secure for them the administration of justice and an increased prosperity.[12]

His message was to urge a proper attention to the development of character, a concern for both personal and public morality, and a commitment to the value of education. In a speech on "Education and National Security," which he delivered in Kyoto after having accepted the call to Korea, Ladd identified four internal enemies of a nation: superstition, injustice, avarice and ambition, and party strife. He argued that education is the only cure for these ills and that no other activity that is carried on in a society is as indispensable for the maintenance of national security.[13] In his work as Ito's guest he proposed to continue his advocacy of these principles and to do so with all the moral earnestness at his command.

[12] *In Korea with Marquis Ito*, pp. 40–41.
[13] *Kyoto Hinode Shimbun*, January 26, 1907, p. 1.

In Japan there had been a stream of invitations to speak to a great variety of audiences, but in Korea Ladd found immediately that he would have to make his own way. He was under a cloud of suspicion, and expressions of interest in his ideas seemed to melt away before a formal invitation to speak had been issued by a society or school. The *Korean Daily News* had raised doubts about Ladd's motives in going to Korea and, during the early weeks of his visit, continued to muddy the waters by its suspicious attitude. While he resented the doubts about his motives and was indignant at any affront to his friend and host, the Resident-General, the suspicion and resistance that he encountered were a natural consequence of the sponsorship and the mission. Here was an American who had long been identified with Japan, and decorated by the Emperor, who was present as a friend and guest of the leading figure in the occupying government, and who proposed to talk to Koreans about the relation of education and morality to national welfare and stability. It was reasonable to conclude from the situation that he had come to smooth the way for the Japanese.

It obviously was inappropriate for Marquis Ito to arrange meetings, and as time passed it began to look as if Ladd might not be able to gain a platform for his message. Finally, he turned to the Seoul Y.M.C.A. Following a number of rather difficult meetings with officials, a series of lectures was announced by that organization. He was to speak on "Education and Social Welfare," "Religion and Social Reform," and "Education as Related to the Stability and Progress of the Nation." The lectures were well attended, but he did not find the Koreans as favorably responsive as the Japanese.

Ladd's work with the Korean people was frustrated by his known relation to Japan and by the tense and distracting conditions in the country. In his autobiography and in his book about Korea, he claimed more of an impact than actually occurred. A minute analysis of the evidence as offered by these books and other reports suggests that, with the exception of lectures under Y.M.C.A. sponsorship and one "mass meeting" in Seoul on April 21 that was attended by over fifteen hundred people, Ladd's lectures were presented to Christian audiences and to the Japanese who were resident in the country. The *Seoul Press* carried reports of his efforts, and it does not appear that he had much success in reaching the common man of the country.

In his lectures to the Japanese community he stressed the importance of Japan's special responsibilities for a humane and elevating role in Korea. He urged a compassion and friendship that arose from religious principle and personal morality rather than from a self-serving national ambition. In Seoul, Pyongyang, and Chemulpo he pressed for policies that met one overriding consideration: Was the course of action going to work for the betterment of the people of Korea, and at the same time foster friendly feelings between Korea and Japan? In all these speeches, however, it is evident that he was working from a prior assumption—namely, that the conditions in Korea, the historical and cultural ties between the two countries, and the clear threat of competing foreign interests justified the Japanese protectorate.[14] That assumption in itself was enough to doom his effort to reach the common man.

It was in his relations with the missionaries that Ladd found the greatest success and the keenest frustration. Their response was a puzzling and difficult problem. He was distressed to find so much resentment toward the Japanese government. Although he realized that there had been incidents in which the Koreans were poorly treated, he was so firmly convinced that the Japanese presence was essential to the improvement of Korean life that he was inclined to

---

[14] Ladd maintained this position consistently through the years, and when the protectorate became outright annexation he accepted the need for this course of action by the Japanese. See G. T. Ladd, "The Annexation of Korea: An Essay in 'Benevolent Assimilation,'" *Yale Review*, 1 (1912), 639–656; also, G. T. Ladd, "The Development of Korea in Most Recent Times," *Journal of Race Development*, 8 (1918), 431–438.

minimize the complaints. The missionaries, however, seemed to magnify them. Ladd was sorry to find that they did not feel inclined to work closely with the Resident-General.

An analysis of the situation convinced Ladd that there were two principal reasons for their lack of cooperation. The first reason was professional. Preoccupied with the problems and the challenge of working with the Korean common man, to the end that *individuals* might become *converts*, the missionaries tended to distrust or ignore the larger governmental and diplomatic questions that were of primary concern to the Japanese officials. They were sympathetic to the problems that individuals faced, and often the actions that were deemed necessary by the government intensified rather than ameliorated those problems.

The second reason was political. Ladd believed that a great share of the Korean response to the missionary movement was politically inspired. It was his theory that large numbers of the destitute and uneducated people were turning to the missions under the false impression that the missions would provide a measure of security in the face of what was widely held to be a dire Japanese threat. The anti-Japanese sympathies of many missionaries also provided the Korean with a feeling that the Christian message was somehow related to his own patriotic impulses.

Ladd conferred with many of the missionaries, patiently explaining his own conviction that the Christian effort in Korea should be brought into a more sympathetic relation to the work of the Resident-General. He argued that Marquis Ito was primarily interested in promoting the welfare of the Korean people and that the missions and Ito should work together in behalf of the common man. In his book on Korea,[15] he referred to a conference that he arranged between Ito and mission officials in which it was proposed to increase cooperation and dispel rumors that the two forces were at odds. The conference produced assurances by both parties

[15] *In Korea with Marquis Ito*, pp. 63–64.

that cooperation and good will would characterize their common effort to better the lives of the Korean people. The agreement was made public,[16] and Ladd felt satisfied that the new alliance, however long it might last, was a tangible achievement of his mission.

With the passage of each week, Ladd found it more difficult to sustain the non-political role that he had assigned himself. The political activists were trying to reach him, hoping that he would become a useful tool in their machinations; also, with a widening circle of acquaintances, he became more vulnerable to the rumors and plots that were sweeping back and forth across the Korean scene. He realized that the success of his entire mission depended upon his maintaining a position that was free of politics. In order to keep his role clearly before the people, he reminded each audience that he was in Korea as an individual who was principally concerned with the lives and welfare of other individuals, and that he would continue a policy of non-involvement in the internal affairs of the country.

When a rumor or plot was brought to his attention he usually referred his informant to the person or agency that was officially sanctioned to deal with the problem. Though he frequently consulted with Marquis Ito he did not view his own role as that of an informant; apparently Ito never expected him to function in this manner. It was not easy to ignore the scandalous reports that were brought to his attention, and while Ladd found the inner workings of the political machinery a fascinating spectacle, after two months in Korea he was relieved to be rid of his delicate role.

Though he worked at his assignment with his usual intensity and dedication, the problems in Korea were so complex that the amateur statesman often wondered whether his efforts were of value. The moral principles behind his work were not open to doubt; and certainly he did not question the relevance of these principles to

[16] "Marquis Ito and Christian Missionaries," *Seoul Press*, May 4, 1907.

the problems of a nation. In an interview with Ito toward the end
of his visit he expressed his belief in

> . . . a Universal Moral Spirit, who shaped the destinies of man
> and of nations and who used us all in his service—if we so
> wished—to our own well-being and to the good of humanity.
> God, it seemed to me, had bound together Japan and Korea in
> such sort, both naturally and politically, that they could not
> willfully separate their interests, whether for weal or for woe.[17]

History might question whether God "had bound together Japan
and Korea," but Ladd was convinced that their destinies were inseparable, as were the destinies of all nations under the rule of a
universal moral spirit.

What Ladd sought was an instrument by which the overwhelming problems of Korea could be solved. He found that instrument
in the personality and character of Marquis Ito. His admiration for
Ito and a deep respect for the quality of his friendship grew steadily during their association. He found in Ito a living expression of
the virtues that he so much admired in the Japanese way of life.
Here were patience, tact, a reserved but genuine and discriminating friendliness, a sense of history and an appreciation of culture, a
deep understanding of religious values, and a steadfast commitment to the improvement of human welfare. He saw Ito as a noble human being in whom all of these qualities were joined with a
practical and realistic sense of national purpose, an idealist who
was trying to put his ideals to work in the solution of a great human
problem.

The Ito-Ladd friendship developed out of mutual respect and
was sealed under fire in Korea. It is almost impossible to consider
the meaning of that relationship apart from the human problems
and the political issues by which it was dramatized. For Ladd, Ito's

---

[17] "Autobiography," pp. 633–634.

George Trumbull Ladd

work in Korea symbolized an age-old test of ideals. The sincere idealism of the man captured his loyalty and he wanted very much to help in what he felt was a painful but glorious struggle to breathe life into the ideals that they shared.[18]

Was Ladd wrong in his view of the Korean situation and of Ito's role in it? This is, of course, an exceedingly difficult question. There has been a difference of opinion about the long and eventful involvement of Japan in Korea; furthermore, scholars have differed concerning Ito's role as Resident-General. Ladd's view of the whole matter was by no means disinterested, and certainly he was not prepared by training or experience to move easily and knowledgeably through the intricacies of international diplomacy and national politics. As might be expected, he was right and wrong and unfailingly himself.

Ladd was not "the cat's paw of Japan," but he was a consistently loyal champion of the Japanese cause in Korea. While he could be critical of the government, more often than not his criticism was but a slight qualification of his arguments in support of Japanese policy. Behind his friendly support of Japan there was an undiluted confidence in the integrity and noble purposes of the Emperor[19] and the Resident-General, a conviction that Japanese in-

---

[18] One reviewer of Ladd's book on Korea observed that it is valuable "for its unconscious reflection of the personality of the author and of Prince Ito." The book does reveal an apparent similarity of philosophy and a shared belief in the central importance of ideals in the solution of human problems. As the review notes, the book is "confessedly apologetic" on behalf of the Resident-General. See K. Asakawa, review of G. T. Ladd's *In Korea with Marquis Ito*, *Yale Review*, 17 (1908–1909), 350–352.

[19] In an article written after the Emperor's death, Ladd wrote: "He will go down in history, not as a great war lord, a leader to victory of great armies and a powerful navy, although two foreign wars—one of them of immense proportions—were successfully carried through under his rule. He will be known as the great and good Emperor of Japan, who, beginning as a boy of fifteen, without any training for his increasingly complicated responsibilities and problems of government, himself grew in wisdom, insight, and force, and at the end of nearly a half-century of rule, died with his Empire vastly enlarged and wonderfully improved in enlightenment and in all the benefits of modern civilization, himself respected and adored by all classes;

240

tervention in the affairs of Korea was essential to her development, and a belief that the improvement of Korea required the indefinite postponement of conflicting foreign interests in the affairs of the country.[20]

He realized that the application of Japanese power sometimes led to heavy-handed suppression and even brutality, but he did not view the situation with the outrage that was widely reported by other observers.[21] In commenting upon Ladd's justification of the Japanese policies in light of the documented accounts of the suffering of the Korean people, Conroy asked:

> How could Ladd have been so blind? The answer would seem to be that he was not blind, he was merely being realistic. "Midst fairly settled" practices of international relations a weak and troubled country like Korea, strategically located in a world political arena, had to be controlled by a stable power, benevolently if possible, but firmly, if necessary. Not only Professor Ladd, but other sensible, and influential, foreigners reached the same conclusion.[22]

Conroy sketched Ladd's position with respect to Ito's regime and suggested that his analysis should not be dismissed as readily as some have done; rather, he held that Ladd "was a penetrating student of human behavior and that his evaluation of Ito's regime was entirely consistent with the conclusions he derived from years

and what is still better, tenderly loved and sincerely mourned by the great body of the common people." "The Man Who Ruled Japan," *New York Evening Post*, August 3, 1912, p. 2.

[20] See G. T. Ladd, "The Japanese Administration in Korea," in *China and the Far East*, ed. G. H. Blakeslee (New York: T. Y. Crowell & Co., 1910), pp. 397–435.

[21] Opposing views are presented by F. A. McKenzie in his book *The Tragedy of Korea* (New York: E. P. Dutton & Co., 1908); and H. Hulbert, *The Passing of Korea* (New York: Doubleday, Page & Co., 1906).

[22] H. Conroy, *The Japanese Seizure of Korea: 1868–1910, A Study of Realism and Idealism in International Relations* (Philadelphia: University of Pennsylvania Press, 1960), p. 347.

of scholarly inquiry into that general subject."[23] He argued that Ladd's view was practical and realistic,[24] and that

> Ladd was not intellectually dishonest, nor was he merely taken in by Itō's hospitality. Nor can it be said that he suffered myopia because of writing too soon, before the brutal aspects of Itō's administration began to show themselves. Indeed, he reiterated his favorable evaluation of it after the bitter Korean antagonism to the Japanese had been made manifest in Itō's assassination and the Japanese had used extreme, repressive measures in effecting the annexation.[25]

Conroy's evaluation of Ladd's position was essentially correct. Ladd was aware of the suppression and the suffering, both of which became more severe after Ito's assassination. But he was an idealist who was practical enough and, it must be admitted, sufficiently attached to Japan to seek some effective means of bringing order to the scene. The means would be provided by the power and diplomacy of Japan, and specifically by the humane hand of Ito.

It is not necessary to claim that Ladd was right or wrong, or that such national intervention is ever justified. What can be claimed is that he held these views and worked assiduously and loyally to help Japan stabilize the Korean problem.

His support of Ito expressed his concurrence with the Resident-General's effort to achieve Japan's goals without annexation. He considered Ito to be a moderate and humane statesman who was struggling against almost insuperable problems in Korea and steady pressure by some groups in Japan for the use of more force

[23] *Ibid.*, p. 342.

[24] In characterizing Ladd's philosophical position Conroy stated that "even while criticising its more extreme aspects he was much influenced by the pragmatism of William James" (*ibid.*, pp. 342–343). It is more accurate to view Ladd's basic position and James's pragmatism as arising out of the same general background of intellectual and historical forces. The pragmatic threads in Ladd's philosophy were not placed there through James's influence.

[25] *Ibid.*, p. 343.

and less patient diplomacy. Ito may not have been as humane and benign as Ladd pictured him to be, but he was one of the major forces for moderation at a time when some of his countrymen were urging the excesses of militarism and empire.[26]

Ladd and his wife left Korea on May 29, returning to Japan and the inevitable lecture tour, this time to the northern island of Hokkaido. There followed a long period of retreat in a borrowed seaside house at Hayama during which he worked steadily at the task of writing his book about Korea. The last weeks of his stay in the Far East were highlighted by another audience with the Emperor, an additional decoration with the Second Degree of the Order of the Rising Sun, a long visit by President and Mrs. Thwing of Western Reserve University, and a large number of farewell receptions.

That fall, as he left Japan, Ladd correctly assumed that he would never again see his beloved second home. With a sad satisfaction he departed for Hawaii and a month that was filled with lectures and a final revision of the Korea manuscript. After an absence of sixteen months he returned to New Haven, enjoyed a quiet Thanksgiving dinner in his own home, and began a fourteen-year period of restless retirement.

[26] Ladd's position was criticized, but it was also subjected to the distorting effects of excessive partisan enthusiasm. See A. Kinnosuke, "The Korea of Today," review of G. T. Ladd's *In Korea with Marquis Ito, Pacific Era,* 1 (1908), 405–408.

$$Chapter \cdot 15 \cdot$$

$$The \ Quiet \ Years$$

Retirement was an affliction for which no remedy could be found. After a remarkably full and intense professional life, spiced by struggle and sweetened by occasional victory, Ladd found himself reduced to a "bearable" existence as "day after day, in the house and in the garden, slipped by at an even pace and with an almost wearisome quietness." He complained of the "monotony and diminishing sense of usefulness that accompanied a life so much confined within the walls of the study." Retirement had come too soon; there was more and better work yet to be done; definite plans for teaching were left unfulfilled.

"I love teaching," Ladd protested,

> . . . and I crave the face-to-face encounter with human minds, with the living presence, which the "speaking teacher" alone enjoys. I like to know my pupils as men; to watch their development and to cultivate their growth and friendship under me; to trace and, if possible, assist the success of their careers in after life.[1]

[1] "Autobiography," pp. 667–668.

244

But the teaching career was over and the face-to-face encounter with the living presence was limited to speaking engagements at colleges, universities, conferences, and civic functions. There was talk of a special teaching appointment at Western Reserve and at Kyoto University, but apparently the talk did not produce formal invitations. The habits of decades are not easily extinguished; each fall there was a sense of keen expectancy and renewal as the students began to appear on Prospect Street. The old campaigner watched them from his study window, doubting the wisdom of a system that converted teachers of the world into emeritus observers of the academic scene.

He was deprived of his pupils, but he still had his pen. Life became a quiet rhythm of movement between the garden and the study, broken only by occasional lecture trips. The zip and challenge were missing, but the rhythm was productive. During the twelve years that elapsed between his return from Japan and the conclusion of serious writing two years before his death, Ladd produced twelve books, thirty-three articles, and his 794-page unpublished autobiography. William James is quoted as having observed in 1896 that "Prof. Ladd writes too much!"[2] but he had no way of knowing what was still to come. Ladd's daughter viewed the matter as a member of the family when she commented that "at home my father was a frugal and conserving New Englander in every way but one—he used too much paper!"[3]

Even in retirement, cascades of words poured out of the frugal New Englander, filling page upon page and book upon book in a ceaseless stream. Students remember Ladd in his office at Yale, writing rapidly on folio paper and letting each completed page drop to the floor as he hurried on to the next.[4] Surrounded by his reference books, he sat in an ample rocking chair that had an oversized

2 M. Matsumoto, "Memories of Professor Ladd," *Shinri-Kenkyū*, 20 (1921), 244.
3 An interview with Mrs. Walter A. Barrett of Fort Wayne, Indiana, April 1, 1962.
4 M. Matsumoto, "Memories of Professor Ladd," p. 244; also, H. Kawabe, "In Memoriam for Professor Ladd," *Shinri-Kenkyū*, 20 (1921), 259.

writing tablet on the right arm. Whether in his office or in his study at home, he drew upon an enormous store of organized notebooks in which he collected relevant materials for future books and articles. The words poured from his pen, but the writing process was anchored in a prodigious, systematic scholarship; and it was supported by great personal discipline and self-control.

> In the work of composition, I have tried to cultivate habits of regularity and self-control, and not to yield to the subjection of whimsical moods and external disturbances. For one of rather precarious health, of nervous constitution, and hypersensitive temperament, this conquest is no easy thing; it can never be complete; and it ought not to be complete. A man who becomes a book-making machine is no better, and less lovely, than several other kinds of human machines. But almost anyone can acquire a rather business-like way of authorship, if only he will take the necessary pains.[5]

Though he may not have been a book-making machine, Ladd certainly took the necessary pains to establish a record that was impressive in quantity, if not uniform in quality. It is of interest that in 1898 the inveterate writer complained in a paper delivered before his colleagues in the A.P.A. that "an increasing amount of premature publication on the subject of psychology"[6] was one of the hindrances to the progress of the field. It seems evident from a study of his autobiography that he realized he was writing too much and knew that the quantity of his writing might lessen the impact of his work. It was a risk that he would just have to take.

The retirement years brought quietness without peace. Forswearing whimsical moods and external disturbances, Ladd worked

[5] "Autobiography," p. 692.

[6] "On Certain Hindrances to the Progress of Psychology in America," *Psychological Review*, 6 (1899), 129. The theme was echoed in his autobiography when he wrote: "I have considered it as bordering on a species of immorality to publish immature books" (p. 691).

at his scholarship and writing as if his whole career depended upon it. It was during these years that he produced his three books on Korea, Japan, and India. They were a direct product of his travels, of course, as were the 1907 book, published in Japan, on the application of virtue to business life, and the 1911 book *The Teacher's Practical Philosophy*. The latter book was an adaptation and elaboration of the lectures delivered to thousands of Japanese teachers during the visit of 1906–1907. It was not a profound work, but it did state clearly and with conviction Ladd's view that teaching is a species of conduct, an ethical activity which, perhaps more than any other, is the means for assuring the primacy of ethics in any society.

The theme of the book was of interest to many who felt that education was becoming divorced from ethics and morality. Ladd was satisfied with the reception that greeted this publication and must have noted with pleasure the observation of one reviewer that "Professor Ladd's book is characterized by a deep moral seriousness throughout, and it is this attitude of the author that makes the book the best work on the principles of education known to the present writer."[7]

In the fields of psychology and philosophy he was not attempting to break new ground. This final period of his life was a time of summary, revision, and integration. With the exception of the 1911 revision of *Elements of Physiological Psychology*, a great deal of which was accomplished by his junior collaborator, Robert S. Woodworth, the books of this period were issued with a popular or semi-popular audience in mind.

Knowledge, Life and Reality was written during the two years following the return from Japan. It was given the subtitle, "An Essay in Systematic Philosophy." Apparently he intended to treat in one volume those topics that he considered most representative of

[7] E. Jordan, review of G. T. Ladd's *The Teacher's Practical Philosophy, Philosophical Review*, 22 (1913), 232.

his distinctive system. The book drew upon all his previous works; it summarized the favorite topics, revealed the familiar worries, and faithfully recreated the style of thought and style of writing that had characterized forty years of scholarship. But it was more impressive as a summary of Ladd-the-philosopher than as a representation of systematic theory. By 1909 Ladd had said what he had to say about philosophy. There were few surprises left for the reader.

The years from 1911 to 1915 were devoted to journal articles and to the preparation of his quartet of "What" books. *What Can I Know?* was published in 1914, followed in 1915 by *What Ought I to Do?*, *What Should I Believe?*, and *What May I Hope?* These four books were Ladd's effort to simplify and popularize philosophy and psychology by bringing his theories and arguments to bear upon the practical problems of living. As the titles suggest, the books were written from a personal standpoint. The author expected that they would be illuminating for individual lives; he made no claim that they would present new thinking about substantive problems of the two fields.

What Can I Know? and *What Ought I to Do?* were anticipated by the large, technical, and highly abstract works on the *Philosophy of Knowledge* and the *Philosophy of Conduct*. Written in what was, for Ladd, a remarkably attractive and readable style, *What Can I Know?* presented the relation of the powers of reflective thought to the business of life. Though it drew upon classical theories of epistemology, it also revealed that Ladd was a psychologist, in its stress on the problems of special ability, temperament, habits and training, and the fallibility of knowing. It was a good example of the productive joining of philosophy and psychology that characterized his life work.

What Ought I to Do? conveyed a special interest in problems of responsibility and duty. It showed the unusual fervor that was evident in *Philosophy of Conduct*[8] and, as one reviewer commented:

[8] See our discussion of *Philosophy of Conduct*, pp. 168–171.

> The author's moral enthusiasm, though never allowed to interfere with the argument, adds greatly to its effectiveness. It inspires his style, which at times takes on the character of sustained eloquence.[9]

His eloquence grew out of a conviction that was second to none in its strength and immutability—namely, that the moral life of man was the quintessential expression, the living embodiment, of a compatible union of philosophy and psychology.

What Should I Believe? sketched the relation of beliefs, as judgments of value, to personal life and the problems of ethical living. The informed intellect with its function of reason was seen as purifying and supporting the "higher beliefs." In this respect, the causes and circumstances of belief were viewed as the necessary conditions of ethical behavior. A distinction was made between the external proof and the internal meaning of belief. Ladd was enough of a psychologist to appreciate the internal and personal framework that a person brings forward in judging the validity of belief, and he was functional enough to care about the relevance of personal validity to the solution of problems of living.

The final book in the quartet was somewhat removed from the theme of the other three. It was Ladd's "leap in the dark," a rather daring effort to jump from a springboard of reasonable theory into a sea of dark but inviting speculation. The book was subtitled "An Inquiry into the Sources and Reasonableness of the Hopes of Humanity, Especially the Social and Religious." He admitted in the preface that the phenomena of "hoping" were not amenable to scientific treatment. The work dealt with many of the issues that he had treated in his two-volume book on the *Philosophy of Religion*; while it was a more readable account than had been presented in the heavy volumes on religion, it was not an especially compelling job. For one thing, he wrote his way into a number of

[9] H. N. Gardiner, review of G. T. Ladd's *What Can I Know?* and *What Ought I to Do?*, *Yale Review*, 5 (1916), 220.

highly dubious positions without allowing time and space for ample documentation. The positions stood naked before the reader, provocative but unbelievable.

One stark example will illustrate the problem. Throughout his life Ladd had toyed with the question of the separability of mind and matter at death. It was no small question. When he grappled with it in *What May I Hope?* it developed into his longest and bravest chapter. Discussing "The Hope of Immortality" he raised the old issue of the relation between the mind and the body, and once more considered the localization of cerebral functions as a demonstration that function is not always and permanently located in a specific area of the brain. He then observed that in the final stages of "soul-destroying" disease, as seen in the progressive paralysis of the insane, mental life may unexpectedly return to normal vigor "as though it had by one supreme effort broken loose from the barriers which had been closing round it through the decadence of the brain."[10] Ladd decided that there was "a reasonable hope" of immortality, but he did not claim that there was evidence for the maintenance of personal identity.[11]

In 1918 he published *The Secret of Personality*. The book drew heavily upon his earlier works, and while it was not a scissors-and-paste production, it must have sounded familiar to those who knew his position on psychological issues. Perhaps the most important point about the book was the fact that he wrote it. Aware of the growth of interest in personality, he wanted to have his say on the

[10] *What May I Hope?* (New York: Longmans, Green & Co., 1915), p. 238. Acknowledging that this "seems to be a relatively new piece of evidence," one reviewer commented in a mild understatement: "If this is accepted, the materialists may be boldly challenged for an explanation." H. N. Gardiner, review of G. T. Ladd's *What Should I Believe?* and *What May I Hope?*, *Yale Review*, 5 (1916), 895.

[11] Ladd's interest in the doctrine of immortality was expressed in a number of publications during his retirement years. In one article he argued that a decline in belief in the doctrine reflected "a lack of interest and appreciation for . . . eternal and unseen things" and suggested that this was an unjustified by-product of science. See G. T. Ladd, "Is Faith in God Decadent?" *Harvard Theological Review*, 5 (1912), 296.

topic while there was still time. From the book's frequent references to anthropology, it was evident that Ladd had some knowledge of the new perspectives that were developing out of cultural anthropology and sociology.[12]

The Secret of Personality argued that human will, subject to the individual's self-control, is at the center of personality. Stressing self-theory, the discussion was predominately functional and dynamic in tone. Ladd held that religious aspirations and the hypothesis of immortality are integral to the development of a mature personality; in his highest form, man is a creature of ideals who strives to bring his actions into conformity with a vision of the ideal-real. He was not as explicit as he might have been concerning the secret of personality, but he apparently felt that the secret was a religious mystery that could only be fully understood by faith. The alluring title of the book implied that secrets would be revealed between the covers, but unfortunately Ladd stopped writing before the revelation. It was the only book that he published that left the reader wishing for a fuller discussion.

The thirty-three articles and reviews that were published between 1906 and 1919 were consistent with long-standing interests. While they revealed little in the way of new insights, they did dramatize the role that Ladd had played with such fervor and sincerity. His bibliography expressed a continuing interest in religion, philosophy, psychology, the mind-body problem, education, and Japan. But not even his deep involvement in scholarship could prevent the steady growth of a sense of remoteness from the world.[13] Friends and adversaries were passing away, and he knew that he was becoming an old man; as long as he could still read and write, however, he would refuse to allow his favorite problems to become the exclusive property of younger men.

[12] He was always rather skeptical about sociology and usually referred to the field as "the so-called science of sociology." By 1918 he may have begun to appreciate its importance.
[13] See "Autobiography," pp. 785–786.

He did not grow old gracefully, falling back upon contented reminiscence and the genial goodness of grandchildren. Pen in hand, he dueled with his infirmities as if he believed that they could be subdued by sheer hard work. Relaxation was only a temporary state of suspended penmanship to be filled by reading and by work on the inevitable notebooks that must be organized in preparation for the next article or book. He was not a "book-making machine." He was simply a man who, in spite of age and the daily inconvenience of having to eat and sleep, just could not stop being what he was.

He kept on being what he was, prodigiously, with convictions, and without humor, and meanwhile the world that he cared about continued to change. In the fall of 1909, Ladd's old friend Resident-General Ito was assassinated, and the troubled relations between Japan and Korea were thrown into an intense crisis. It was not Ito's assassination that brought about the Japanese annexation of Korea, but the annexation was made even more certain by the break-up of his regime. Ladd was deeply affected by the violent death of his friend. He wrote in his journal on October 26, 1909:

> Bright and clear overhead, but in mind and heart destined to be one of the blackest days of all my life. I had just got started working over a chapter in the new edition of The Elements of Physiological Psychology, when the telephone called me to hear the dreadful news: Prince Ito has been assassinated![14]

Though he had believed in Ito's moderate policies and had argued against the seizure of Korea, when annexation occurred he did his best to explain and to defend the action. His 1912 essay on "benevolent assimilation" was a bravely pro-Japanese effort; it was not a piece of fluffy propaganda, but it defended the Japanese ac-

[14] *Ibid.*, p. 682.

tion in every way possible.[15] His 1914 article on the annexation[16] and the two larger efforts of 1915[17] and 1916[18] continued his role as one of the leading American champions of Japanese affairs. His opinion was sought on a variety of subjects, but there appears to have been a special interest in his views on the best way of improving friendly relations between Japan and the United States.[19]

In the field of education, he had said it before and he would say it again—this time as the featured speaker at the inaugural proceedings of Acadia University in Nova Scotia:

> To make . . . higher education too easy for the multitude, too attractive as a means merely of improving one's social position or increasing one's earnings, is to run the serious risk of embarrassing or burying the really worthy and capable beneath a crowd of the unworthy and the incapable. To provide the means for doing this is surely not the duty of either the State or of private individuals.[20]

Education should be provided for all, to the extent that each is able to profit by it; but it should not be diluted needlessly and it should not be diverted from its central function, the enrichment and uplifting of human lives and the ethical advance of society.

[15] "The Annexation of Korea: An Essay in 'Benevolent Assimilation,'" *Yale Review*, 1 (1912), 639–656.

[16] "A Year of 'Benevolent Assimilation,'" *Journal of Race Development*, 4 (1914), 374–379.

[17] "Japan in the Orient, Part I—Korea," *Journal of Race Development*, 6 (1915), 113–144.

[18] "Japan in the Orient, Part II—Relations to China," *Journal of Race Development*, 6 (1916), 237–269.

[19] One of the best illustrations of Ladd's role as an "unofficial consultant" on Japanese-U.S. relations is a letter from the editor of the *Japanese-American Commercial Weekly* of New York. Stating that "we cannot hand down to our future generations a mutilated romantic relation between Japan and the United States," he asked Ladd how they could perpetuate the existing friendship. Ladd's correspondence concerning Japan was extremely heavy. See Nakahara to Ladd, August 16, 1913, in possession of Miss Cornelia T. Ladd of Cleveland Heights, Ohio.

[20] "The University and the State," *Acadia Athenaeum*, 37 (1910), 6.

In the field of religion he also had said it before, but the retirement years provided opportunities to say it again:

> Now the significant thing . . . for one who understands human nature in any worthy way—take it in the individual man or take it in the social whole, as you will—is simply this: The miseries of mankind can not be cured, they cannot even be much ameliorated, without the uplift of righteousness and without the courage and consolations of a faith in the righteousness and goodness of God.
>
> .   .   .   .
>
> Out of the ages, and from every quarter, come messages of hope and promises of success to all who have the faith in God as perfect Ethical Spirit, who cherish the passion for righteousness which this faith engenders, and who lead the life which this faith commands.[21]

There really was nothing more to be said. God was "perfect Ethical Spirit," it mattered whether or not one believed in Him, the tide was running inexorably onward, and immortality was a "reasonable hope."

But other inexorable tides were running and it mattered, at least to psychologists and philosophers, whether or not one believed in *them*. Freud had been to Clark University in 1909 and psychoanalysis was finding a footing in America; William James's pragmatism was marching on; Dewey and the functionalists were pushing into new problems; Gestalt theory was gathering warm adherents following Wertheimer's efforts in 1912; and J. B. Watson was making 1913 into his own special year with the birth of behaviorism. The second decade of the new century found Ladd in his seventies, an old man on the sidelines who was tirelessly addressing himself to "central problems."

[21] "Strategic Points for Moral Progress," *Addresses Before the New York State Conference of Religion*, series 9 (1911), 23, 31.

With these new currents gaining strength, Ladd's precious central problems became mere spindrift on a very large sea. Where were the idealists who would join him between the two fields of philosophy and psychology to protect the tender buds of regnant human ideals? After all,

> Pragmatism and the new realism may serve for a day or two to prune away some of the inconsistencies and exaggerations of the current forms of idealism. But when the time of pruning and chastening is past—and it soon will be—a new and improved idealism will come to the fore.[22]

Who would rise with Ladd against a member of the new breed who "deprecates the admission of metaphysics within the sacred precincts of a scientific psychology?"[23] Freud he simply ignored, but as for behaviorism, the inevitable offspring of materialism, "It is the proof of how American psychology has degenerated; we can make nothing out of it."[24] How does one bring a doctrine to bear upon central problems when he can make nothing out of it?

It was possible to make something out of pragmatism, however, and Ladd could not pass up the opportunity. He felt that pragmatism was "too much like a playing on words, and a playing to the galleries,"[25] and after some hesitation he submitted an article to the *Hibbert Journal*, giving it the title "Certain Assumptions of Pragmatism." The editor of the journal changed the title, however, to what was probably a better description of the article.

In "The Confusion of Pragmatism" Ladd criticized the method and the aim of philosophy, the assumed nature of truth, and "the scope and sanctions of the ideas of value" that were advocated by

[22] G. T. Ladd, "A Defense of Idealism," *Mind*, 23 (1914), 487.
[23] "The Ontological Problem of Psychology," *Philosophical Review*, 20 (1911), 363.
[24] G. T. Ladd, as quoted in N. Oshima, "My Recollections of Dr. Ladd," *Shinri-Kenkyū*, 20 (1921), 356.
[25] "Autobiography," p. 698.

George Trumbull Ladd

the pragmatist. (When he wrote of the pragmatist he was writing of William James, of course, and the critical article bore a striking resemblance to his lengthy 1892 critique of James's *Principles of Psychology*.) He understood the importance of "practical consequences" and "practical differences" as implications, if not criteria, of philosophy, but he wanted to know:

> What sort of practical? *Practical* for whom, and when, and where? *Consequences* of what sort, how measured, how determined, how realised, how known? *Differences* also, of what sort, how estimated, how motived, by what possible means to be adjusted or arranged?[26]

He argued that "clear reflective thinking" was the only possible means for establishing answers to such questions, and that reflective thinking as he had advocated it was the only true method of philosophy. Such a method embraced pragmatism, but pragmatism could not possibly encompass the larger and, in Ladd's view, more fundamental problems of the field.

The notion that truth was to be tested against the proof of consequences, with what he considered to be a de-emphasis of proper rationalism, convinced Ladd that "pragmatism turns out to be, with respect to ethical and religious contentions and conclusions, either a pretty thorough-going agnosticism or a highly emotional idealism."[27] He wanted to defend both rationalism and idealism against an instrumental or utilitarian viewpoint. Finding nothing "helpfully new" in pragmatism, he announced his readiness to "cling to the rationalistic method of intellectualizing our idealism."

> This germ of idealism, which perennially springs out of reason, it is the chief business and highest aim of philosophy to comprehend, to cultivate, to expound and justify by compar-

26 "The Confusion of Pragmatism," *Hibbert Journal*, 7 (1909), 790.
27 *Ibid.*, p. 799.

ing it with all the other fundamental facts and abiding growths of human experience.[28]

In response to Ladd's critical article, James wrote as follows:

Chocorua, N.H., July 21, 1909

Dear Ladd,

I have just read your article in the Hibbert Journal, and find the change refreshing, from charges that pragmatism is irrationalism incarnate, to the accusation that it is only rationalism in an eccentric pose. On the whole I get more comfort from the concessions in your article than from the strictures that accompany them, so I have nothing to say in rejoinder, for I believe that the dispute will end by straightening itself out *ambulando*. . . . I hope you are enjoying your *otium* as much as I am, though I trust you are not so much in the sere and yellow leaf.

Very truly yours,

Wm. James.[29]

When he wrote this letter James was near the end of his life, but Ladd had well over a decade remaining. During that decade he continued his efforts to protect "this germ of idealism" from the pragmatists, empiricists, and a growing company of materialistic monists.[30]

On both philosophic and human terms, the defense of idealism was a painful and, from all appearances, a losing battle during the final years of life. Developments in philosophy and psychology were not friendly to the position that Ladd ceaselessly promoted;

[28] *Ibid.*, p. 800. This underlying assumption also is detected in Ladd's review of James's *The Meaning of Truth, Philosophical Review*, 19 (1910), 63–69.

[29] "Autobiography," pp. 698–699.

[30] See G. T. Ladd, "Rationalism and Empiricism," *Mind*, 22 (1913), 1–13; and "A Defense of Idealism," *Mind*, 23 (1914), 473–488.

while he championed ideals, spirit, and religious and moral values, the mental science that he had helped to launch seemed bent on converting the mind into muscles and glands. It may not have been a lonely struggle, for there were others who considered his position to be of value, but the struggle seemed lonely enough to be depressing. Even more depressing was the anguished condition of a world caught up in the Great War. All the glories of philosophy were dulled by the inhumanity of the conflict. Where were ethics and idealism, and where was that essential nobility of man from which came the optimism of the idealist and his abounding human faith? For Ladd, the war years were both an intellectual and a moral torment. In an interview with the writer his daughter recalled that "my father was personally obsessed with the meaning or lack of meaning of that war. He never got over it."

His torment over the war did not disable him enough to quiet his pen, however, and he lashed out at Germany in two articles of indignation and conscience.[31] They were not major efforts and neither was a great piece of political commentary, but they revealed Ladd's continuing interest in the world of human affairs and his characteristic willingness to make judgments and take positions even though the problems were extremely complicated. One of the last examples of his social and political comment was a statement released to the press concerning the League of Nations. He castigated President Wilson and the Democrats and labeled the League covenant "a blunder."[32] His Republicanism shone radiantly through the statement.

Confronted by the turmoil of the war, the distressing success of rival philosophical and psychological doctrines, and the irreversible toll of age, Ladd must have taken courage from the conclusions

[31] "The Human Mind *Versus* the German Mind," *Hibbert Journal*, 14 (1916), 300–319; and "The Spectacle of Incorrigible Germany," *New York Times Magazine*, August 26, 1917, pp. 5–6.
[32] "League Covenant a Blunder, Says Professor Ladd," *New Haven Journal-Courier*, October 25, 1920, p. 1.

that were drawn in his book *What May I Hope?* Life was pointed upward, and though the trials and disappointments often seemed overwhelming, from a faith in the perfect Ethical Spirit there may come "messages of hope and promises of success." It was profoundly important to Ladd not only that the universe was there, but that it was *friendly*. He believed that "the Universe is indeed lifting and leading the race toward the goal of a redeemed humanity." Secure in the reciprocating friendliness of the universe, man should strive for the ideal good:

> And if he cannot depart this life with a triumphant vision for the future, he is at least entitled to have placed upon his tombstone, "I have lived and loved and laboured. All is well."[33]

And now it was all over. By 1919 age had stilled his pen, and for Ladd this must have been an unwelcome but incontrovertible sign that the end was near. In the spring of that year he told a former student that he had become more feeble and that he could no longer read "the philosophical sort of books."[34]

A year later he fell while taking a bath and lost consciousness for an extended period. Though he achieved a partial recovery, his daughter recalled that "Father didn't come downstairs during the last year. He wouldn't stay in bed, but would read on a couch in the sitting room upstairs."[35]

Ladd died on the evening of August 8, 1921. When word reached faraway Japan, his former student, the eminent psychologist Matataro Matsumoto, began work on a long statement that ended with words of personal sorrow: "Alas, my dear Professor! He has now gone; but his will lives all through me."[36] It was the ultimate tribute to the speaking teacher who had hoped to be a teacher of the world.

[33] "Is the Universe Friendly?" *Hibbert Journal*, 10 (1912), 343.
[34] N. Oshima, "My Recollections of Dr. Ladd," *Shinri-Kenkyū*, 20 (1921), 362.
[35] Interview with Mrs. Walter A. Barrett, April 1, 1962.
[36] M. Matsumoto, "Memories of Professor Ladd," p. 256.

Chapter · 16 ·

The Ladd Legacy

The death of George Trumbull Ladd brought to a close a life of uncommon versatility, passion, and muted drama. It was versatile in ranging from the Christian ministry to physiological psychology to social and political criticism; it was dramatic in the events of a religious heresy, a personal confrontation with the faculty and administration of a great university, and an extensive involvement in foreign lands; and it was passionate in the persistence of labor and in the zealous commitment to a noble cause. But, above all, it was a life of enlightened passion.

Across five of the most formative decades of American intellectual history the frail but tenacious son of the Western Reserve tended the fires of idealism and carried the banners of the human spirit. By deliberate choice he guided his life and his career through the uneven currents of theology, philosophy, and the new mental science. He knew that he had something of value to contribute to the world of ideas that churned about him as he finished his student days at the time of the Civil War; he knew also that the mission he felt compelled to undertake would carry him into perilous, if not impossible, circumstances. But the commitment to ideas was total, and Ladd yielded himself without reservation to the fortunes of a career that might be foredoomed.

In certain respects the career *was* foredoomed. His decision to mediate between the old and the new forms of learning set Ladd upon a course that was unlikely to satisfy the purists in either camp; moreover, the effort to mediate was based upon a belief that a reconciliation of conflicting points of view was possible. The developments of later years revealed that forcing an unnatural reconciliation of conflicting positions was a thankless and sometimes fruitless struggle. Perhaps the outstanding example of this mediational problem was Ladd's unsparing effort to force mentalism and a dualistic metaphysics upon the positivists of the new science.

For all its built-in problems and frustrations, the career of mediator offered an abundance of opportunities. The time and the place were right for a Ladd—for someone who would try to bridge, synthesize, and weld the increasingly disparate trends of nineteenth-century philosophy and science. And it was opportune to attempt this great task through a critical scholarship that was at the same time friendly toward classical learning, still the dominant force in academic institutions, and knowledgeable concerning the new and largely foreign science of man. It was the time for a liberal classicist who knew theology; for an idealist who was a hardheaded rationalist; for a theorist who appreciated the importance of laboratory science and who was a keen observer of man in his natural habitat; for a brave, articulate spokesman; and for one man who, combining all of these, would remain faithful to his convictions and bring them to bear upon his work throughout the formative decades of a new field.

The versatility and drama of Ladd's career were nourished by an inextinguishable passion. A superficial examination of the career fails to reveal the depth and intensity of his emotional commitment to life. The hefty books are humorless; the inability to make small talk reveals the impatience and inhibition of his social relationships; and the erudition and formality of his lectures suggest a dry dispassion. As one becomes better acquainted with the man behind the prodigious work, however, one begins to appreciate the quality of this commitment to life. Ladd's personal involvement in his mission was suffused with feeling and an unquenchable thirst for empathic understanding of his fellow man.

It was the passion of the Puritan. The frontier boy for whom life was serious business and religion the means of purification became a man of conscience and convictions. His world view changed with age and experience, but the basic cast of his mind and character was set in the Western Reserve. The virtue of hard work, the never complete struggle to match performance with religious ideals, a confidence in the reality of the unseen, and an overriding sense of guilt concerning transgressions (and particularly the sin of doing less than one might have done!)—all were permanently etched in his mind and character.

In looking back across the years, Ladd acknowledged that there had been a change in the feelings that were related to the conduct of his life: "Perhaps this change may be defined as *away from* the more Puritanical *toward* the more cosmopolitan view of life."[1] He did become more sophisticated and cosmopolitan as he grew older and it is interesting to know that the change was accompanied by an alteration in his feelings. "It was no small thing for the middle-aged former minister to begin smoking professorial cigars and tipple a little when convenient!"[2]

The Puritan conscience remained, however, and the religious and metaphysical convictions provided a framework for new knowledge and for the conduct of life. The zealous performance of duty arose from a fundamental assumption about the *truth* of his convictions. His viewpoint was not only an interesting intellectual

[1] "Autobiography," p. 784.
[2] An observation by his daughter, Mrs. Walter A. Barrett, during an interview with the writer, April 1, 1962.

derivation—it was a compelling vision of a society made noble through acceptance of his own informed ideals. In the history of psychology he may not have been "the last of the Church Mohicans,"[3] but certainly he was the Jonathan Edwards of the new mental science.

Throughout his life the humorless Puritan found personal relations with others a difficult, and at times an almost incomprehensible, problem. The amenities were a chore, small talk a waste of time, and the unnecessarily warm approach of others a violation of privacy that often appeared tinged with hypocrisy. He was unbending in his heavy formality and abrupt when he encountered shallow thinking or shoddy workmanship. His restraint and formality often impressed others as arrogance or insensitivity. Preoccupied with the serious business that always was at hand, he had little time or inclination to reveal the more human and tender part of his nature. Ladd's daughter recalled:

> When my husband asked for my hand in marriage, Father's only response was, "Have you ever had T.B.?" When assured that he had not, Father went in and shut the library door![4]

And yet, behind the abruptness and seeming insensitivity, there was strong loyalty and affectionate concern for the welfare of the family and close friends. Letters to his family were an easier avenue for expressing the feelings that were habitually guarded in face-to-face encounters. The letters he wrote his son at the time that he was graduated from Johns Hopkins Medical School, married, and began practice in Cleveland were open, friendly, and solicitous.[5]

Late in life Ladd admitted that he had not been able to enjoy the wide friendship that appeared so natural in the lives of others. In

[3] A. A. Roback, *History of Psychology and Psychiatry* (New York: Philosophical Library, 1961), p. 174.
[4] Interview with Mrs. Walter A. Barrett, April 1, 1962.
[5] Letters in possession of Miss Cornelia T. Ladd of Cleveland Heights, Ohio.

a tepid self-defense he made some remarks concerning the "sacredness of friendship," observed that he may have had "a natural lack of personal winsomeness," and dismissed the matter by quoting a colleague: "Prof. Ladd, you are just naturally bound to be a lonely man."[6] Apparently he was able to accept the opinion, and that was that.

The restrained and serious mien complicated Ladd's relations with students. His classes would have been more popular, especially with the undergraduates, if he could have thawed out enough to break the deadly stream of weighty lecturing. In his ministry, and in the teaching and lecturing assignments, he worried about the success of communication; he knew that he could not be a popular or entertaining lecturer, yet he wanted desperately to be accepted and appreciated as a speaking teacher. His success as a teacher, and it was notable, was a product of an exhaustive supporting scholarship and the moral earnestness of his style of speaking. The force of intellect and the obvious sincerity of his belief in the importance of what he had to say made him a successful teacher almost in spite of himself.

In previous chapters we have seen that Ladd's personal characteristics played an important part in his dismissal by Yale. He was inclined to be dogmatic and domineering, and the unexpected high success of his work in Japan strained even further his relations with his colleagues. The faculty felt that his acceptance abroad increased his already firm self-confidence:

> The faculty found it impossible to love him, but they had to respect his intellectual capacity and his undeviating loyalty to scholarly standards. His research in a field which in the 90's was relatively new disturbed them and they failed to understand it. But he never sought popularity for himself or his lectures. I think that faculty members did their best to be fair to

[6] "Autobiography," p. 788.

him; but they were never particularly glad to have him around, nor was he an effective member of faculty committees or faculty gatherings determining policy.[7]

Respect, but not love. He was "just naturally bound to be a lonely man," and he made the most of his loneliness. Had he been a warmer colleague and a bit less outspoken he probably would not have been fired at the end of his career—or have driven himself so furiously and productively for fifty years.

Ladd's entry into the new mental science was dramatic in the quiet way that significant events tend to occur in the history of ideas. It was dramatic in the courageous decision to move into a field for which he had had little formal preparation, and in the rigorous self-denial and disciplined good judgment that he exhibited in the years of study that led to *Elements of Physiological Psychology*. One can sense the excitement and optimism that he experienced when he realized the potential value of the new science. The theologian-minister who was a classical scholar was caught up in the fresh views of Wundt, Weber, Fechner, Helmholtz, and Lotze,[8] and he knew that his own intellectual dissatisfaction could be remedied by an all-out effort to see "what the new mental science had to offer." There would seem to be no other case in the early history of American psychology that more fully symbolized the web of diverse personal and intellectual conditions that shapes the background of a new field of learning.

The field of psychology would have been launched without Ladd's contributions, but then the same thing can be said about any

[7] Personal communication to the writer from former Yale President Charles Seymour, November 13, 1961.

[8] Ladd acknowledged his indebtedness to these men, but he denied the frequently published claim that he was a disciple of Lotze. Concerning his entry into the field of psychology, he observed that "it was not the reading of Helmholtz, or Fechner, or Weber, or Wundt, that led me to the study of this subject; it was the interest in the subject which led me to the study of these authors." G. T. Ladd, "A Disclaimer and an Explanation," *Philosophical Review*, 25 (1916), 641.

early figure in its history. The point is that Ladd was there, that he made the important contributions that he did, and that his presence in the field was a telling comment on the diverse roots of the new venture. American psychology was not launched by psychologists, but by men. They were men who came from a variety of backgrounds, but they shared one important characteristic—they were not satisfied with existing theories about mental life. In their dissatisfaction they found a common challenge. They believed that the mind of man could be approached profitably in the spirit, and through adaptation of the methods, of science. In this way, of course, the nature of philosophy, theology, and other fields of learning would be changed.

The audacity of it all! These men were beginning to push into areas that were sacred. They were questioning, doubting, and proposing new views about man that bid fair to reverse some of the thinking that had prevailed for hundreds and even thousands of years. From the vantage point of a field now fully launched and legitimate, it is difficult to appreciate the extent to which the new mental science challenged the old views and accepted methods of scholarship. The brass instruments and testing devices in the Yale Psychological Laboratory were a tangible threat to an ancient and revered tradition of learning. No wonder theologians, philosophers, and even President Hadley of Yale found the new field a disturbing innovation.

It is ironic that Ladd, who had entered psychology in a spirit of mediation and with deep convictions about the older views, should have been the one to produce the enormous American handbook of the new field. It was a tour de force and in itself a sufficiently significant piece of work to make his career a matter of permanent importance in the history of the field. But when one considers the entire sweep of his life and career it becomes even more apparent that he deserves the honor of a lasting recognition. His teaching career at Yale was a substantial, and in the end a rather colorful, thread in the pattern of early American academic institutions; his work in Japan, India, and Korea was a notable contribution to the spread of a functional and socially relevant psychology and philosophy; his lecturing and scholarship in the field of religion and in practical matters of church government were a force for liberality; but surmounting all his unusually varied achievements there looms the bulk of his scholarly and literary remains, testifying to the life of a man of principle who was determined to make reason serve ideals.

The bulk of Ladd's publications reveals the impressive versatility of the man. He published too much, and it was not of uniform quality, but the surprising thing is that most of it was very much worth while. When one becomes accustomed to the literary style and resigned to the rolling wordiness, one begins to appreciate the rather consistent quality of the message. Ladd had something to say—at length and always seriously—and he had his say on most of the problems of philosophy, psychology, and religion. Whatever the subject of discussion, the underlying assumptions remained the same. His publications became a predictable and valuable point of reference in a period when American scholarship was experimenting productively with a great variety of views. For many years, and almost every year, there would be a new book by Professor Ladd against which to rethink old problems and wonder anew about those that were still troublesome and unsolved. A great many people found his moderate viewpoint compelling; his critics knew well just what he believed and they knew also that he would not leave them in peace.

Writing in 1912, Ladd concluded his autobiography with a summary comment concerning the point of view that he had tried to promote and defend during his long career. He observed that brief summaries are likely to be unintelligible or illusory, "but that if they are to be given at all, perhaps they are best given by the one whose opinions they are." He then went on to record "some rela-

George Trumbull Ladd

tively fixed opinions" from a half-century of reading, reflection, and study:

> What we call *knowledge*, but by calling it this, only vaguely distinguish it from faith, opinion, and even in not a few cases, conjecture,—seems to me a matter of development, both in the individual and in the race, which involves all the mental activities, and admits of endless degrees, approximating only, but ever at a distance from, the fullness of the facts and laws that truly characterize Reality. The centre of its assurance lies in the consciousness of the Self and of its object, as here and now present, real and reciprocally active in every cognitive event. The very nature of knowledge, and of every cognitive experience, refutes the scepticisms which would cut the mind off from all commerce with reality; while it gives no warrant for scientific "cocksureness" or philosophic immodesty and pride. In the last analysis the validity of knowledge depends upon the assumption that in every cognitive event mind answers to mind; and that the terms of its answer, while constituting limitations, are barriers against error rather than bars separating the soul from all truth.
>
> As to the nature of the cognitive subject, of the mind that knows, or thinks it knows, contributions from all the allied positive sciences are too gratefully and trustingly received by the psychologist, though always with reservation of his rights of criticism. These all, however, only show under what conditions, and as dependent on what terms of interaction, the self-active being we call the human mind develops its own *sui-generis* nature, as set in the larger Nature of which it forms a part.
>
> As to method in philosophy, I need not hesitate to avow myself a "rationalist"; if only the term include what it justly may, and in fact is bound to include. For man is *rational*, not simply because his faculties of prevision and powers of calculation and of syllogistic reasoning so greatly surpass those of the lower

animals. His intellectual emotions and aspirations, his moral, artistic, and religious sentiments and ideals, are integral and inalienable parts of his rational equipment. Considered in this broad way, reason is in man the sole organon of knowledge or defensible opinion, whether its source be reflection, insight, unanalyzed experience, or so-called revelation. For science and philosophy there is no other method secure, not to say possible, than the rationalistic method. But all man's thinking, observing, and experimenting, should be, and in the long run is bound to be,—as well as the resulting growth of reason, and the accumulating achievements of rational procedure,—contributory to an improved conduct of life. While, then, dissenting from the vagaries and deficiencies of every form of so-called Pragmatism, I desire to be permanently classed among those thinkers who, like the great Greek masters Plato and Aristotle, and indeed like the greater thinkers of all ages, have made the object of their striving to effect a more harmonious union between the theoretical and the practical interests of man. This has always been the effort of what we may—not unfitly—call the "classical philosophy." Or to express the thought in a more modern way: I have striven as best I could to expound the validity and the value of the intellectual, moral, aesthetical, and religious ideals of humanity, in the light, and through the facts and laws, of the modern positive sciences.

But have I succeeded in this effort at mediation and increased harmony? That is not for me to say. Perhaps, just now, it is not for any one to say, with a confidence approaching perfection. Certainly, this form of "classical philosophy," or Idealism as expounded and defended by the rationalistic method and in the name of the positive sciences, is not the kind of reflective thinking at present in vogue. One who consistently advocates it is not unlikely to find himself in the position of Socrates, of whom it was said: "He will be summoned before the judges, and he will fare there much as would a physician who should be accused by a confectioner before a jury of children." But as surely as reason reigns—the Universal Divine Reason in the Macrocosm, and in the end more and more, the finite but divinely bestowed and cultured reason in the microcosm, man, this kind of philosophy will come to its own again. And whether any particular name is connected, by however slender a thread, with the leading-in of its fuller appearance, is not the matter of utmost concern.[9]

The summary was not well written (Ladd was then over seventy years of age and only six books and seventeen articles away from the end of his career), but it did reaffirm the basic assumptions that he had brought to his work at the beginning of his career. The success of his "effort at mediation and increased harmony" was a matter of great importance to him, and it is not surprising that he wondered how well he had done. Taken as a whole, his writings and personal documents convey the distinct impression that he felt his mission had been successful, but that general developments in philosophy and in the positive sciences masked the significant contribution that he had made. He may have been right. While the assessment of success is a complicated question, the masking effect of contrary developments would seem indisputable.

It is appropriate that Ladd's greatest success came in that aspect of his work which was closest to his heart. The breadth and variety of his teaching and scholarship; the fairness and general tolerance of his position on philosophical, psychological, and theological issues; the timely effort to systematize the materials of a new field—all these factors were united in the larger struggle to mediate between the diverse trends of human learning and to promote the development of mental science. It was precisely in his announced function as a generalist and mediator that he was most influential; and it is in this function that history finds personal contributions to be most elusive.

[9] "Autobiography," pp. 790–792.

In the eighties and nineties, Ladd was a towering figure, through his academic leadership, in the introduction of the new psychology. This was the period in which physiological, experimental, genetic and abnormal psychology gained recognition in the college curriculum of this country, and Ladd did much to bring this recognition. Yet, he was not primarily a psychologist and did no experimental work in any of the fields which he so ably introduced. He came into psychology through philosophy, and had come into philosophy through theology. History will probably recognize him as an organizer rather than an inspirer, or an original contributor in specific problems.

While always regarded as more or less dry, his books and lectures were characterized by remarkable clearness, accuracy, thoroughness, broadmindedness and chasteness of style and a pleasing absence of the irrelevant. His definitions were those of a logician; his scientific perspective was that of a philosopher; his power of appeal was that of the forceful teacher. The fidelity and constructive analysis with which he interpreted the findings of research men in physiology, physics, medicine and genetics gave dignity and permanence to his work. The encyclopedic character of his work shows him at his best in his power to organize for himself and put in teachable form these new and diverse approaches to the study of the human mind. His "Elements of Physiological Psychology" and "Psychology Descriptive and Explanatory" will live as classics from that period.[10]

Seashore made a special point of Ladd's capacity to unify the contributions of numerous thinkers in the field of psychology and to quiet the turbulent waters "by certifying and formulating as a philosopher, as a preacher and as a teacher what was 'wholesome' and giving it a setting in academic psychology." He spoke of Ladd's efforts as "the power of a great thinker to interpret and organize new and relevant facts."

[10] C. E. Seashore, "George Trumbull Ladd," obituary, *Science*, 54 (1921), 242.

George Trumbull Ladd

A similar analysis was made by Armstrong, who characterized the qualities of Ladd's intellectual temperament as "broad and sound scholarship based on unremitting study, sympathy with the methods and the results of modern critical inquiry, and yet firm confidence that constructive conclusions necessarily follow from thorough reflection."[11] The essentially constructive tone of Ladd's work, especially in the valuable rendering of texts for the new field of psychology, was made evident in Hicks's evaluation. He considered *Psychology: Descriptive and Explanatory* a more important and original work than *Elements of Physiological Psychology* and noted especially the effort to come to terms with "the old and vicious doctrine of 'faculties.' "[12]

Titchener, whose elaborate criticism of Ladd's theories was considered in Chapter 9, did not believe that Ladd had been a great psychologist. He did acknowledge, however, the "competent and assiduous" nature of the man and the "very distinct service to the cause of psychology in this country" that was rendered by his many publications. He said of *Elements of Physiological Psychology*:

> Coming, as it did, from a professor of philosophy at Yale who had been a Congregational minister, it gave the young science an air of respectability (I can think of no better word) which was of high advantage in its struggle for life.[13]

Ladd may not have been a great psychologist in the germinal and incisive way that Wundt, James, Freud, and Watson were great, but in his time and within the field as he helped to launch it he was an extremely important figure. The translator and systematizer and textbook writer who could provide the doubtful new field with an

[11] A. C. Armstrong, "George Trumbull Ladd," obituary, *Philosophical Review*, 30 (1921), 639.

[12] G. D. Hicks, "Prof. G. T. Ladd," obituary, *Nature*, 108 (1921), 23.

[13] E. B. Titchener, "George Trumbull Ladd," obituary, *American Journal of Psychology*, 32 (1921), 600.

"air of respectability" among other disciplines and within the emerging pattern of higher education was a man to be highly valued. He was regarded as one of the three senior men of American psychology at the time that the field began to recognize itself as a new and permanent profession.[14]

Ladd's seniority in the field in the closing years of the nineteenth century was not merely a matter of chronological age. His early entry into the field was a mark of some distinction, and both his presence and the nature of his psychology reflected the state of the science in the days of his study and informal preparation. It is of more importance to recognize, however, that in terms of the date of initial major contributions, Ladd preceded both Hall and James. The publication of *Elements* in 1887 placed him in the front ranks of American psychology, and this position was enhanced by the publication of *Psychology: Descriptive and Explanatory* in 1894. His seniority in the field was the result of substantive and highly valued contributions to its early development. With James and Hall he must be honored as one of the three pioneers of American psychology.[15]

He was a pioneer and a self-starter, entering psychology without the stimulus of a master teacher and without formal training in the field. Ladd, James, and Hall, as the first generation of American psychologists, were professionally self-propelled, and it was the peculiar genius of each man to find his own way forward. As self-starters, they have been termed *"les enfants du bon Dieu."*[16] Whatever their origin, the field needed them to get itself started; they

[14] Ladd, James, and Hall were involved in the formation of the American Psychological Association in 1892, and Fernberger observed that, in choosing its early presidents, the association began by honoring its three senior men—Hall (1892), Ladd (1893), and James (1894). See S. W. Fernberger, "The American Psychological Association, a Historical Summary, 1892–1930," *Psychological Bulletin*, 29 (1932), 83.

[15] See J. M. Cattell, "Psychology in America," *Science*, 30 (1929), 337.

[16] M. D. Boring and E. G. Boring, "Masters and Pupils Among the American Psychologists," *American Journal of Psychology*, 61 (1948), 531.

appeared upon the scene in the natural and inevitable way that often seems to characterize the appearance of the right men at the right time. But it is the splendid fortune of only a few to preside at the birth of a new field of learning.

Ladd's psychology was enormously important at the time that it appeared, but it was a contribution that became more diffuse and intangible as the field was enriched by new methods, new theories, and compelling new personalities. It was destined to appear increasingly outdated, and even quaint, to those who prided themselves on the sterling purity of a psychology that had won its freedom from philosophy and metaphysics. Psychology no longer honored mediators; the search for common ground somehow implied a compromise of hard-won principles, and if there was anything that the new field desired it was an uncompromising and uncluttered chance at its own destiny. But that was not all. The forces that pushed psychology along looked urgently forward and there was little inclination to examine the history that had been so recently in the making. With an exciting future ahead, the past seemed of questionable relevance.

Toward the close of his work at Yale, Ladd began to feel that psychology was moving away from "right principles." He acknowledged the importance of the steps that the field was taking in the name of science, but he regretted the increasing insularity of psychology "in a sea of big human questions." Science, yes; but science in the conscious service of man was what was needed. He saw psychology moving toward purity and irrelevance, simultaneously improving its opportunity for methodological control of complex variables and increasing its remoteness from man. There was a world to understand and improve, and it seemed that the psychologist was more and more inclined to make a new, but inhuman, religion of his promising field. In Ladd's view, the new religion was linked to certain assumptions about man and society that prevailed in still another robust new religion—that of commercialism. Filled with concern about man's social ills, and worried about the irrelevant tendencies of psychological science, he cried out:

> Do not tell me that modern commercialism, backed up how-
> ever much with the discoveries of the modern physico-chemical
> sciences, without the motive forces of morality and religion, is
> going to regenerate the world![17]

The career had gone full circle. It was, after all, the regeneration
of the world that he cared about. In his Milwaukee pastorate he
had flailed the Common Council for its failure to hold to right
principles, and then, decades later and after the adventures of a circuitous route through the brambles of a new science, he had resumed his prophetic stance and warned anyone who would listen
about the fate of a society, and of a science, that eschewed the principles of morality and religion.

In the years since his death Ladd's contributions to American
psychology and philosophy have received little attention. There
have been occasional references to his work,[18] but in most cases he
has been treated as an early figure of only marginal importance.
Histories of psychology have given him credit for minor contributions, often restricting reference to his work as a writer of early
textbooks. Boring's discussion of Ladd suggests more accurately
than most the extent of his contributions and the range and variety
of his interests.[19] One permanent reminder of his work has been
provided by his alma mater, Western Reserve University, with the
creation in 1957 of a distinguished professorship in psychology
that bears his name.[20]

Perhaps the current growth of interest in the history of psychology will bring about a more general appreciation of Ladd's life and

[17] "Autobiography," p. 488.
[18] Contrasting examples are the lengthy doctoral dissertation of V. A. Fochtman,
submitted in 1928 to the Ludwig-Maximilians-Universität-München, and entitled
"Das Leib-Seele-Problem bei George Trumbull Ladd und William McDougall," and
brief reference to Ladd's work on the movement of the eyeballs during sleep in "A
Third State of Existence," *The New Yorker*, September 18, 1965, p. 58.
[19] E. G. Boring, *A History of Experimental Psychology* (New York: Appleton-
Century-Crofts, Inc., 1957), pp. 524–527, 546.
[20] Since the time of its creation, the Ladd professorship has been held by Dr.
George Wilson Albee.

work. While his relation to the origins of the field deserves more attention than it has received, the Ladd legacy is in no way confined to psychology. It is the legacy of a life of ideas and purposeful action that defied the boundaries of any discipline or profession. By its singular reach and deep humanity, Ladd's life spoke of the urgent calling that has illuminated the lives of informed and passionate men through the ages. It was a life of consistent devotion to high ideals. In the words of one of his Japanese students, "Whatever judgment may be passed on his ideas, it must be admitted that he did what he intended to do, most faithfully to the end."[21]

[21] N. Oshima, "My Recollections of Dr. Ladd," *Shinri-Kenkyū*, 20 (1921), 360.

Bibliography

Materials concerning the life and work of George Trumbull Ladd are widely scattered, but certainly there is an ample supply. In addition to Ladd's own publications, the large unpublished autobiography provides a valuable account of the most important periods of his life. Letters and other personal documents are in the possession of the Ladd family. The archives of Case Western Reserve University and of the Lake County (Ohio) Historical Society contain sources that illuminate the early years. The period spent in Edinburg, Ohio, is sparsely sketched in the *Book of Records* (1869–1871) of the Edinburg United Church. The years in Milwaukee are more fully documented in the *Book of Records* (1866–1894) of the Grand Avenue Congregational Church, and in frequent articles in the *Milwaukee Sentinel* for the period 1871–1879.

The Yale University Library has several volumes of essays, speeches, journal articles, and lecture reports that were collected by Ladd's second wife. Sources concerning the years at Yale are found in the Letters and Papers of President A. T. Hadley, in the Henry P. Wright Collection of Letters and Papers, 1898–1911, and in the Papers of Henry Walcott Farnam on Yale Affairs. The *Yale Daily News* and the *Yale Alumni Weekly* contain occasional reports of Ladd's activities during the period of his service on the faculty. The library also has an excellent, though incomplete, collection of the many books that Ladd published. Numerous articles about him are to be found in issues of the *New Haven Journal-Courier* for the years of his residence in that city.

Ladd's own publications are a useful source for the periods that were spent in Japan, Korea, and India. In addition, the work in Japan is well documented in the *Hinode Shimbun* (Kyoto), in the *Dōshisha-Bungaku*

Bibliography

(Kyoto), and in the journals *Shinri-Kenkyū* and *Rikugōzassi*. The Korean work is reported in issues of the *Seoul Press* that appeared in the spring of 1907, and the travels in India are sketched in the *Times of India* (Bombay) and the *Bombay Catholic Examiner* during the period of his visit in 1899–1900.

THE WRITINGS OF GEORGE TRUMBULL LADD
(Listed Chronologically)

BOOKS

The Principles of Church Polity. New York: Charles Scribner's Sons, 1882.
The Doctrine of Sacred Scripture. 2 vols. New York: Charles Scribner's Sons, 1883.
Lotze, H. *Outlines of Metaphysic.* Trans. & ed. by G. T. Ladd. Boston: Ginn, Heath & Co., 1884.
Lotze, H. *Outlines of Practical Philosophy.* Trans. & ed. by G. T. Ladd. Boston: Ginn & Co., 1885.
Lotze, H. *Outlines of the Philosophy of Religion.* Trans. & ed. by G. T. Ladd. Boston: Ginn & Co., 1885.
Lotze, H. *Outlines of Aesthetics.* Trans. & ed. by G. T. Ladd. Boston: Ginn & Co., 1886.
Lotze, H. *Outlines of Psychology.* Trans. & ed. by G. T. Ladd. Boston: Ginn & Co., 1886.
Lotze, H. *Outlines of Logic and of Encyclopaedia of Philosophy.* Trans. & ed. by G. T. Ladd. Boston: Ginn & Co., 1887.
Elements of Physiological Psychology. New York: Charles Scribner's Sons, 1887.
What Is the Bible? New York: Charles Scribner's Sons, 1888.
Introduction to Philosophy. New York: Charles Scribner's Sons, 1890.
Outlines of Physiological Psychology. New York: Charles Scribner's Sons, 1891.
Primer of Psychology. New York: Longmans, Green & Co., 1894.
Psychology: Descriptive and Explanatory. New York: Charles Scribner's Sons, 1894.

Primer of Psychology. Braille edition. Louisville, Ky., 1895.

Philosophy of Mind. New York: Charles Scribner's Sons, 1895.

Philosophy of Knowledge. New York: Charles Scribner's Sons, 1897.

Outlines of Descriptive Psychology. New York: Charles Scribner's Sons, 1898.

A Theory of Reality. New York: Charles Scribner's Sons, 1899.

Essays on the Higher Education. New York: Charles Scribner's Sons, 1899.

Philosophy of Conduct. New York: Charles Scribner's Sons, 1902.

The Philosophy of Religion. 2 vols. New York: Charles Scribner's Sons, 1905.

The Doctrine of the Virtues as Applied to Business Life. Tokyo: Tokyo Higher Commercial School, 1907.

In Korea with Marquis Ito. New York: Charles Scribner's Sons, 1908.

Knowledge, Life and Reality. New York: Dodd, Mead & Co., 1909.

Rare Days in Japan. New York: Longmans, Green & Co., 1910.

Elements of Physiological Psychology. With R. S. Woodworth. New York: Charles Scribner's Sons, 1911.

The Teacher's Practical Philosophy. New York: Funk & Wagnalls Co., 1911.

"The Autobiography of a Teacher." Unpublished manuscript. Written 1910–1912. Pp. 794.

What Can I Know? New York: Longmans, Green & Co., 1914.

What Ought I to Do? New York: Longmans, Green & Co., 1915.

What Should I Believe? New York: Longmans, Green & Co., 1915.

What May I Hope? New York: Longmans, Green & Co., 1915.

The Secret of Personality. New York: Longmans, Green & Co., 1918.

Intimate Glimpses of Life in India. Boston: R. G. Badger, 1919.

Japanese Translations

Shotō Shinri-gaku (Primer of Psychology). Trans. by Nobutada Oda. Tokyo: Fuzanbō, 1897.

Shinri satsu yō (Outlines of Descriptive Psychology). Trans. by Rikizō Nakashima. Tokyo: Sanseido, 1898.

Ladd-shi ninshiki-ron (Ladd's Philosophy of Knowledge). Trans. by Rikizō Nakashima. Tokyo: Fusanbō, 1898.

Bibliography

Kyōiku-gaku ni ōyō shitaru Shinri-gaku (Psychology Applied to Education). Trans. by Kazutami Ukita. Tokyo: Bungakusha, 1900.
Seiriteki Shinri-gaku (Outlines of Physiological Psychology). Trans. by Senjiro Watanabe. Tokyo: Chugai Shuppansha, 1901.
Ladd-shi Kyōiku-gaku (Ladd's Science of Education). Trans. by Kazutami Ukita. Tokyo: Sanseido, 1907.
Rinri tetsu-gaku (Philosophy of Conduct). Trans. by Naoharu Oshima. Tokyo: Sanseido, 1912.

ARTICLES AND PAMPHLETS

"The Origin of the First Three Gospels," *Bibliotheca Sacra,* 26 (1869), 1–37.
"What Is the True Doctrine of Christ's Second Coming?" *New Englander,* 33 (1874), 356-383.
Memorial Sermon of Deacon Samuel Brown. Milwaukee: Hawks & Hinsdale, 1875.
"Cherubim," *Bibliotheca Sacra,* 33 (1876), 32–51.
"The New Theology," *New Englander,* 35 (1876), 660–694.
"The Origin of the Concept of God," *Bibliotheca Sacra,* 34 (1877), 1–36.
"The Difficulties of the Concept of God," *Bibliotheca Sacra,* 34 (1877), 593–631.
"The Concept of God as the Ground of Progress," *Bibliotheca Sacra,* 35 (1878), 619–655.
The Unknown God of Herbert Spencer and the Promise and Potency of Professor Tyndall. Milwaukee: I. L. Hauser & Co., 1878.
"Final Purpose in Nature," *New Englander,* 38 (1879), 677–700.
"An Essay in Systematic Theology," *Bibliotheca Sacra,* 36 (1879), 706–729.
"History and the Concept of God," *Bibliotheca Sacra,* 37 (1880), 593–639.
"Nature, the Supernatural and the Miraculous," *Christian Philosophy Quarterly,* 2 (1882), 75–102.
"Suggestions Toward a Reconstructed Theory of Sacred Scripture," *Conference Papers* (General Conference of the Congregational Churches in Connecticut), 1882, 138–146.
Congregationalism and Foreign Missions. Boston: Franklin Press: Rand, Avery & Co., 1882.

The Ideal Christian Church. Torrington, Conn.: Register Book & Job Print, 1882.

"Revelation," *Journal of Christian Philosophy,* 2 (1883), 156–178.

"Inspiration," *Journal of Christian Philosophy,* 2 (1883), 225–249.

"Oehler's Old Testament Theology: A Review," *New Englander,* 43 (1884), 364–376.

"The Interpretation of the Bible and the Doctrine of Sacred Scripture," *Andover Review,* 2 (1884), 18–34.

"The Question Restated," *Andover Review,* 4 (1885), 1–16.

"Education, New and Old," *Andover Review,* 5 (1886), 1–18.

Review of Lotze's *Microcosmus, New Englander and Yale Review,* 45 (1886), 318–332.

"The Development of the American University," *Scribner's Magazine,* 2 (1887), 346–360.

"Dr. Cattell on *Elements of Physiological Psychology,*" *Mind,* 13 (1888), 308–312.

"On Body and Mind," *Mind,* 13 (1888), 627–629.

"Letter from Professor George T. Ladd, of Yale University," *Christian Advocate,* July 4, 1889, pp. 3–4.

"Ethics of Art," *Independent,* October 24, 1889, pp. 2–3.

"The Psychology of the Modern Novel," *Andover Review,* 12 (1889), 134–157.

"The Place of the Fitting-School in American Education," *Scribner's Magazine,* 6 (1889), 298–304.

"Ethics in Yale University," *Ethical Record,* 2 (1890), 217–220.

"Influence of Modern Psychology upon Theological Opinion," *Andover Review,* 14 (1890), 557–578.

"The Biblical and the Philosophical Conception of God," *Essays* (misc. pamphlets & articles), vol. 2 (1891). Sterling Library, Yale University, New Haven, Conn.

Sermon preached in Battell Chapel, September 25, 1891. *New Englander and Yale Review,* 55 (1891), 465–476.

"A Contribution to the Psychology of Visual Dreams," *Mind,* 1 (1892), 299–304.

"Philosophy of Religion," trans. M. Matsumoto, *Rikugōzassi,* 137 (1892), 245–246.

Bibliography

"Psychology as So-called 'Natural Science,'" *Philosophical Review*, 1 (1892), 24–53.

"The Nature, Origin, Essence and Method of Philosophy," trans. M. Matsumoto, *Rikugōzassi*, 139 (1892), 340–345.

"Philosophy of Religion," trans. M. Matsumoto, *Rikugōzassi*, 140 (1892), 366–383.

"The Development of Attention in Infancy," *Childhood*, June, 1893, pp. 197–200.

Presidential address before the New York meeting of the American Psychological Association, *Psychological Review*, 1 (1894), 1–21.

"Direct Control of the Retinal Field," *Psychological Review*, 1 (1894), 351–355.

"Is Psychology a Science?" *Psychological Review*, 1 (1894), 392–395.

Review of Ormond's "Basal Concepts in Philosophy," *Psychological Review*, 1 (1894), 415–416.

"What is Mental Philosophy?" *Chautauquan*, 14 (1894), 157–162.

"Experimental Psychology in America: Founding of Laboratories in the Universities," *Science*, 2 (1895), 626–627.

"The Consciousness of Identity and So-called Double Consciousness," *Psychological Review*, 2 (1895), 159–161.

"A Communication," *Psychological Review*, 2 (1895), 394–397.

"Lotze's Influence on Theology," *New World*, 4 (1895), 401–421.

"Mental Characteristics of the Japanese," *Scribner's Magazine*, 17 (1895), 79–93.

"Consciousness and Evolution," *Psychological Review*, 3 (1896), 296–300.

"A Color Illusion," *Studies from the Yale Psychological Laboratory*, 6 (1898), 1–5.

"On Certain Hindrances to the Progress of Psychology in America," *Psychological Review*, 6 (1899), 121–133.

"The Philosophical Basis of Literature," *Philosophical Review*, 8 (1899), 561–588.

Lectures on the Philosophy of Religion. Madras: Natesan, 1900.

"Imperialism in Japan," *Nation*, 71 (1900), 283–284.

"A Death Ceremonial of the 'Kapola Bania' Caste," *Journal of the American Oriental Society*, 22 (1901), 227–236.

"Present Religious Tendencies in India," *American Journal of Theology*, 5 (1901), 217–239.

The Essentials of Christianity. Tokyo: The Student YMCA Union of Japan, 1901.

"Education and the Unity of the Race," *East and West*, 1 (1901), 125–140.

"A Communication to the Editor," *Dial*, 33 (1902), 386–387.

"Legal Aspects of Hypnotism," *Yale Law Journal*, 11 (1902), 173–194; and *Report of New York State Bar Assoc.*, 25 (1902), 182–212.

"The True Functions of a Great University," *Forum*, 33 (1902), 33–45.

"The Disintegration and Reconstruction of the Curriculum," *Forum*, 33 (1902), 165–178.

"The Degradation of the Professorial Office," *Forum*, 33 (1902), 270–282.

"How Shall the College Curriculum Be Reconstructed?" *Forum*, 35 (1903), 130–148.

"The Present Moral and Religious Crisis," *East and West*, 2 (1903), 387–400.

"The Present Crisis in Morals in the Churches," *Addresses Before the New York State Conference of Religion*, series 1 (1903), 1–8.

"Modern Apologetics," *American Journal of Theology*, 7 (1903), 523–543.

"Prolegomena to an Argument for the Being of God," *Philosophical Review*, 12 (1903), 130–137.

"Direct Control of the 'Retinal Field': Report on Three Cases," *Psychological Review*, 10 (1903), 139–149.

"Brief Critique of 'Psycho-physical Parallelism,' " *Mind*, 12 (1903), 374–380.

"The Religious Consciousness as Ontological," *Journal of Philosophy, Psychology, and Scientific Method*, 1 (1904), 8–13.

"A Suggestive Case of Nerve-Anastomosis," *Popular Science Monthly*, 67 (1905), 319–328.

"The Mission of Philosophy," *Philosophical Review*, 14 (1905), 113–137.

"The Development of Philosophy in the Nineteenth Century," *Philosophical Review*, 14 (1905), 403–428 (part 1); 563–575 (part 2). Also printed in *Congress of Arts and Sciences, Universal Exposition, St. Louis, 1904.* Boston: Houghton Mifflin Co., 1905.

"The Child's Capacity for Religion," in *The Child and Religion: Eleven Essays*, ed. Thomas Stephens. New York: G. P. Putnam's Sons; London: Williams & Norgate, 1905.

"On the Business Morals of Japan," *Century Magazine*, 76 (1908), 395–400.

Bibliography

"America and Japan," *International Conciliation*, document 7, series 1 (1908), 3–15.

"The Confusion of Pragmatism," *Hibbert Journal*, 7 (1909), 784–801.

"Ethics and the Law," *Yale Law Journal*, 18 (1909), 613–624.

"The Moral Need of Religious Solidarity," *Addresses Before the New York State Conference of Religion*, series 7 (1909), 7–29.

"Suggestions from Two Cases of Cerebral Surgery Without Anesthetics," *Popular Science Monthly*, 74 (1909), 562–567.

"The Japanese Administration in Korea," in *China and the Far East*, ed. George H. Blakeslee. New York: T. Y. Crowell & Co., 1910. Pp. 397–435.

"The University and the State," *Acadia Athenaeum*, 37 (1910), 1–27.

Review of William James's *The Meaning of Truth*, *Philosophical Review*, 19 (1910), 63–69.

"The Ontological Problem of Psychology," *Philosophical Review*, 20 (1911), 363–385.

"Strategic Points for Moral Progress," *Addresses Before the New York State Conference of Religion*, series 9 (1911), 10–32.

"The Annexation of Korea: An Essay in 'Benevolent Assimilation,' " *Yale Review*, 1 (1912), 639–656.

"The Man Who Ruled Japan," *New York Evening Post*, August 3, 1912.

"Is the Universe Friendly?" *Hibbert Journal*, 10 (1912), 328–343. Also printed in *Living Age*, 273 (1912), 97–106.

"Is Faith in God Decadent?" *Harvard Theological Review*, 5 (1912), 283–298.

"The Need of Administrative Changes in the American University," *Popular Science Monthly*, 80 (1912), 313–325. Also published in *University Control* by J. McKeen Cattell. New York: Science Press, 1913. Pp. 349–369.

"The Study of Man," *Science*, 37 (1913), 275–290.

Review of John Watson's *The Interpretation of Religious Experience*, *Philosophical Review*, 22 (1913), 539–546.

"Rationalism and Empiricism," *Mind*, 22 (1913), 1–13.

"Facts in the Souls of Men," *Everybody's Magazine*, 31 (1914), 131–135.

"A Defense of Idealism," *Mind*, 23 (1914), 473–488.

Introduction to Henry Davies' *Art in Education and Life: A Plea for the More Systematic Culture of the Sense of Beauty.* Columbus, O.: R. G. Adams & Co., 1914.

"A Year of 'Benevolent Assimilation,'" *Journal of Race Development,* 4 (1914), 374–379.

"Japan in the Orient, Part I—Korea," *Journal of Race Development,* 6 (1915), 113–144.

"Japan in the Orient, Part II—Relations to China," *Journal of Race Development,* 6 (1916), 237–269.

"The Human Mind *Versus* the German Mind," *Hibbert Journal,* 14 (1916), 300–319.

"Trials of an Old-fashioned College Treasurer," *Yale Review,* 5 (1916), 382–396.

"A Disclaimer and an Explanation," *Philosophical Review,* 25 (1916), 639–641.

"The Spectacle of Incorrigible Germany," *New York Times Magazine,* August 26, 1917, pp. 5–6.

"Why Women Cannot Compose Music," *Yale Review,* 6 (1917), 789–806.

"The Development of Korea in Most Recent Times," *Journal of Race Development,* 8 (1918), 431–438.

"A Case of Multiple Personality," *Yale Review,* 8 (1919), 318–333.

"Mental Characteristics of the Japanese," *Encyclopedia Americana* (1920 ed.), vol. 15, pp. 635–640.

"Philosophy," *Encyclopedia Americana* (1920 ed.), vol. 15, pp. 768–777.

"Four Elements of a Great Art," *Essays* (misc. articles & pamphlets), vol. 1. Sterling Library, Yale University, New Haven, Conn.

"The Art of Almsgiving," *Essays* (misc. articles & pamphlets), vol. 1. Sterling Library, Yale University, New Haven, Conn.

"The Doctrine of Christian Song," *Essays* (misc. articles & pamphlets), vol. 1. Sterling Library, Yale University, New Haven, Conn.

"The Moral Value of a Well-planned Secondary Education," *Essays,* (misc. articles & pamphlets), vol. 1. Sterling Library, Yale University, New Haven, Conn.

"The Strength and the Weakness of Idealism," *Essays* (misc. articles & pamphlets), vol. 3. Sterling Library, Yale University, New Haven, Conn.

Bibliography

"Syllabus of Lectures on Psychology to be Delivered in the Sir Cowasji Jehangier Hall of the Bombay University, November 30 to December 15, 1899," *Essays* (misc. articles and pamphlets), vol. 3. Sterling Library, Yale University, New Haven, Conn.
"The Future of Japan," *Essays* (misc. articles & pamphlets), vol. 4. Sterling Library, Yale University, New Haven, Conn.
"What Do Dreams Mean?" *Essays* (misc. articles & pamphlets), vol. 4. Sterling Library, Yale University, New Haven, Conn.
"Japanese-America," *Essays* (misc. articles & pamphlets), vol. 4. Sterling Library, Yale University, New Haven, Conn.
"American Critics on Japan," *Essays* (misc. articles & pamphlets), vol. 4. Sterling Library, Yale University, New Haven, Conn.

SELECTED SOURCES

Adhikari, P. B. *An Analysis of Ladd's "Primer of Psychology."* Lahore: The Tribune Press, 1903.
Albrecht, F. M. "The New Psychology in America: 1880–1895." Unpublished Ph.D. dissertation, Johns Hopkins University, 1960. Pp. 235.
Anderson, R. S. *Japan: Three Epochs of Modern Education.* Washington: U.S. Department of Health, Education, and Welfare, 1959. Bulletin No. 11.
Angell, J. R. *Psychology.* New York: Henry Holt and Co., 1904.
Armstrong, A. C. "George Trumbull Ladd," obituary, *Philosophical Review,* 30 (1921), 639–640.
Asakawa, K. Review of G. T. Ladd's *In Korea with Marquis Ito, Yale Review,* 17 (1908–1909), 350–352.
Atkins, G. G., and Fagley, F. L. *History of American Congregationalism.* Boston: The Pilgrim Press, 1942.
Baldwin, J. M. *Between Two Wars: 1861–1921.* vol. 1. Boston: Stratford, 1926.
Barr, N. C. Review of G. T. Ladd's "Rationalism and Empiricism," *Philosophical Review,* 22 (1913), 569–570.
Blix, O. B., *et al.* (eds.). *One Hundred Years of Christian Service, 1847–1947.* Milwaukee: Grand Avenue Congregational Church, 1947.

Boardman, M.A. *Historical Sketch.* Milwaukee: Grand Avenue Congregational Church, 1907.

Boring, E. G. *A History of Experimental Psychology.* New York: Appleton-Century-Crofts, Inc., 1957.

————. "The Influence of Evolutionary Theory upon American Psychological Thought," in *Evolutionary Thought in America,* ed. S. Persons. New Haven: Yale University Press, 1950.

Boring, M. D., and Boring, E. G. "Masters and Pupils Among the American Psychologists," *American Journal of Psychology,* 61 (1948), 527–534.

Buchner, E. F. "Teachers of Philosophy Among Yale Graduates," *Education,* 21 (1901), 549–556; 618–627.

Calo, G. "L'Etica di Giorgio T. Ladd," *Rivista Filosofica,* March–April, 1906, pp. 3–34.

Cattell, J. M. "Early Psychological Laboratories," *Science,* 67 (1928), 543–548.

————. "Psychology in America," *Science,* 30 (1929), 335–347.

————. "The Founding of the Association and of the Hopkins and Clark Laboratories," *Psychological Review,* 50 (1943), 61–64.

Cherry, P. P. *The Western Reserve and Early Ohio.* Akron: R. L. Fouse, 1920.

Cleaveland, N., and Packard, A. S. *History of Bowdoin College.* Boston: James Ripley Osgood and Co., 1882.

Conroy, H. *The Japanese Seizure of Korea: 1868–1910. A Study of Realism and Idealism in International Relations.* Philadelphia: University of Pennsylvania Press, 1960.

Cross, W. L. *Connecticut Yankee.* New Haven: Yale University Press, 1943.

Dewey, J. "The Reflex Arc Concept in Psychology," *Psychological Review,* 111 (1896), 357-370.

Fairbrother, S. H. Review of G. T. Ladd's *Philosophy of Conduct, Mind,* 12 (1903), 259.

Fay, J. W. *American Psychology Before William James.* New Brunswick: Rutgers University Press, 1939.

Fechner, G. *Elements of Psychophysics.* vol. 1. Trans. by Helmut E. Adler. New York: Holt, Rinehart, & Winston, Inc., 1966.

Bibliography

Fernberger, S. W. "The American Psychological Association, a Historical Summary, 1892–1930," *Psychological Bulletin*, 29 (1932), 1–92.

Fochtman, V. A. "Das Leib-Seele-Problem bei George Trumbull Ladd und William McDougall." Unpublished Ph.D. dissertation, Ludwig-Maximilians-Universität-München, 1928. Pp. 113.

Fullerton, G. S. "Discussion of Professor Ladd's APA President's Address," *Psychological Review*, 4 (1897), 402–405.

Gabriel, R. H. *Religion and Learning at Yale.* New Haven: Yale University Press, 1958.

Galloway, G. Review of G. T. Ladd's *Philosophy of Religion*, *Mind*, 16 (1907), 133.

Gardiner, H. N. Review of G. T. Ladd's *What Can I Know?* and *What Ought I to Do?*, *Yale Review*, 5 (1916), 220.

———. Review of G. T. Ladd's *What Should I Believe?* and *What May I Hope?*, *Yale Review*, 5 (1916), 895.

Garvey, C. R. "List of American Psychology Laboratories," *Psychological Bulletin*, 26 (1929), 652–660.

Hall, G. S. Editorial on "Experimental Psychology in America," *American Journal of Psychology*, 7 (1895), 3–8.

———. Reply to letters written by Ladd, James, Baldwin, and Cattell, *Science*, 2 (1895), 734–735.

———. Review of G. T. Ladd's *Elements of Physiological Psychology*, *American Journal of Psychology*, 1 (1887), 159–164.

Hatch, Louis C. *The History of Bowdoin College.* Portland, Maine: Loring, Short & Harmon, 1927.

Hawthorne, J. "The Horrors of the Plague in India," *Cosmopolitan*, 23 (1897), 231–234.

Henmon, V. A. C. Review of G. T. Ladd and R. S. Woodworth's *Elements of Physiological Psychology*, *Psychological Bulletin*, 9 (1912), 239–242.

Hicks, G. D. "Prof. G. T. Ladd," obituary, *Nature*, 108 (1921), 23–24.

Hinman, E. L. Review of G. T. Ladd's *Knowledge, Life and Realty: An Essay in Systematic Philosophy*, *Philosophical Review*, 19 (1910), 440–442.

Hulbert, H. *The Passing of Korea.* New York: Doubleday, Page and Co., 1906.

Hume, R. E. Review of G. T. Ladd's *Intimate Glimpses of Life in India,* *Yale Review,* 11 (1921–22), 412–415.

James, W. "A Plea for Psychology as a 'Natural Science,' " *Philosophical Review,* 1 (1892), 146–153.

———. *Principles of Psychology.* vols. 1 & 2. New York: Henry Holt and Co., 1890.

———. *Psychology.* Cleveland: The World Publishing Co., 1948.

———. Review of G. T. Ladd's *Psychology: Descriptive and Explanatory,* *Psychological Review,* 1 (1894), 286–293.

Jones, W. T. *A History of Western Philosophy.* New York: Harcourt, Brace and Co., 1952.

Jordan, E. Review of G. T. Ladd's *The Teacher's Practical Philosophy,* *Philosophical Review,* 22 (1913), 231–232.

Kawabe, H. "In Memoriam for Professor Ladd," *Shinri-Kenkyū,* 20 (1921), 257–261.

Keenleyside, H. L., and Thomas, A. F. *History of Japanese Education.* Tokyo: The Hokuseido Press, 1937.

Kinnosuke, A. "The Korea of Today," review of G. T. Ladd's *In Korea with Marquis Ito, Pacific Era,* 1 (1908), 405–408.

Le Clair, R. C. (ed.). *The Letters of William James and Theodore Flournoy.* Madison: University of Wisconsin Press, 1966.

Lensen, G. A. (ed.). *Korea and Manchuria Between Russia and Japan, 1895–1904.* Tallahassee: The Diplomatic Press, 1966.

Long, C. S. "Professor Ladd Rebuked from Japan," *Methodist Review,* November, 1889, p. 910.

Matsumoto, M. "Memories of Professor Ladd," *Shinri-Kenkyū,* 20 (1921), 242–256.

Matthews, A. *Ohio and Her Western Reserve.* New York: D. Appleton & Co., 1902.

McKenzie, F. A. *The Tragedy of Korea.* New York: E. P. Dutton and Co., 1908.

Mezes, S. E. Review of G. T. Ladd's *Philosophy of Conduct, Psychological Review,* 1 (1904), 18.

Mitchell, M. J. "Religion as a Factor in the Early Development of Ohio," *Mississippi Valley Historical Review,* 9 (1917), 75–89.

Bibliography

Miyake, I. "Remembrances of Professor Ladd," *Shinri-Kenkyū*, 20 (1921), 262–264.

Müller-Freienfels, R. *The Evolution of Modern Psychology.* Trans. by W. Beranwolfe. New Haven: Yale University Press, 1935.

Murchison, C. (ed.). *A History of Psychology in Autobiography.* 3 vols. Worcester, Mass.: Clark University Press, 1930–1936.

Murphy, G. *Historical Introduction to Modern Psychology.* New York: Harcourt, Brace and Co., 1949.

Nakashima, R. Review of G. T. Ladd's *Psychology: Descriptive and Explanatory. Rikugōzassi,* October, 1894, 532–537.

Neesima, J. H. *The Founding of the Doshisha and Doshisha University.* Kyoto: Doshisha University, 1960.

Oshima, N. "My Recollections of Dr. Ladd," *Shinri-Kenkyū,* 20 (1921), 352–363.

Paxson, F. L. *History of the American Frontier, 1763–1893.* New York: Houghton Mifflin Co., 1924.

Perry, R. B. *The Thought and Character of William James.* vols. 1 & 2. Boston: Little, Brown and Co., 1935.

Phelps, W. L. *Autobiography with Letters.* New York: Oxford University Press, 1939.

Pierson, G. W. *Yale College—an Educational History, 1871–1921.* New Haven: Yale University Press, 1952.

Pillsbury, W. B. *The History of Psychology.* New York: Norton, 1929.

Porter, N. *The Elements of Intellectual Science.* New York: Charles Scribner's Sons, 1883.

Pruette, L. *G. Stanley Hall: A Biography of a Mind.* New York: Appleton, 1926.

Riddle, A. G. *History of Geauga and Lake Counties, Ohio.* Philadelphia: Williams Brothers, 1878.

Roback, A. A. *History of American Psychology.* New York: Library Publishers, 1952.

————. *History of Psychology and Psychiatry.* New York: Philosophical Library, 1961.

Ruckmich, C. A. "The History and Status of Psychology in the United States," *American Journal of Psychology,* 23 (1912), 517–531.

————. "The Use of the Term *Function* in English Textbooks of Psychology," *American Journal of Psychology*, 24 (1913), 99–123.

Schneider, H. *A History of American Philosophy*. New York: Columbia University Press, 1946.

Seashore, C. E. "George Trumbull Ladd," obituary, *Science*, 54 (1921), 242.

Titchener, E. B. "George Trumbull Ladd," obituary, *American Journal of Psychology*, 32 (1921), 600–601.

————. *Systematic Psychology: Prolegomena*. New York: Macmillan Co., 1929.

Waite, F. C. *Western Reserve University—the Hudson Era*. Cleveland: Western Reserve University Press, 1943.

Walker, W. *The Creeds and Platforms of Congregationalism*. New York: Charles Scribner's Sons, 1893.

Wasson, W. W. *James A. Garfield: His Religion and Education*. Nashville: Tennessee Book Co., 1952.

Watson, J. *The Philosophy of Kant*. New Haven: Tuttle, Moorehouse & Taylor, 1884.

Watson, R. *The Great Psychologists—from Aristotle to Freud*. 2nd ed. New York: J. B. Lippincott Co., 1968.

Weigle, L. A. "The Religious Education of a Protestant." In *Contemporary American Theology*. 2nd series. New York: Round Table Press, 1933.

Winchell, A. *The Doctrine of Evolution*. New York: Harper & Bros., 1874.

Wundt, W. *Principles of Physiological Psychology*. vol. 1. Trans. by E. B. Titchener. New York: Macmillan Co., 1904.

Index

Index

Index

Metaphysics, 1, 6, 10, 32*n*., 43, 63, 164
  dualistic, 130
  Ladd's psychology, 141
  Lotze, 108
  and physiology, 76
  and psychology, 125
  and science, 78, 199
Methodist Review, 90
Microcosmus (Lotze), 110
Military service, 30
Mills, Dorothy W., *xi*
Milwaukee, Wis., 3, 50–66
Milwaukee Sentinel, 52–55
Mind, 76, 124, 136, 150
  as epiphenomenon, 125
  independence of, 145
  mind-body relationship, 127–130
  nature of, 9
Ministry, 41
  Edinburg United Church, 44–50
  Grand Avenue (Spring Street)
    Congregational Church, 50–66
Miracles, 77, 78
Missionaries, in India, 193, 194
  in Japan, 187–188
  in Korea, 229, 236, 237
Monism, 128–130, 166
Moral freedom, 167
Morality, 170
  in science, 8
Moriyama, J., *xi*

Nagasaki, 225
Nagasaki, Count, 190
National Science Foundation, *ix*
Nationalism, in Japan, 187
Nature, as real-ideal unity, 154
"Nature, the Supernatural and the
  Miraculous" (article, Ladd), 77
Neesima, Joseph Hardy, 176
Nerve-commotion, 137, 139
Nerve-physiology, science of, 123
Nervous system, 102
New Connecticut, 11
New Englander, 61
New Haven, 74, 79, 152, 172, 182, 243
New Testament, 17
"New Theology, The" (article, Ladd),
  61, 62

New York City, 36, 217
New York State Bar Association, 117
Newell, L. Jackson, *xi*
"No Ague in Milwaukee" (letter),
  54–55
Nova Scotia, 40, 253

Oberlin College, 49
Okamoto, S., *x*
Old Testament, 89
Optics, and final purpose, 76
Order of the Rising Sun, Ladd's receipt
  of, 2, 189, 243
Ordination, requirements for, 84, 85, 92
Orient, The (Bowdoin student
  newspaper), 71
Origin of Species, The (Darwin), 97
Orthodoxy, 62, 92
Osaka, 180
Outlines of Descriptive Psychology,
  (Ladd, Japanese ed., 1898), 186
Outlines of Physiological Psychology
  (Ladd, Japanese ed., 1901), 195
Outlines of Psychology (Lotze), 107

Painesville, Ohio, 13–16, 22, 23, 25
Parallelism, 129
Paris, France, 2, 185, 196
Park, Professor Edwards A., 37, 39
Perkins, F. Theodore, *vii*
Personality, 250, 251
Phelps, William Lyon, 113
Philosophical anthropology, 110
Philosophical Review, 119, 124
Philosophy, 29, 30, 32, 51
  in America, 156–158
  background, 1–10
  at Bowdoin, 67–82
  "Development of Philosophy in
    the Nineteenth Century," 154
  Lotze, 108
  and other disciplines, 156
  at Yale, 9, 110
Philosophy of Conduct (Ladd, 1902),
  169–171, 248
Philosophy of Kant, The (J. Watson),
  110
Philosophy of Knowledge (Ladd,
  Japanese ed., 1898), 186

Index

This book was set in twelve-point Garamond. It was composed and printed by Oberlin Printing Company, Oberlin, Ohio, and bound by The C. J. Krehbiel Company, Cincinnati, Ohio. The paper is Bradford Book. The design is by Nan C. Jones.